Texas Jurist

*The Life, Law
and
Legacy
of
B.D. Tarlton*

Perry Cockerell

Copyright © 2022 Perry Cockerell

ISBN: 978-1-7345702-9-8
Library of Congress Control Number: 2022920704

Alliance Publishing, LLC
Dallas, Texas

Printed in the United States of America.

All rights reserved. No part of this book may be reproduced, transmitted, or stored in any form or by any means, graphic, electronic, or mechanical, including photocopying, taping, and recording, without prior written permission from the publisher.

Contents

Introduction — v

One: The Hurricane — 1
Two: The Tarltons — 3
Three: The Tarlton Plantation — 9
Four: The Civil War — 21
Five: A Miracle in Grand Coteau — 29
Six: After the Civil War — 49
Seven: Waxahachie, Texas — 65
Eight: Death in Waxahachie — 73
Nine: Hillsboro, Texas — 77
Ten: District Judge Abbott — 93
Eleven: District Judge J.M. Hall — 95
Twelve: Private Practice — 97
Thirteen: 1890 — 113
Fourteen: Eastland County — 117
Fifteen: Texas Commission of Appeals — 123
Sixteen: Second Court of Civil Appeals — 135
Seventeen: The Court Officially Opens — 149
Eighteen: The 1892 Election — 169
Nineteen: 1893 — 173
Twenty: 1894 — 177
Twenty-One: 1895 — 181
Twenty-Two: 1896 — 185
Twenty-Three: 1897 — 187

Twenty-Four: The Election of 1898	191
Twenty-Five: The Tarlton Opinions	205
Twenty-Six: Private Practice	213
Twenty-Seven: Law School Professor	225
Twenty-Eight: The Hurricane	243
Twenty-Nine: The Death of Tarlton	247
Thirty: Legacy	259
Thirty-One: Why Did Conner Run Against Tarlton?	275
Epilogue	289
Acknowledgements	293
Notes	297
Index	317

Introduction

New students who enter the University of Texas School of Law cross a threshold in the university's law library. As they enter, they see a large portrait of a distinguished gentleman with white hair, a black suit, and a bow tie. He silently watches thousands of young men and women enter the library named after him. They are the future Texas lawyers who come to the library of one of the finest legal institutions in the country and see a man in the painting.

What was his story? What were his accomplishments? Why does his picture hang in the library?

As they come and go, searching for knowledge and dreaming about their future in the field of law, they may wonder who this man was. By the time they graduate and become licensed attorneys in Texas, they will come to know him; they have studied him and learned why his portrait hangs in the school and the library is named after him.

Benjamin Dudley (B.D.) Tarlton served two terms in the Texas House of Representatives, one year as an Associate Justice on the Texas Commission of Appeals, one six-year term as Chief Justice of the Second Court of Civil Appeals in Fort Worth, and fifteen years as Professor of Law at the University of Texas.

B.D.'s family was not Catholic, but he embraced the Catholic faith after being educated in a strong Catholic school and community in Grand Coteau, Louisiana, having studied for seven years at St. Charles College, an all-boys Catholic school run by the Jesuits.

As a young boy, B.D. grew up on a sugar plantation in St. Mary's Parish in Louisiana. His father, Dr. John Tarlton, and his uncle Dr. Leo

Tarlton were medical doctors who closed their medical practices in Mobile, Alabama, in 1848 to move to the parish to acquire sugar plantations. Dr. Tarlton acquired a second plantation in St. Landry Parish and owned as many as 150 slaves between the two plantations.

The Tarlton family lived through a tumultuous time in American history, witnessing the Civil War and experiencing the most violent period during Reconstruction in Louisiana. B.D. Tarlton was twelve years old when the Civil War broke out. *The Battle of Grand Coteau* occurred when he and his brothers were students at St. Charles College in the same city. Two of his older brothers joined the Confederacy and served until the end of the war. He witnessed his parents, Dr. John Tarlton and Frances Caller Tarlton, shut down their sugar plantations during the Civil War. Union troops actually entered the Tarlton plantation in St. Mary's Parish in 1864 in an event captured by a reporter who depicted the scene in a drawing for publication.

After the Civil War ended, the legend passed down was that Dr. Tarlton was a witness to the *Miracle of Grand Coteau* in 1866 when Mary Wilson, a young novice at the Sacred Heart Academy, was cured miraculously. The Tarlton boys were being educated at St. Charles College just walking distance from the academy when all effort was made through intercessory prayers and novenas to John Berchmans for intervention. Wilson was cured and John Berchmans was canonized a saint in 1868. The event passed down was that Dr. John Tarlton, an Episcopalean, converted to Catholicism. If he did not, B.D. Tarlton and his older brother Toulmin Tarlton became Catholic and graduated from St. Charles College.

While studying at St. Charles College, B.D. became interested in priesthood but changed his mind and chose law school instead. He developed an interest in real estate, real estate law, and real estate litigation. This interest may have been out of necessity to find a legal way to help his parents endure the ongoing litigation. B.D. saw his parents endure eight years of litigation to foreclosure the mortgages on the plantations in St. Mary's and St. Landry's parishes. Two of the cases went to the Louisiana Supreme Court and were decided in 1870 while B.D. Tarlton was attending law school at the University of Louisiana.

After graduating from law school, B.D. stepped in to purchase some of parents' property at a tax foreclosure sale. During Reconstruction of Louisiana, which was still being occupied by Federal troops, B.D. believed, as did many attorneys in St. Landry Parish, that the taxes imposed by the government of Republican Governor William Kellogg were illegal and that Kellogg's election was not valid. Democrat John McEnery, Kellogg's opponent, refused to concede the 1872 election. The state remained in conflict for two years while both candidates claimed to be governor. Tarlton lived during a time when a real *coup d'etat* of the Kellogg government was conducted by White League paramilitary operatives in the Democrat Party, who removed Kellogg from power only for him to be forcibly returned to power by Republican U.S. President Ulysses S. Grant.

In 1874, at age twenty-five, B.D. ran for the Louisiana legislature as a candidate of the Democrat-Conservative party only to lose in a crowded race of twelve candidates to forty-one-year-old E.D. Estillette, the incumbent, who would become Speaker of the House in Louisiana in 1876. B.D. took on the establishment. He would oppose an incumbent or the system itself if he had cause.

In March 1876, B.D. closed his legal practice in Grand Coteau and moved to Waxahachie, Texas, following his family who had resolved all their litigation and had moved to Ellis County, Texas, in December 1873. In downtown Waxahachie, the Tarltons started over by purchasing a property known as the "Lacey Home" on a ten-acre tract of land. But after the closing Dr. Tarlton refused the make his first payment on the property when he realized that a mechanic's lien claimant, who performed work on the property had a judgment lien which was not final and on appeal and was not paid off at the closing. There was no mention of the lien in the deed to him. The dispute generated multiple lawsuits over the next seven years to foreclose the mortgage liens on the property. The case of *Tarlton v. Daily* lasted for seven years, from 1874 to 1881, before it was decided by the Texas Commission of Appeals, the court where B.D. Tarlton would eventually serve as an associate justice. The case was proof that Texas needed intermediary courts of appeals to handle appeals that the Texas Supreme Court would not hear.

In Texas, B.D. found work in Hillsboro in Hill County when he partnered with Texas State Representative Jo Abbott, who later became the district judge and United States Congressman. Following Abbott's footsteps, B.D. served two terms in the Texas Legislature. After Abbott took the judicial bench in Hill County, B.D. established a family-owned law firm with his brother Green Duke (G.D.) Tarlton and brother-in-law Wright Chalfont Morrow.

After years of handling cases before District Judge J.M. Hall, B.D. became an experienced trial and appellate attorney, handling civil and criminal appeals and reversing many of Judge Hall's decisions. In 1880 B.D. challenged Hall for his district court seat, but he lost to the incumbent judge. It was his second loss for public office.

B.D. personally experienced litigation when his law firm became embroiled in a title dispute in the case of *Tarlton v. Kirkpatrick* over land his firm acquired in Hill County. Over a fifteen-year period, the case was tried two times and appealed two times, resulting in two opinions from the Fort Worth and Dallas courts of appeals that would ultimately rule in favor of the Tarlton firm.

Tarlton knew the value of having friends in the right places. He rose in prominence after befriending attorney Jo Abbott in Hillsboro, Texas, and later Governor James S. Hogg, who noticed Tarlton's articulate abilities during his service in the Texas legislature. In 1891, the governor appointed B.D. as a justice to Panel B on the Texas Commission of Appeals. There he and two other appointees issued more than fifty opinions in one year—the last year of the court's existence. In 1892, the governor appointed Tarlton as the first Chief Justice of the Second Court of Civil Appeals established in Fort Worth.

Chief Justice Tarlton served for six years on the new court and wrote over 400 opinions during his first and only term. Tarlton was denied reelection when District Judge Truman H. Conner of Eastland County challenged him in the Democratic primary in the spring of 1898. Tarlton lost in an era when primary races were decided by the elected delegates to the Democratic

Convention, who were allowed to commit their votes in advance of the convention. The size of the Second Judicial District, which included 118 counties, enabled Conner to reach out to the western counties as far as El Paso and obtain more than a sufficient number of delegate pledges to defeat Tarlton before the convention convened. Conner won by painting Tarlton as a member of the elite in Fort Worth, the city that had deprived him of the nomination in 1895 when Justice Head stepped down. When the Governor selected Sam Hunter from Fort Worth over Conner from Eastland, Conner declared war in 1898 and went after the top seat to topple Chief Justice Tarlton.

Was Conner's challenge truly based on a lack of representation on the court? Was his stated reason the *real* reason he ran against Tarlton? What enabled Conner to obtain the delegate pledges so easily prior to the convention? Before the Democratic Convention was held in July 1898, Tarlton withdrew his name from nomination and allowed Conner to take the prize without a challenge on the convention floor. Tarlton had lost two prior races for public office. He was not going to lose a third race.

In January 1899, after six years on the court, former Chief Justice Tarlton established a private practice in Fort Worth with Ben Ayers, an influential and jovial attorney who worked to bring the Second Court of Civil Appeals to Fort Worth, the new transportation hub for the state and nation.

In 1904, Tarlton became the first president of the Tarrant County Bar Association and accepted a teaching position at the state university, now the University of Texas School of Law. He left Fort Worth for Austin, leaving behind the questions of why this man could not serve another term and why the Democratic delegates rejected one of the most important judicial figures in Texas history. Tarlton's loss and Fort Worth's loss of Tarlton were bitter pills to swallow. His loss still hurts today.

During his fifteen years in the classroom, Tarlton became a welcome colleague among his peers and a beloved mentor of his law students at the University of Texas School of Law. Accolades, honors, and positions of leadership followed Tarlton until his untimely death in 1919.

While B.D.'s father, Dr. John Tarlton, was a plantation owner and slave owner who believed in state's rights and secession and opposed the 15th

Amendment (right to vote) he spawned a legacy that was quite the opposite of him. His family lineage fought for civil rights and against racial discrimination in all forms for over 100 years, continuing to this day. His son, B.D. Tarlton was respected and beloved by all and was for women's rights before there was women's suffrage. B.D.'s son, B.D. Tarlton Jr., who attended law school during his father's tenure as professor, practiced law in Hillsboro and settled in Corpus Christi to become a successful criminal defense attorney, handling the defense of capital murder cases and earning a reputation in his own right fighting against civil injustice and the Ku Klux Klan in the 1920s.

B.D. Jr.'s daughter, Mary Frances "Sissy" Farenthold, became a well-known and highly respected politician, attorney, and civil rights activist who ran twice for governor of Texas and was nominated for vice-president of the United States. Before passing away in September 2021, Sissy Farenthold shared her beliefs as to why her grandfather lost to District Judge Truman Conner in 1898. Interviewed many times in 2020 and 2021, she maintained the real reason for his loss to Judge Conner. This book will explore the Tarlton-Conner race in 1898 and what might have caused Judge Conner to openly challenge her grandfather for the chief justice position and to wrestle the nomination from the sitting incumbent.

This book is B.D. Tarlton's story and that of his family, past and present. It is a search for the man who died 103 years ago but is remembered as if he were alive today. This book is about religion, love, war, peace, conflict, law, and within all of this, there is a miracle.

Perry Cockerell
February 2022

ONE

The Hurricane

By September of 1919, B.D. Tarlton and his wife, Suzanne Marie Littell, had experienced successful lives. They were parents of four living children: Frances, Elizabeth, Genevieve, and Benjamin Dudley Jr. While visiting their daughter Genevieve Daugherty and her husband James Daugherty and their four children in Beeville, Texas, they took the train to Corpus Christi to visit their son B.D. Tarlton Jr., a licensed attorney practicing law downtown. After checking in the Breakers Hotel, they enjoyed the view of the Texas gulf coast from their hotel room.

B.D. grew up in south Louisiana, not far from the Louisiana coast, so he felt at home. His son B.D. Jr. graduated from the University of Texas School of Law in 1911, where his father was a professor of law. The son of one of the most famous professors at the school was making a name in his own right. At sixty-nine years of age, one month shy of his seventieth birthday, B.D. relaxed with his wife in the coastal city to enjoy the waters. His health in decline, he and Susan had visited Colorado in the previous year in hopes that the climate would renew his vigor.

On August 31, 1919, a hurricane east of the Windward Islands began slowly moving towards Key West, Florida. On September 10, 1919, the hurricane struck ten ships and a small island located in its path. The force continued to move into the Gulf of Mexico, but forecasters lost the storm at that point.[1] With no modern satellite imagery and no categorical measurements for storms, no one knew the massive storm was moving towards Texas.

On Saturday, September 13, 1919, swells from the storm rolled into Port Aransas and Corpus Christi. A Port Aransas engineer messaged the Corpus Christi Weather Bureau that water was coming into an office located fifteen feet above mean low tide. Word of the storm caused residents to seek higher ground towards a bluff above downtown, while others made their way to Army Hospital No. 15 on North Beach, the Nueces Hotel between Chaparral and Water streets at Peoples Street, and the four-year-old Nueces County Courthouse.

Theodore Fuller, ten years old at the time, noticed large schools of fish in the Corpus Christi Bay. He later recalled: "There were so many flounders to be seen right up against the shore. Novice fisherman with no knowledge of gigging were spearing them with cooking forks."[2]

Around 4 a.m. on Sunday, September 14, 1919, the hurricane smashed into the Texas coastline at 115 miles per hour, surging water sixteen feet into the city and decimating the business district. By today's standards, it was a Category 3 hurricane that measured fifty miles long. B.D. was not fearful. He weathered many a storm in his life and in the courtroom …

TWO

The Tarltons

THE TARLTON FAMILY ROOTS CAN be traced as far back as the thirteenth century to Liverpool, England.[3] The early Tarlton settlers who arrived in Maryland and New Hampshire are divided into six ancestors who spelled their last name in two ways. The Tarltons who lived before 1800 in Maryland omitted the "e" in their name.

B.D. Tarlton's grandfather Jeremiah Tarlton was born in St. Mary's County, Maryland, in 1761. At an early age, Jeremiah Tarlton and his brother Caleb Tarlton joined the Continental Army and served with the Greene & Morgan Military Service.[4] From February 4 and May 22, 1778, Jeremiah Tarlton served as a private in the 2nd Maryland Regiment. He received a pension from his service in the Continental Army with the rank of corporal.

In 1786, twenty-five-year-old Jeremiah migrated to Frederick County, Maryland, where he began to buy property in Washington and Alleghany counties. He married Mary Herbert Briscoe on June 29, 1786, and the couple had eight children: Ralph Briscoe, Ann, Alfred, Emily, John (the father of B.D. Tarlton), Catherine, Meredith, and Llewellyn Pitt, and Amanda.[5]

In 1806, Tarlton moved his family to a farm east of Georgetown, Scott County, Kentucky, where other Tarlton descendants had migrated. A distant cousin in the county had the same name but was of the Catholic faith. To distinguish the two, the families referred to them as "Jeremiah, the Catholic Tarlton" and "Jeremiah, the Protestant Tarlton." B.D.'s family descended from "Jeremiah, the Protestant."

The Tarltons were lovers of good horses, and Jeremiah had the best racehorse in Kentucky in his time. Jeremiah owned one slave while in Frederick County in 1790. The Briscoe family, however, had many slaves.

In 1833, Jeremiah died of cholera at the age of seventy-two. When he died he held eighteen slaves.[6] The two Jeremiahs represented family traits passed down to successive generations: the Tarltons were wealthy, educated landowners, public servants, and members of the Catholic and Protestant faiths, into which they were either born or had experienced a conversion of faith. Members of the Catholic and Protestant faith were often within the same immediate family.

Dr. John Tarlton

John Tarlton, the third son of Jeremiah Tarlton and B.D.'s father, was born on August 24, 1800, in Carroll Manor, three miles from Hagarstown, Maryland. From age six, John Tarlton grew up in Scott County, Kentucky. His parents were wealthy enough to send him to Transylvania University in Lexington, Kentucky, to become a medical doctor.

Transylvania University, a private liberal arts college, was established in 1780 and affiliated with the Disciples of Christ. Located in a heavily forested area in Lexington, Kentucky, the name "Transylvania" means *Across the Woods* in Latin. Tarlton arrived when the school included a medical school, law school, divinity school, and a college of arts and sciences.[7]

"It was the Harvard of the West," said Sissy Farenthold, Dr. Tarlton's great granddaughter, in January 2021.

Many famous politicians were educated at Transylvania University, including Stephen F. Austin, a founder of Texas, and William A. Trimble, a U.S. Senator. Both men graduated in 1810. David Rice Atchison, who would become a U.S. Senator of Missouri, also attended the university. Solomon W. Downs, future U.S. Senator of Louisiana, graduated in 1823. Other alumni include Jesse D. Bright (future Lieutenant Governor and U.S. Senator of Indiana), George Wallace Jones (U.S. Senator of Iowa from 1848 to 1859), Edward A. Hannegan (U.S. Senator of Indiana from 1843 to 1849), and Jefferson Davis, who attended the university in 1821 before transferring to West Point in 1823.

John Tarlton graduated from the university in 1825. His dissertation was on *Bilious Remitting Fever* which caused great suffering in Philadelphia in 1780. The term bilious remitting fever can refer to yellow fever, a serious disease during its day and one that Dr. Tarlton would confront in his medical practice in Louisiana after becoming a sugar planter. The yellow fever virus originated in Africa and came to the Western Hemisphere during the slave trade era. The first epidemic was reported in 1648 in Yucatan. Jumping years later to 1870, after Dr. Tarlton was an established physician in Grand Coteau, Louisiana, he and his partner, Dr. Edward Millard, instituted a quarantine in the nearby town of Opelousas, Louisiana, preventing anyone who had been infected from traveling into the town. To calm the public, Dr. Tarlton and Dr. Millard announced in the local newspapers (printed in English and French) that they had not treated a patient with yellow fever.

"Yellow fever took the lives of many people back then. I spoke at the university [Transylvania] in 1990, and they gave me a copy of his thesis," Sissy Farenthold recalled.

After graduation, Dr. Tarlton moved to Sumpter County, South Carolina, where he practiced medicine and met his first wife, Caroline Mary Belser.[8] The couple married on January 27, 1827.[9] Shortly thereafter, Dr. Tarlton moved his family to Mobile, Alabama, a rapidly growing port town.[10] Over the next nine years, the family had five children:

Alfred Jeremiah, born December 12, 1827, and died October 18, 1837.
Mary Martha, born September 1, 1829, and died October 15, 1834.
Emma Louise, born July 27, 1832, and died March 7, 1837.
Caroline Mary Belser, born January 12, 1834, and died March 27, 1855.
John Belser, born December 16, 1836, and died March 31, 1907.

Only John Belser Tarlton lived into adulthood.

In Mobile, Dr. Tarlton established his medical practices with his brother, Dr. Leo Tarlton. Dr. Tarlton also became an entrepreneur. In 1837 he collaborated with his brother, Alfred Tarlton, in forming A&J Tarlton for the purpose of transacting a general Commission, Provision & Forwarding Business. It apparently became common for physicians to engage in other forms of business to earn sufficient income. Dr. Tarlton may have considered medicine as a secondary practice.

Death of Caroline Belser Tarlton

On February 4, 1837, Caroline Belser Tarlton died. The *Camden Journal* reported her death:

> Died in the village of Jacksonville near Mobile, on the 24th inst., Mrs. Caroline Mary Tarlton, age 27, consort of John W. Tarlton. A member of the Baptist Church left a husband and children. Mobile Register.

At age thirty-six, Dr. Tarlton was now a widower with three minor children: Alfred Jeremiah, age ten, Caroline Mary Belser, age three, and John Belser, a three-month-old infant. How could he care for a three-month-old infant while being a full-time practicing physician?

Six months later Alfred Jeremiah, the oldest, died. Word must have circulated in Mobile of the relatively young eligible medical doctor with young children. Before long, Dr. Tarlton became acquainted with Jane H. Toulmin Caller, thirty-eight years old and two years older than he. Dr. Tarlton was attracted to Jane Caller, and she could have been his wife, except that she was married to Green Duke Caller, whose health and financial circumstances were uncertain. Moreover, she and Green Duke Caller had a twenty-two-year-old daughter, Frances Ann Caller, who was not married. Jane Caller needed security, and Dr. Tarlton needed a wife; his children needed a young mother.

"He courted the mother and married the daughter," said Sissy Farenthold, based on stories passed down after years of family gatherings.

On March 24, 1838, Dr. John Tarlton and Frances Caller were issued a marriage license in Mobile County, Alabama, and were married. Their marriage benefited the Tarlton and Caller families. Dr. Tarlton and his wife Frances Caller and Jane Caller formed a companionship that would endure the rest of their lives.

The following year after their marriage, a great fire occurred in Mobile in the business district where Tarlton and his brother's office was based. His last known place of business was at the corner of Royal & Dauphin streets.

In September 1841, Dr. Tarlton and Frances Tarlton had their first child, Emma Jane.[11] Three years later, on April 20, 1844, they had their second child, Frances Celia.

In 1844, Frances Tarlton's father, Green Duke Caller, died and an estate was opened up. Dr. Tarlton was the co-executor of the estate along with Theophilus L. Toulmin (1796-1866).

Theophilus L. Toulmin served as Justice of the Peace and Sheriff of Mobile and commissioned a Lt. Colonel to General of the 4th Division, 9th Brigade of the Alabama Infantry in 1826 and promoted to General in 1829. Toulmin was a close friend of Green Duke Caller and a fellow Kentuckian. Dr. Tarlton was an admirer of Theophilus Toulmin and would pass his name down to his firstborn son of Dr. Tarlton and Francis Caller.

THREE

The Tarlton Plantation

IN 1803, THE UNITED STATES acquired the Louisiana territory in the Louisiana Purchase at the cost of $15 million dollars. The acquisition was a great accomplishment for President Thomas Jefferson because it doubled the size of the United States. The purchase involved negotiating a transfer of Spain's interest in the property to France, who would then transfer the rights to the United States. The French did not occupy all of the Louisiana Territory that extended far north, but the acquisition gave the United States the preemptive right to purchase the land. The area in what is now Louisiana became a major center of Cajun and French Creole culture as well as the Catholic religion that penetrated Louisiana.

Louisiana had a surging sugar and cotton industry that expanded from the 1830s until the beginning of the Civil War. The Tarltons moved to St. Mary Parish, a parish established in 1811 and named after Mary, the Mother of God for those of the Catholic faith. The parish had almost 9,000 residents.

St. Mary Plantation

In 1846, Dr. Tarlton and his brother Dr. Leo Tarlton closed their medical practice in Mobile, Alabama, and moved the Tarlton families to St. Marty Parish, Louisiana. What would prompt the two doctors to close their medical practice and head to Louisiana?

"The sugar cane was like a gold rush," said Erin Shirley, Chair of the Morgan City Archives Commission in Morgan City, Louisiana. "The land was cheap; the labor was cheap. I imagine that people who had money to invest would want to do that. The land was available, and they came from more populous areas to less populous areas. All of the major settlers came from the northeast to here."

When the Tarltons arrived in St. Mary Parish, the area was known as Tiger Island, named after the wildcats in the area. The city was later called Brashear City and eventually Morgan City as it is known today after Charles Morgan, a steamship magnate who dredged the Atchafalaya Bay, making the city a port and trade center.

The general area in Louisiana was also known as the Attakapas district, named after the Attakapas Tribe, an indigenous tribe who lived along the Gulf of Mexico and were devastated by infectious diseases after the Europeans made contact. There are only 450 tribal members left of the Attakapas Tribe living in the southern region of Louisiana and Texas.

Erin Shirley believes that the the Tarltons settled initially in Belle Isle in St. Mary Parish. The two brothers, Dr. John Tarlton and Dr. Leo Tarlton, purchased separate plantations in the parish. Dr. John Tarlton settled in an area of land between current day Morgan City and Amelie and along the Bayou Boeuf, a river that runs to the city of Franklin, the parish seat. The Bayou Boeuf carried steamboats of sugar and cotton for trade in Franklin, which was an inland port.

In February 1848, Dr. Tarlton and John Dooly and his wife, Cynthia, purchased 1,200 arpents of property from William C.C.C. Martin and Sophia Lamp, his wife.[12] Martin was not a sugar farmer but is believed to have been a land speculator who acquired the property for resale. Dr. Tarlton named his property the "Tarlton plantation." Figure 1 shows the properties identified by surveys in the name of Robert Martin.

Dr. Tarlton's mortgage on the property was $15,000 and was payable in five promissory notes ranging from $2,000 to $3,000 that were due each April from 1849 through 1854. Dr. Tarlton's wife, Frances Caller, invested $7,400 of her dowry into the acquisition.

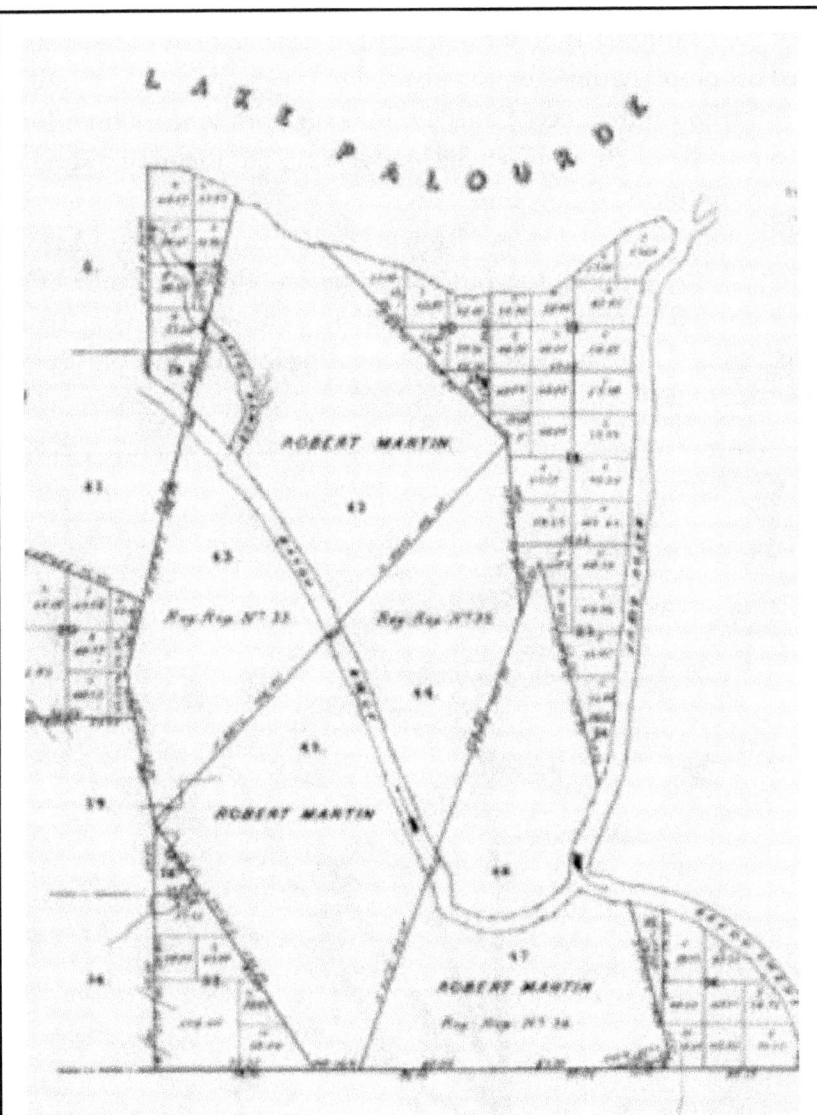

Figure 1 Location of original land grants. Dr. John Tarlton owned property on both sides of the Bayou Boeuf in sections noted as No. 43, 44, and 45. The Morgan City Archives show that Dr. Leo Tarlton, Dr. Tarlton's brother, purchased property in Centreville in St. Mary Parish and would become Mayor of the city of Franklin, the seat of St. Mary Parish.

Dr. Leo Tarlton acquired his plantation near Franklin, Louisiana, and named his property the "Augusta plantation."

Dr. Tarlton and Frances Caller Tarlton's firstborn son, Toulmin Tarlton, was born on April 10, 1847, in St. Mary Parish, but there is no specific location for his birth.

B.D. Tarlton was born on October 18, 1849 and is said to have been the first Tarlton born on the Tarlton plantation. The origin of B.D.'s first name is from Benjamin Franklin. The origin of his middle name has been lost to history. Growing up and while attending St. Charles College, he was known as Dudley.

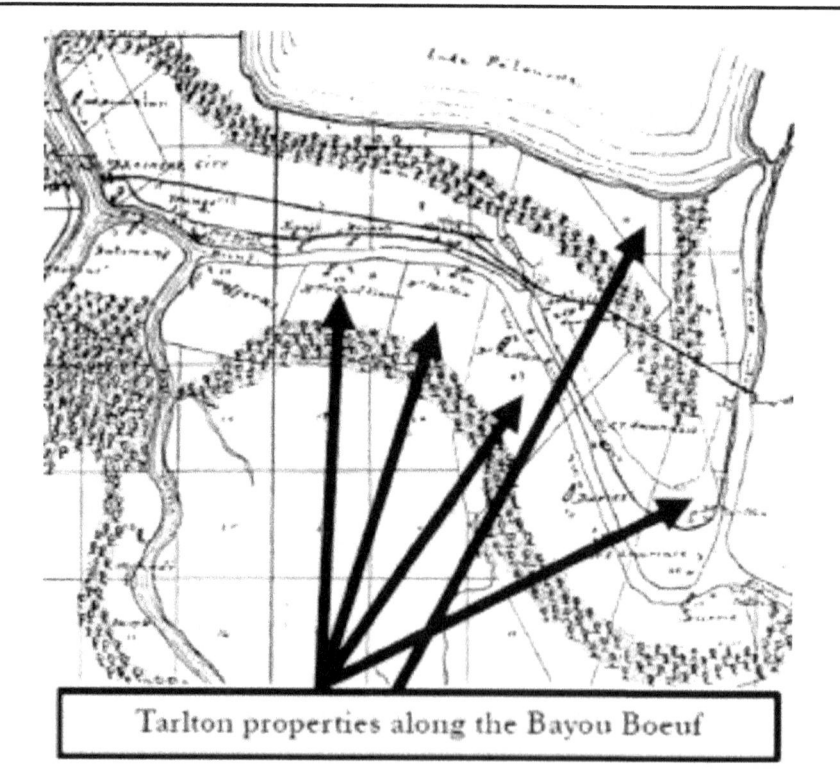

Figure 2 This graphic is an 1864 Confederate map and shows the Tarlton properties located on both sides of the Bayou Boeuf, a river that runs to the city of Franklin, an inland port and the seat of St. Mary Parish. Dr. Tarlton became one of the largest plantation owners in St. Mary Parish.

Figure 3 Comparing this aerial photo to Figure 2 shows the approximate location of the Tarlton estate in St. Mary Parish along the Bayou Boeuf. A state highway runs through the middle of the property. The Bayou Boeuf serviced the steamboats transporting sugar and cotton to Franklin, Louisiana. The Amelia Belle Casino, a riverboat casino, is now located on the Bayou Boeuf.

In 1850, Dr. Tarlton's profile changed from prominent doctor and businessman to an outspoken citizen regarding many issues, including states' rights and slave ownership. In that year he became a delegate to the Democrat state convention. By this time Dr. Tarlton owned nearly 80 slaves.

In 1851, part of the land he acquired was seized after a judgment creditor discovered John Dooly's ownership interest in the property. After learning of the dispute, on June 18, 1851, Dr. Tarlton took out a notice in the newspaper that he "was determined not to pay more than the proportion of the price that the real quantity of land bears to the quantity sold."

On June 21, 1851, Sheriff Ethan Allan posted notice that in *Case No. 125, John Dooley v. A. Lirette Sheff et al, Fifth District Court, Parish of Terrebonne*, he would sell the property at a public sale on August 2, 1851. Dr. Tarlton was greatly offended by the discovery of a judgment lien creditor with a claim against his property after his purchase.

B.D.'s brother Green Duke Tarlton, named after his maternal grandfather, Green Duke Caller, was born on February 20, 1852. Growing up he was known as Duke.

Peter Richardson Tarlton was born July 24, 1854, and Frank Ross Tarlton was born on March 15, 1857.[13]

Frances Celia Tarlton died on September 14, 1848, at the age of four, one month before B.D. was born. Emma Jane died on Sept. 27, 1853, at the age of twelve. With diseases rampant without cure, many children never survived into adulthood.

Purchase from Elizabeth McWaters

In June 1857, Dr. Tarlton purchased two additional tracts of land from Mrs. Elizabeth McWaters. The first tract was a sugar plantation a mile long along the Bayou Boeuf and included the building and improvements, mules, oxen, cows, hogs, farming utensils, and plantation tools "now employed on the said plantation." The second tract was 80 acres and included "slaves for lifetime." The deed named the slaves:

> Henry Johnson, a man aged about 35 years, his wife Adeline, aged about 26 years, and her four children: Louis, aged about 13 years; Maria, aged about 10 years; Kitty, aged about 5 years; and Susan,

about 2 years. Tom, a man aged about 32 years, his wife Irving, aged about 31 years. Bill, a man aged about 30 years, His wife Francis, aged about 24 years, and her son Edmund, aged about 4 years old. George, a man aged about 24 years, his wife May, aged about 24 years, and her three children: Jimmy, about 9 years; Usilda, aged about 6 years; and Tifford, aged about three years. Naw, a man aged 45 years warranted only in title, his wife Fancy, aged 22 years old, and his three children: Albera, aged 10 years; Clara, 6; and Ellick, 3 years. Hanker Vinson, a man aged 25 years. Dan, a man aged about 28 years. Seven, a man aged 22 years. Eliza, a woman aged about 28 years old, and her two children: Polk, 4 years old; Olivier, one year. Mary Stanley aged about 22 years.

Figure 4 Dr. John Tarlton with Frank Ross Tarlton in 1858.

McWaters acquired the plantation from Dr. Ethan Allen in December 1856 and was in no position to operate it. She needed someone to take over her mortgage payments to Dr. Allen. She needed the income from the sale of the plantation to purchase her own homestead. Dr. Tarlton paid $75,000 for the plantation and agreed to assume McWaters' liabilities to Dr. Allen. Dr. Tarlton made a $10,000 down payment and assumed four promissory notes for $5,000 and three others for $6,666.66, which fell due on January 1 of the years 1858 through 1861. Dr. Tarlton agreed to hold Mrs. McWaters harmless of her note to Dr. Ethan Allen, who was obligated to Adland Carlin for his mortgage on the plantation. The agreement was that when $40,000 of the $75,000 had been paid, then the debt of Dr. Allen to Adland Carlin would be paid.

Dr. Tarlton agreed to release the dowry claim of his wife, Frances Caller, in the property and this would become an issue in later years. The deed provided:

> And now to these presents, personally came and intervened Madam Francis Caller of lawful age, wife of the said Dr. John Tarlton who declared unto me the said Recorder, that it is her wish and intention to release in favor of the said Elizabeth McWilliams widow of Aaron McWaters deceased the property herein mortgaged from any right claims, mortgages and privileges to which she may be entitled, whether by virtue of her marriage with the said Dr. John Tarlton or otherwise.

Mrs. McWaters then purchased her own plantation with cattle, work animals and farming implements, from Homer Smith. She endorsed the four notes of Tarlton to Smith and gave an additional note of $872.32. She subrogated Smith to the notes payable by Dr. Tarlton. This meant that Smith could sue Dr. Tarlton directly for payment on the note and hold McWaters responsible as well.

The purchase of the plantation shows how financing arrangements in the 1800s were potentially unstable transactions. Each property owner was dependent on the subsequent owner for their income. This property transaction was subject to three prior mortgages: Adland Carlin looked to Dr. Ethan Allen, who looked to Elizabeth McWaters, who looked to Dr. Tarlton for payment of the mortgage. If anyone of the property owner (mortgagor) failed to pay his mortgagee, then the prior mortgagee could foreclose the mortgage in order to be paid. Foreclosure of a mortgage was by a lawsuit that could take years to finalize. Even if the judicial sale occurred, the payment for the mortgage would come from a credit bid against the debt. The real payment comes from the new purchaser willing to purchase the property with seller financing or cash.

In 1858, Dr. Tarlton purchased a second adjoining tract from Dr. R.B. McKay, who purchased the property from William C.C.C. Martin, the same man who sold Dr. Tarlton his first estate in 1848. McKay sold his property to Dr. Tarlton after the area suffered from a hurricane and his damages were too great. The combined estates made Dr. Tarlton one of the largest sugar producers in the region.[14]

On July 9, 1858, Dr. Tarlton took out an ad in the *Times Picayune* seeking a partner to assist with the properties after the damage from the hurricane:

A Rare Chance for a Sugar or Cotton Planter who has lost his crop by High Water

PARTNER WANTED for one or more years, having from 50 to 75 hands, to cultivate a large Sugar Plantation, in Attakapas, above overflow and risks of high water. With such a one, a full crop, say 500 arpents of cane and 300 of corn, can be planted the coming year., The mill and machinery quite sufficient to take off 1000 hhds. A suitable man, with such a force can make a very profitable arrangement, the owner not having sufficient force to work the lands. Abundance of corn to serve the place; mules, plow, carts and oxen, for one-half that force, on the plantation. An application will be considered if made early to FELLOWES & CO. New Orleans,

Or to dr. John Tarlton Jy7-6t&4tW
Alligator P.O., Parish, St. Mary. La.

The notation of 50 to 75 "hands" could have been a reference to the number of slaves working the plantation. In the research of this book, Sissy Farenthold never said not to write about the fact that her grandfather owned slaves, but only to "be prepared."

Boundary Dispute

In April 1859, Dr. Tarlton became involved in a boundary dispute with his neighbor James N. Wofford over his property. The Wofford tract is observable in the graphic at Figure 2. Dr. Tarlton sued Wofford, but a judgment was rendered in the case against him. Dr. Tarlton could have posted a bond and appealed the judgment but failed to file the appeal bond. In 1860, Dr. Tarlton attempted to file the bond, but the Louisiana Supreme Court dismissed his case in *Tarlton v. Wofford* for failing to timely appeal.[15]

St. Landry Plantation

In 1857, the Tarltons looked north to St. Landry Parish to establish a new residence. With the young boys becoming older, they needed to be educated. The nearest school was St. Charles College in Grand Coteau, located in St. Landry Parish. With the assistance of Jane Toulmin Caller, his mother-in-law, Dr. Tarlton purchased 1,400 acres of land in St. Landry Parish from William Hardy for $26,000. Dr. Tarlton made a $6,000 down payment and signed two promissory notes of $10,000, payable to Jane Toulmin Caller, who endorsed the notes to John F. Smith. Jane Toulmin Caller became responsible for the debt to Smith by reason of her endorsement.

Ronald Finch, who conducts research for the Ellis County Museum, in Waxahachie said that, in the 1860s "Dr. Tarlton became outspoken and participated in a public debate regarding *Squatter's Sovereignty*, which was the platform of Democrat presidential candidate Stephen Douglas, that placed the issue of slavery to the citizens of new states."

	1863-1864	
Names	Place of residence	Age
Edmon Mouton	Lafayette	15
Voorhies Arthur	St. Martin	13
Voorhies Charles	"	13
Voorhies William	"	15
Guidry Valerie	"	
Gautier Charles	"	13
Daigle Isidor		
Mouton Alcide	Lafayette	16
Guidry John	Grand Coteau	
Mouton Edward	Lafayette	16
Cauret Octave	Opelousas	14
Broussard Cleophen		
Tertrou Louis	St. Martin	
Fournet Jack		
Fournet Alexander		
Critien Francis		14
Eugine Decuir	new Iberia	
Decuir Adolphe		
Metrot Henry		
Mistrote Leonse		
Latiolais Jacques	Lafayette	
Montagne Ernest	St.	
Thompson Will		
Decuir Alfred		
Broussard Francis	Breaux Bridge	
Broussard	"	
Wiltz Sidney	New Orleans	14
Grevenburg George		
Ducust Laurebt	Ducrest St Martinville	
Thomas Robert	St Crest Martin St. Martinville	
Morse Henry J.		
	1864-1865	
Tarlton Dudly	Austin Jef. Grand Coteau	15
Tarlton Duke	Hillsboro, Texas "	13
Petitin Armand	"	11
Laury Joseph.	"	14
Luary Frank	"	12
Barry Edgar	"	11
Thomas Robert		
Posey William	new Orleans Opelousas	15
Dupre Laurent	"	15
Walet John	St. Martin Coteauelle	15
Gardiner George	Bellview	16
Francis P. Cuevers	Grand Coteau	15
Broussard Joe	"	15
Bernard Edward	Lafayette	14
Riu Paul	"	14
Mouton Paul		15
Dunbar Millard	Grand Coteau	15
Tolidano Christapher	Opelousasm	13
Guidry Ignacious		
Broussard Francis	Breaux Bridge	16
Broussard Aimars	"	14

Figure 5 The 1863-1864 list of students at St. Charles College shows B.D. Tarlton and G.D. Tarlton in attendance. B.D. went by Dudley, and G.D. went by Duke. Toulmin Tarlton's name is not included because in 1863 he left school and joined the Confederacy until the end of the war.

St. Charles College

Founded in 1837, St. Charles College was run by the Jesuits, the Fathers of the Society of Jesus, who came from France and migrated to Louisiana through Kentucky.[16] In 1852, the college began offering degrees, academic honors, and almost year-round schooling and boarding for the boys. Known as a literary institution, the college had a goal to inform the minds and improve the hearts of their pupils. Pupils of every religious denomination were admitted, provided that, with a view to order and uniformity, they are willing to attend the exercises of Catholic worship. The course of instruction included Latin, Greek, English, French, Spanish, Rhetoric, History, Geography, Book-Keeping, Mathematics, Chemistry, and Moral and Natural Philosophy.

The school year consisted of one session, from October 20 to August 20. Total fees included $160 per year for board and tuition, plus $88 for other costs such as washing, medical fees, stationery, entrance, vacation (if spent at the college), music, and drawing. The students wore a black or dark blue frock coat, pantaloons of the same color, and white for summer. The school had thirteen faculty and staff members.

The board of trustees were filled with members of the Society of Jesus. Twice a year the school sent a report to parents stating their child's conduct, progress, rank in class, and examination results conducted twice a year. The Tarltons were not Catholic. This educational experience would be priceless for their boys.

Sacred Heart Academy

Sacred Heart Academy, an all-girl's school located in Grand Coteau, was established in 1821 under the direction of the French Saint Rose Philippine Duchesne, who founded the Society of Sacred Heart in the United States. Duchesne arrived in New Orleans in 1818 and traveled into the area known as St. Charles in the Missouri Territory. From there she established communities and schools on the land formerly owned by France prior to the Louisiana Purchase in 1803.[17] The school was within walking distance of St. Charles College.

FOUR

The Civil War

On January 26, 1861, two months after the election of Abraham Lincoln as president, the Louisiana Legislature voted to secede from the Union. Louisiana sent thousands of Confederate soldiers out of state. In the first year of the conflict 25,000 men enlisted, and through volunteers and conscription, between 50,000 and 60,000 Louisianans served in the Confederate army.[18]

By April 1862, New Orleans had been captured in decisive battles at the *Battle of Fort Jackson and St. Philip* from April 18–28, 1862, and in the *Capture of New Orleans* from April 25 to May 1, 1862. In retreat, the Confederates moved the capital of Louisiana to Opelousas, only ten miles from Grand Coteau. Numerous battles would be fought for the next two years throughout Louisiana.

Dr. Tarlton's eldest son, John Belser Tarlton, his son by his first wife, joined the Confederacy at the beginning of the war. John Belser Tarlton graduated in 1858 from the Louisiana Centenary College and received a commission as a lieutenant. In January 1859, he married Leila de la Houssaye.[19] He would serve until the end of the war.

St. Mary Parish was captured by the Union forces in *The Battle of Fort Bisland* from April 12 to 13, 1963. The Confederate forces abandoned the fort, and Union forces controlled the area until the end of the war.

The Battle of Grand Coteau

During the first months of 1863, General Nathaniel P. Banks prepared to lead 30,000 Union troops into the Teche Country of Southern Louisiana and into the Attakapas District. There they would settle in the fields of Sunset outside of Grand Coteau while taking on minor battles with the Confederates.

Figure 6 Depiction of The Battle of Grand Coteau by Judith Gosse Illustration & Graphic Design.

"Apprehension and uncertainty were the order of the day throughout Louisiana and much of the South," wrote Trent Angers in his book, *Grand Coteau, The Holy Land of South Louisiana.* The nuns at Sacred Heart Academy and the Jesuit priests at nearby St. Charles College in Grand Coteau and the parents at the of the children being cared for in both places had no idea if the institutions would close or be captured by the Union. The nuns were aware that the Academy could be obliterated in a matter of hours and they could starve to death.

Before the Union Army advanced into Louisiana, Mother Amelie Jove, in charge of the Sacred Heart Academy learned that one of the Union generals leading his troops to the South had a daughter at another Sacred Heart school in Manhattanville, New York. She wrote to Mother Aloysia Hardey, the head of the school in Manhattanville, who had been a former student and novice of the Sacred Heart Academy at Grand Coteau. She contacted General Banks' wife, asking her to write to her husband and request that he look after the nuns and students and spare the academy from any harm. Mrs. Banks wrote to her husband making the request and General Banks honored her request.[20]

On May 4, 1863, General Banks issued a protective order preventing an attack on the Sacred Heart school and St. Charles College. His order stated that violators would be punished by death.[21] Not only did he spare the school he provided the nuns with generous amount of food to help them out through the war.

The Battle of Grand Coteau, or the *Battle of Bayou Bourbeaux,* occurred on November 3, 1863, when the people of Grand Coteau heard bugles and drums as 5,000 Union troops marched through the countryside while being attacked by as many as 400 Confederate soldiers who opened fire with cannons and muskets, using guerrilla tactics and snipers, only to disappear into the woods before they could be engaged by the opposition. The Union soldiers retreated in disarray.[22]

The nuns at the Sacred Heart Academy, witnessing the battle from the second floor of the balcony of the academy, spent hours on their knees praying and petitioning the Lord to spare them the destruction of the war. The engagement pitted Brigadier General Thomas Green and Union Brigadier Stephen G. Burbridge against each other.

Confederate Major General Richard Taylor issued orders to Green to attack the Union camp after receiving three infantry regiments on November 2, 1863. The regiments were led by Confederate Colonel Oran M. Roberts, who would later become Texas Governor and Chief Justice of the Texas Supreme Court.

The Union suffered casualties of 26 killed, 124 wounded, and 566 captured or missing. The Confederates admitted a loss of 22 killed and 103 wounded.

Figure 7 Colonel Oran M. Roberts became Texas Governor and Chief Justice of the Texas Supreme Court.

According to William Criss, Ph.D. of Corpus Christi, an appellate attorney, historian, and Secretary of the Texas State Bar Appellate Section, "O.M. Roberts is the most influential Texas politician about whom no book-length biography has ever been published. This is because few modern historians would want to invest the time to catalog the career of a man who was on the wrong side of every issue in Texas politics other than the foundation of the University of Texas. A pro-slavery secessionist who never disavowed his Confederate sympathies, a segregationist, and a foe of populist and progressive reformers at every turn, Roberts compounded his errors by promoting the lost cause view of recent history that romanticized slavery and disunion."

By March 1864, General Nathaniel P. Banks, commander of the occupied areas of Louisiana, summoned a constitutional convention on the orders of President Lincoln. This was an attempt for Louisiana to re-join the Union. Only 19 of the 48 parishes in Louisiana sent delegates. The convention abolished slavery, granted the right to vote to all white males, gave tax money to educate both white and Black children, established a minimum wage, and created a nine-hour workday. It did not act on voting and civil rights for newly freed people.[23] The Louisiana legislature adopted a constitution that ended slavery, but it only eliminated slavery in thirteen parishes controlled by the Union.

On July 2, 1864, Dr. Tarlton and Frances Caller had their tenth child: Fanietta Tarlton, the fifteenth child of Dr. Tarlton. She would marry Wright Chalfont Morrow, who would move to Texas to become law partners with B.D. and G.D. Tarlton in Hillsboro.

During the Civil War, the slaves on the St. Mary's plantation did not leave. In September 1864, Union soldiers entered the Tarlton plantation, and the event was recorded by a newspaper journalist who happened to be on there when the troops arrived and drew a scene of what took place. The drawing was published in the *Frank Leslie's Illustrated Newspaper* on September 10, 1864.[24] The newspaper reported:

SCENE AT TARLETON'S PLANTATION, BAYOU TECHE

Our special Artist depicted the actual scene, which to many will seem a mere caricature of Southern negro life. An old negro with a violin, his master's probably, came into the Union camp, and after redating the cause of his coming, walked away. Shortly afterwards, says our Artist, I found him under a tree, with some of his able brothers around him listening to his performance on the violin, the younger dancing as though such music was too good to be lost and of too salutary a nature to be enjoyed in quiet. But the most comical point of the whole was the presence of two mules, seen in the midst, looking on with an air of quiet drollery perfectly irresistible.

The Tarlton plantation, being on the Bayou Boeuf where the sugar or cotton could be moved to the steamboat on the river and transported. The pictures in Figure 8 showing a steamboat match the current area of the Tarlton plantation along the Bayou Boeuf. Today the Amelie Belle Casino, a riverboat casino, similar to that depicted above is located near Amelie, Louisiana.

During the Civil War and with his sugar plantations no longer operating, Dr. Tarlton could not or chose not to pay the mortgages due on the St. Landry plantation and the additional tract that he purchased from Elizabeth McWaters in St. Mary Parish. Such a decision would come with significant consequences. McWaters was indebted to Dr. Ethan Allen and to Homer Smith for the purchase of her new homestead. She totally depended on Dr. Tarlton to make his payments for the St. Mary's property.

Because Dr. Tarlton couldn't make his mortgage payments, Dr. Allen and Homer Smith began foreclosure proceedings against the St. Mary's property that Dr. Tarlton purchased from McWaters.

Figure 8 Actual scene at the Tarlton plantation in September 1864, prior to the end of the Civil War. By this time slaves were free because the Louisiana Legislature adopted the 13th Amendment prior to it being ratified by the United States.

The St. Landry property was subject to a mortgage to John Hardyman, the administrator of the estate of William Hardy, who sold the St. Landry property to Dr. Tarlton.

The first suit was filed in October 1865 by Dr. Ethan Allen against Dr. Tarlton and Elizabeth McWaters[25] to recover on the notes from McWaters that were endorsed by Dr. Tarlton and to foreclose the mortgage on the St. Mary's property. The case went to trial, and a judgment was entered against McWaters and Dr. Tarlton. The judgment was appealed to the Louisiana Supreme Court in *Allen v. Tarlton*.[26]

Homer Smith filed suit on his debt against McWaters and Dr. Tarlton to enforce his vendor's lien against the property he sold to McWaters and to recover on the notes that McWaters gave to him that were endorsed by Dr. Tarlton. The case of *Smith v. McWaters*[27] went to trial, and a judgment was entered against McWaters and Dr. Tarlton. This judgment was also appealed to the Louisiana Supreme Court.

John Hardyman, Administrator of the Estate of William Hardy, filed suit against Jane Caller and Dr. Tarlton to recover $20,000 for the purchase of the St. Landry property.[28] The attorney handling the suit was John E. King, partner of E.D. Estillette, the State Representative for St. Landry and St. Mary parishes. The litigation went on for two years, and in January 1868, the sheriff posted notice in *The Opelousas Courier* that he would sell Dr. Tarlton's property in St. Landry Parish consisting of 1,400 acres and improvements on February 1, 1868, by a sheriff's sale.[29]

There were at least four other lawsuits filed against Dr. Tarlton seeking the recovery of debts that were due to creditors whose debts were not secured by real estate. Those suits were settled.

FIVE

A Miracle in Grand Coteau

In 1985 Theresa Tarlton, the daughter of Sissy Farenthold, and her cousin Geraldine McGloin were driving to a friend's home in Corpus Christi, Texas. Theresa remembers both of them exiting the car and then walking to someone's home. Behind them was the Corpus Christ Bay with the ocean breeze circulating.

"Did you know that your great-grandfather witnessed a medical miracle?" Geraldine asked.

"Really," said Theresa. "What about that Geraldine?"

"Well, this was in Louisiana in Grand Coteau."

"Wasn't that where Bon Pa went to school?"

"Yes. When he witnessed the miracle, it convinced him, and he became a Catholic, and also the family became Catholic."

"I never knew such a thing. My goodness, I never knew we weren't Catholic. For the longest time I thought we just went back forever, but apparently not," said Theresa.

Geraldine D'Unger McGloin, was the daughter of Gerald Paul D'Unger and Mary Justine Bluntzer. She graduated from Incarnate Word Academy and worked much of her life for United Way in Houston and later as the Director for Incarnate Word in Corpus Christi. She was a member of the Nueces County Historical Society and Corpus Christi Area Heritage Society and worked to preserve the early history of Corpus Christi. She was a regular contributor to the local diocesan paper, the *South Texas Catholic*. Geraldine died in 2013.

"She knew what she was talking about," said Theresa. "She was something else. Our great Aunt Rachel [Hebert] was trained as a historian and a writer and Geraldine learned from her. As a little girl, she would accompany her to the Library of Congress where Aunt Rachel would do research. She knew the genealogy backwards and forwards. So, we really need her, we've missed her so much."

Geraldine did know what she was talking about. It is not every day that an apparition appears to cure the sick. Not many people realize that an approved miracle by the Vatican occurred on December 14, 1866 in Grand Coteau, Louisiana. Mary Wilson, a twenty-year old novice at the Sacred Heart Academy was cured by John Berchmans after numerous prayers and two novenas were performed. A Novena is derived from the Latin word for nine, or "novena" and involves nine days of prayer. She was cured on the last day of the second novena. Berchmans was canonized as a saint in 1888.

The miraculous event occurred when the Tarlton boys, Toulmin, B.D. and G.D. Tarlton were attending the nearby St. Charles College within walking distance of the academy. In 1866, Toulmin Tarlton would have been 19 years old. B.D. Tarlton would have been 17 years old and G.D. Tarlton would have been 14 years old.

The Tarlton boys experienced an excellent Catholic education at St. Charles College, the Civil War, and now they were about to experience something remarkable – a miracle that would change the Tarlton family for generations.

Grand Coteau is the site of Sacred Heart Academy, St. Charles College, and the St. Charles Borromeo Catholic Church (now over 200 years old). The area has been known throughout history as a center for spiritual retreats and Catholic education and is considered to be "ground zero" for Catholicism. The holy ground of Grand Coteau has attracted countless people of deep faith and fervent prayer, including some who have risen to sainthood. Three formally declared saints and two other people en route to sainthood spent time in Grand Coteau or made significant contributions to the community, particularly in education.[30]

Rose Philippine Duchesne brought the Society of the Religious of the Sacred Heart from France to North America in the 1800s. She was canonized in 1988.

Katherine Drexel founded the Sisters of the Blessed Sacrament for Indians and Colored Peoples and donated money to build, repair, or renovate schools for Black children in Grand Coteau. In 2000, Drexel was declared to be a Saint.

Cornelia Connelly was the founder of an order of teaching sisters called the Society of the Holy Child Jesus. She lived at the Academy of the Sacred Heart from 1838 to 1842 and established a new order in Derby, England, serving English and Irish immigrants. She died in 1879 and in 1992 was declared "venerable."

Henriette Delille was the founder of a congregation of teaching sisters called the Sisters of the Holy Family. She was a free woman of color in New Orleans and taught the sons and daughters of slaves in the nineteenth century; her congregation educated the descendants of slaves in Grand Coteau in the twentieth century. She was given the title "Servant of God" by the Catholic Church in 1989 as the church began to study her cause for canonization.

John Berchmans was born on March 13, 1599, in Diest, in the Seventeen Provinces which were the Imperial states of the Habsburg, Netherlands. The son of a shoemaker and the oldest of five children, he was named in honor of St. John the Baptist and was said to have appeared at the Academy of the Sacred Heart in 1866, one year after the Civil War, to heal Mary Wilson, the young novice at the academy, of her illness.

At a young age, Berchmans had only one ambition: to become a priest. He went to confession every week; twice a month, and on the greater feasts, he went to Holy Communion. After Jesus, Mary had the next place in his heart. No one could mention her name in his presence without his face lighting up with a smile; and when he spoke of her, there was an expression in his eye, a sound in his voice, all telling his love.[31]

Figure 9 St. John Berchmans.

In 1615, the Jesuits opened a college at Malines (Mechelen). Berchmans was one of the first to enroll. He wanted to join the Society of Jesus, but his father dissuaded him and sent him to the Franciscan convent in Malines. Berchmans chose the Jesuits and wanted to become a chaplain in the army, hoping to be martyred on the battlefield.[32]

In January 1618, Berchmans made his first vows and began his study of philosophy in Antwerp. After a few weeks, he traveled to Rome on foot and was admitted to the Roman College, where he studied for the next two years. The Roman College was established by St. Ignatius of Loyola in 1551 as a Jesuit College. In his third year, in August 1621, while participating in a study of philosophy at the Greek College administered by the Dominicans, Berchmans was seized by Roman fever succumbed to dysentery. He died on August 13, 1621, at the age of twenty-two.

After he died, a large crowd gathered for several days to view his remains and to invoke his intercession. Phillip-Charles, Duke of Aarschot, the 3rd Count of Arenberg, who ruled the area known as the Spanish Netherlands, sent a petition to Pope Gregory XV to request the process of beatification of Berchmans. Berchman's remains were eventually buried in Sant'Ignazio Church in Rome, which was completed in 1650.

Mary Wilson

Mary Wilson was born in New London, Canada on September 20, 1846, and was raised as a Presbyterian. While on a trip to St. Louis, she became interested in the Catholic Church. She formerly entered the church in

1862 at the age of sixteen when she was accepted as a novice in the Society of the Sacred Heart, despite being in ill health. It was decided that the climate in Louisiana might be better for her so she was sent to the Convent of the Sacred Heart in Grand Coteau.

She arrived at the academy in September 1866. After a month at the academy, Mother Superior Victorine Pizarro Martinez, the superior of the Convent of the Sacred Heart Academy noticed her health becoming worse. She had fever, violent headaches, pain on her side, and would vomit two and three times a day. She could not drink water and had not eaten in days.

Father Felise Benausse, the President of St. Charles College called in Dr. James G. Campbell, a young, twenty-eight-year-old medical doctor to see her. Dr. Campbell attended medical school at the University of Louisiana and served as a surgeon during the Civil War.

What is interesting about Father Benausse's request is that Dr. Campbell was a Protestant physician and St. Charles College already had a staff physician, Dr. Edward Millard, a devout Catholic with thirty years' experience. The request could have been because Dr. Campbell was new to Grand Coteau and the young doctor had offered his assistance to the academy and the college.

Dr. Campbell took out an ad in newspaper on September 22, 1866 about his arrival:

Dr. James G. Campbell

Having removed to Grand Coteau, solicits a share of the public patronage. He will practice in the different branches of Medicine, Surgery and Obstetrics.

Grand Coteau, September 22d, 1866.

Dr. Campbell visited with Mary Wilson for the first time on October 19, 1866. "We were very alarmed," recalled Mother Superior Martinez. Wilson had been hemorrhaging and Dr. Campbell was determined to find where the blood was originating. Dr. Campbell examined her chest to see if the blood had come from her lungs, which was his initial impression. He discovered nothing wrong with her lungs.

"What is your opinion," asked Sister Martinez.

Dr. Campbell decided not to answer. He was not sure and would not give a definitive answer.

The Jesuit priests at St. Charles College suggested praying to St. John Berchmans who had a miracle and needed one more miracle to be declared a saint. The sisters began to dutifully pray for Mary Wilson. The novena would run through October 27, 1866.

On October 20, Dr Campbell went to see Mary again. She had continued to vomit blood during the night. He examined her chest and decided that the blood was coming from her stomach. "A remedy, with the hope of arresting the hemorrhage was given immediately, there was loss of appetite, sometimes fever, with a desire to take nothing at all."

Dr. Campbell returned three days later, on October 23. Her hemorrhaging had continued. He decided to contact Dr. Edward Millard to discuss her case with him.

On October 24, Dr. Campbell saw Wilson again. She had vomited again. Campbell inspected the blood finding it very dark "with the appearance of some gastric fluid." The blood was coming from her stomach.

Mother Superior Martinez said that her spitting of blood was happening daily and that she could only eat very little food. She seemed "to have an unbeatable repugnance for water and rarely drank."

Figure 10 Mother Superior Victorine Pizarro Martinez born in 1815 and died in 1884 at age 69. She is buried at the Cemetery of the Religious of the Sacred Heart in Grand, Coteau, Louisiana.

"It was useless to torture me more," Mary told Dr. Campbell. Wilson was referring to her inability to drink or eat.

Dr. Campbell returned on October 25. He noted that there was no change whatsoever "except that she was gradually growing weaker and now had a disgust for anything in the shape of food or nourishment."

Dr. Campbell had been sick for the past ten days and decided that he needed to leave for Opelousas for treatment. He told the Superior of the Convent that he was "unable in my condition to do justice my patient." Dr. Campbell asked Dr. Millard to take charge of Mary Wilson and he left on his horse for Opelousas for treatment for several days. Dr. Millard took charge of Wilson on October 25, 1866.

Dr. Millard was born in 1815 in Washington, D.C. His parents were Joshua and Ann Manning. He was educated at the Washington Catholic Seminary and Georgetown University where he graduated in 1832. He went to medical school in Baltimore, Maryland. Millard decided to settle in Louisiana. He wrote a letter to his brother, Robert F. Millard of Nacogdoches, Texas, explaining that he wanted "to find a settlement or a location where I may advantageously practice my profession,"

In 1840 he married Ann Eleanor Littell, the daughter of Dr. Moses Littell and Constance Collins Littell. No children were born of the marriage. Dr. Moses and Constance Littell also had a son, Issac F. Littell, who married Mary Eliza Haw. They couple had five daughters, Constance, Sarah Celeste, Suzanne Marie, Mary Eleanor, and Mary E.

Dr. Millard became prominent in St. Landry's Parish. Not only was he a medical doctor in high standing, but he ran for political office in St. Landry Parish and was a member of the constitutional convention of 1870 and a member of the General Assembly in Louisiana. He and his wife were substantial contributors to the St. Charles Borromeo Church in Grand Coteau.

Dr. Tarlton must have known Dr. Millard or known of him. By moving his family from St. Mary's Parish to St. Landry's Parish he could resume his medical practice and he could send all of his boys to St. Charles College in Grand Coteau.

The connection between the Millard and Tarlton families would continue to grow. Toulmin Tarlton and B.D. Tarlton would later court and marry the daughters of Isaac Littell who was the brother of Dr. Millard's wife, Ann Eleanor Littell. B.D. would first marry Suzanne Marie "Susan" Littell and Toulmin would marry Constance Littell. Dr. Millard and his wife were in essence family to the Tarltons.

By October 27 and after the novena, Mary's condition continued to worsen. On November 7, Mary had such a violent attack that the nuns decided that she would receive her final sacrament.

"After that her life became a martyr and no remedies could relieve her," recalled Mother Superior Martinez.

But Mary held on through November and into December.

On December 6, Mother Superior Martinez felt the urge to resort to another intercession of the Blessed John Berchmans.

Mary recalled that "one of our dear Mothers brought me a picture of Blessed Berchmans and said that the community was going to make a novena to Blessed Berchmans."

Sister Kate M. Moran did not have the same feelings about a second novena: "I felt confident its issue would prove as unsuccessful as the many preceding ones."

Nevertheless, the nuns began a second novena to John Berchmans.

The next day, on December 7, Mary felt noticeably better, "but relief was of short duration."

On December 8, the Feast of the Immaculate Conception, was extremely difficult for her: "I was worse that I had ever been before. All hopes of getting better abandoned me," she said.

On Sunday, December 9, Father Benausse administered the Indulgence in Articulo Mortis, a "plenary indulgence" that can be performed by a priest when someone is at a point of death. The condition is that they have been in the habit of reciting some prayers during their lifetime. Dr. Millard was with him and prescribed a teaspoon of almond oil, but it gave her nausea and increased her pain.

"The doctor then told us not to seek similar attempts stating it will more likely increase her suffering and that her martyr will not last more than 3 days. To give us some consolation, he even told me that the violent pain will stop completely some time before her death and that her last moments will be calm," wrote Mother Superior Martinez.

On Monday, December 10 Mary felt that she was getting weaker, "and my sufferings were so intolerable that it seemed to me that it was impossible to bear them long."

On Tuesday, December 11, Father Serran gave her the last plenary indulgence.

Sister Moran spent an hour with Mary and recalled that: "on that day her sufferings were great, her half-opened mouth disclosed a mass of clotted blood which omitted a most disagreeable odor; attempting to swallow a potion presented by the nurse her pains became so violent that I thought her last moment had arrived. Her hands and feet were cramped and cold though she had a burning fever,"

Mother Superior Martinez said that prayers for the dying were repeated many times and "we all believed that our dear patient would be taking her last breath. Her limbs were cold and the cramps in her feet and hands were not giving her any rest,"

On Wednesday, December 12, Mary was suffering from her head and blisters. Her mouth was continuously dripping blood, emitting a foul smell, coagulating, and drying on her teeth and tong. Sister Moran visited her and saw that "her eyes were still closed and lids, much inflamed, the pallor of death over the rest of her features. I hourly expected to hear of her demise, and that same day begged and obtained permission to assist at her death."

Father Benausse and Dr. Millard went to see her. Father Benausse found her "very bad. She did not speak" but Dr. Millard assured that she was still conscious but decided that it would be "almost inhuman to force the further administration of medicine, food or drink, and ordered nothing to be given to her, except as her own demand."

Father Benausse gave her absolution "because judging by the patient's pulse, she could live for another two or three days but would certainly die soon." Mother Superior Martinez thought this would be her last absolution.

Even in her condition, later that evening, Mary shared with the sisters a feeling of happiness to be dying at the Sacred Heart Academy. She had difficulty making herself understood due to the condition of her mouth. Her voice was so weak that the simplest movement to swallow gave her excruciating pain.

The most difficult day for Mary was Thursday, December 13. She said that she suffered more without dying and she had not had any water for twenty-four hours.

After finishing the Convent for Confessions of the people of the community, Father Benausse went to see Mary. He observed her "without speech and with her eyes closed, she was conscious, she only responded to my short exhortations with a slight nod and I gave her absolution again." That night the sisters watching over her did not believe she would see another day. She had all the symptoms of coming to death and freezing cold was numbing her limbs.

On Friday, December 14, the last day of the novena, Sister Martinez went into her room at 6 am in the morning to see if Mary could say her communion one last time. Father Serran arrived to give her a part of the Viatique, the Eucharist. Sister Martinez gave her a teaspoon of water, but it caused her much pain. Mother Superior left and went to the chapel to receive Holy Communion.

Mary thought that she was near death: "I, as well as the good Father and all the community, thought this was for the last time, for death seemed assuredly near at hand. The Father said a few words to encourage me, saying that very soon I would enter upon the long voyage of eternity."

Mary said that she "endured the pangs of death. My body was drawn up with pain; my hands and feet were cramped and as cold as death. All my sickness had turned to inflammation of the stomach and throat. My tongue was raw and swollen. I was not able to speak for two days. At each attempt to utter a word, the blood would gush from my mouth."

"Being unable to speak, I said in my heart: 'Lord, Thou Who seest how I suffer, if it be for your honor and glory and the salvation of my soul, I ask through the intercession of Blessed Berchmans a little relief and health. Otherwise give me patience to the end. I am resigned.'"

"Then, placing the image of Blessed John Berchmans on my mouth, I said: If it be true that you can work miracles, I wish you would do something for me. If not, I will not believe in you."

Mary heard a voice whisper: "Open your mouth."

"I did so as well as I could. I felt someone, as if put their finger on my tongue, and immediately I was relieved. I then heard a voice say in a distinct and loud tone: "Sister, you will get the desired habit. Be faithful. Have confidence. Fear not.'"

"I had not yet opened my eyes. I did not know who was at my bedside."

Then, standing by her bedside, she saw a figure. "He held in his hands a cup, and there were some lights near him. At this beautiful sight I was afraid. I closed my eyes and asked: 'Is it Blessed Berchmans?'"

He answered: "'Yes, I come by the order of God. Your sufferings are over. Fear not!'"

"I opened my eyes, but he was gone."

She turned round and said aloud, "But, Mother Moran, I am well!"

She sat up in her bed. "I felt no pain. I was afraid it was an illusion and that my cure was not real. I turned over in my bed without pain. I then exclaimed: "It is true. Blessed Berchmans has cured me."

"My flesh and strength returned instantaneously. I was able to follow all the exercises of community life from that moment. So that, after two months of cruel suffering and great attenuation of bodily strength from the want of food, I was in an instant restored to perfect health without a moment's convalescence and could eat of everything indiscriminately, I who for thirty-eight days previous could not support a drop of water."

Figure 11 Depiction of John Berchmans appearing before Mary Wilson. Drawing by Judith Gosse Illustration & Graphic Design.

At 7:45 am, Mother Superior Martinez returned to the infirmary and made her art of thanksgiving before a small alter in the infirmary. She went to see Mary "and to my surprise or even more stupefaction, I saw this dear child that I just left dying about one hour ago, reached out and said: My brother, if I feel good, I can get up. That surprised me, especially after having seen her difficulty to have had to move her tongue during the Holy Sacrament."

Martinez would not let Mary get up out of the bed. She called for her other sisters (10 sisters) who had asked as a favor to pay her a last visit to come share in the joy caused by her sudden improvement. To leave any doubts about her recovery, Mary asked for a drink and drank without any pain.

"We were astonished," recalls Mother Superior Martinez.

Sister Moran went to see her and "the cure had already taken place, her eyes were bright and her voice, strong."

At 8:30 am Dr. Millard came in and was very surprised to see Mary free from all of her pain. Mary greeted Dr. Millard at the door.

"He was so overcome that he almost fainted," Mary recalls.

"Have you eaten anything?" Dr. Millard inquired.

After examining her Dr. Millard said to her: "Miss, if you are healed, it is not because of me or the medications, but from the power of God."

Dr. Millard then told her about the miracle of Ann Mattingly who was cured of cancer in 1824 hours before her predicted demise.

"The visits to the infirmary did not stop and 30 people from our community were delighted to come see for themselves what our Lord had done for our dear sister. They congratulated her for the prodigious and instant change that had just happened. The day was filled with joys and gratitude," wrote Sister Martinez.

That evening Mother Superior Martinez allowed Mary to get out of her bed while her bed was made. She was fine that evening and sat by the fire and mingled with the nurses.

The next morning, Mary had breakfast like someone in perfect health.

Mother Superior Martinez went to tell Father Benausse of the cure and that it had arrived the day before, Friday after Holy Communion.

He went to see her later that evening around eight o'clock and found her in bed laughing, conversing with ease and showing no sign of illness."

"Who has cured you so?" asked Father Benausse.

"Blessed Berchmans," She said showing him the Blessed image.

"Have you been cured gradually or suddenly?"

"On a sudden, immediately after Communion," she answered.

Upon leaving the infirmary, Father Benausse told Sister Martinez, "she is cured, you have to note that fact. The good Lord has listened to your prayers."

Mary was allowed to leave the infirmary and she rushed to the chapel where she bowed down in front of the Holy Sacrament and surrounded by the community, to give thanks to the heart of Jesus who had led and glorified the Blessed John Berchmans. Martinez wrote in an affidavit said that "in soliciting this recovery, the novena had asked for that miracle to accelerate his canonization."

On Sunday, December 16, Mary heard the Holy Mass in the chapel and Father Benausse gave her Communion. After lunch he saw her for a moment and asked her if she felt as well as if she had never been sick.

Mary answered, "yes, rather better."

Word of the miracle quickly circulated among the Jesuit priests at St. Charles College.

Eleven attestations were prepared by witnesses to the event that were submitted to the Vatican. Attesting to the miracle were Father Benausse, Sister Mary E. Moran, Sister Victoria Martinez, Father Francois M. Nachon, Sister Claire Fleury, Sister Kate M. Moran, Pulcherie Poursine (Novice), Brigette Breaux (Novice), Dr. Campbell and Dr. Millard. Most of the affidavits were written in French.

Dr. Millard wrote in his attestation to the Vatican:

> Not being able to discover any marks of convalescence, but an immediate return to health from a most severe and painful illness, I am unable to explain the transition by any ordinary natural laws.[33]

On January 21, 1867, Dr. Campbell visited Mary and reported in his affidavit that "she was looking very well about and strong and expressed herself better than she had been for years."

On February 22, 1867, Father Benausse submitted his affidavit reporting his observations to the Archbishop of New Orleans. He noted that Dr. Millard had declared several times that he had never seen anything like this in his life and he knew of no natural way to explain this sudden change from a state of very serious illness to a state of perfect health.

Figure 12 Shrine of St. John Berchmans in Grand Coteau, Louisiana, at Sacred Heart Academy.

About one month after her healing, Berchmans appeared to Mary again assuring her that he was pleased with her testimony. The Jesuit revealed to Mary that she would die before the end of her noviceship, and he encouraged her to observe the rule of the Society faithfully.

Mary Wilson died on August 17, 1867 at the age of twenty and was buried in the Cemetery of the Religious of the Sacred Heart in Grand Coteau, Louisiana.

Figure 13 Grave of Mary Wilson (1846 – 1867) in Grand Coteau at the Cemetery of the Religious of the Sacred Heart.

"The Account of the Cure of Miss Mary Wilson," included the thirteen attestations of the fathers, doctors, nurses, and other witnesses. The Archibishop's court approved the attestations, and the conclusions were sent to Rome. On January 15, 1888, Pope Leo XIII canonized John Berchmans, to the Vatican, and the miracle of Grand Coteau being accepted as authentic.

The *Miracle of Grand Coteau* had been passed down among the Tarlton family lines for over 100 years, particularly in the family line of Dr. Toulmin Tarlton, who became a medical doctor like his father, Dr. John Tarlton.

In December 1966 a centennial of the authenticated miracle was held in Grand Coteau. A mass conducted by Bishop Maurice Schexnayder and other Jesuit priests from the St. Charles College included John Louis Olivier, the grandson of Dr. Toulmin Tarlton. John Louis Olivier was the mayor of Grand Coteau and was at one point the longest-serving mayor in the United States. His father was Frank Olivier who married Mary Tarlton Olivier, one of the five children of Dr. Toulmin Tarlton. He was therefore the great-grandson of Dr. John Tarlton.

The event *"Centennial of Miracle in Louisiana Observed,"* was reported in the December 23, 1966 edition of *The Voice*, a publication of the Diocese of Miami covering 16 counties in South Florida. The article concluded with this paragraph:

> Also taking part in the centennial Mass, as the lay reader of the Epistle, was Mayor John Olivier's grandfather, Dr. Toulmin Tarlton, was one of the two doctors who attended Miss Wilson. After Miss Wilson's cure, Dr. Tarlton, an Episcopalian, became a Catholic.

The article was in error. Dr. Toulmin Tarlton was the first- born son of Dr. John Tarlton. He was a 19- year- old student at St. Charles College the time of the miracle in 1866. He followed his father's footsteps and became a medical doctor. The reference above could have only been a reference to Dr. John Tarlton. Along the way the legend becomes confused and Dr. Toulmin Tarlton's name becomes substituted with that of his father, Dr. John Tarlton.

This led to the next question: Did John Tarlton attend to Mary Wilson? Caroline Richard with the Academy of Sacred Heart in Grand Coteau researched whether Dr. Tarlton submitted an affidavit authenticating the cure of Mary Wilson to the Vatican, but she found none.

"Dr. Campbell appears to be the doctor who attended to Mary Wilson before Dr. Millard took over. I do not know whether he was Catholic or not. I'm sorry we don't seem to have anything from Dr. Tarlton," Richard said.

Dr. John Tarlton, being the medical partner of Dr. Edward Millard would have known of the condition of a patient of Dr. Millard, He might have examined her, consulted with Dr. Millard, and collaborated over her care. Dr. Campbell noted that in his affidavit where he wrote that "remedies were agreed upon." Dr. Campbell was most likely in consultation with Dr. Millard from the beginning of his treatment of Mary Wilson. Dr. Millard would likewise be in consultation with Dr. Tarlton.

The Tarlton boys attending St. Charles College would have heard of the condition of Mary Wilson. The Jesuit priests at St. Charles College learned of her condition, suggested the novena to John Berchmans who needed another miracle cure for canonization, and would have suggested prayers for her. One of the priests recorded in a diary in Latin in 1866 of the apparition of John Berchmans.

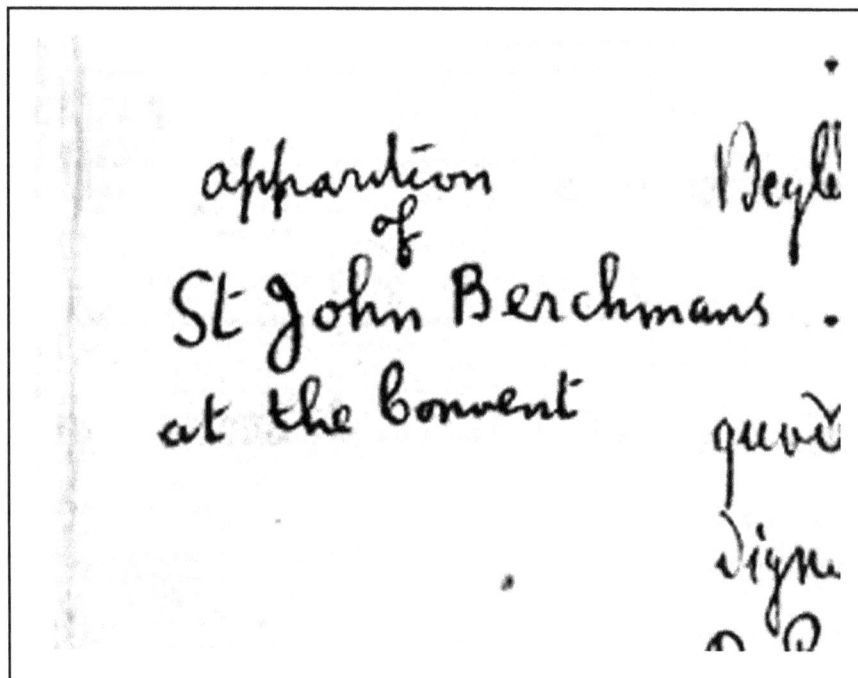

Figure 14 Notes written in English in the margin of a jounral in Latin regarding the apparition of John Berchmans in 1866. John Berchmans was declared a saint in 1888.

The Tarlton boys, like the other boys in the college, could have prayed for her recovery. The boys would not graduate for another three years and would have three years to ponder on the miracle that they lived through. Both Toulmin and B.D. Tarlton became Catholic and practiced their Catholicism their entire life.

Sissy Farenthold knew of the miracle story. "The family were Episcopalian. B.D. was the convert. His Catholicism was genuine. It was only later that I got details of the miracle," Sissy said in January 2021.[34]

SIX

After the Civil War

Graduation from St. Charles College

ON JULY 16, 1869, B.D. passed his final examination at St. Charles College. His older brother, Toulmin Tarlton, passed his final examinations the next day, on July 17, 1869. Toulmin was two years older than B.D. but was set back because in 1863 he left St. Charles College to serve in the Confederacy until the end of the Civil War.

Each August, St. Charles College school had its Annual Commencement Exercise, which included music by the college band and orchestra and a three-act comedy play performed by the students. After the play, the Distribution of Premiums and *Belles Lettres* were awarded to the students for Good Conduct. A *Belles Lettres* is a French phrase meaning "beautiful" or "fine" and the presentation was for fine writing. After graduation, Toulmin Tarlton followed his father's footsteps to become a medical doctor and left for medical school in Mobile, Alabama B.D. left for law school in New Orleans.

University of Louisiana Law School

In 1869, B.D. began law school at the University of Louisiana (now Tulane University). He "seriously contemplated joining the religious order of the Roman Catholic church and devoting his life to the service of his church and Master; but a domestic incident turned the current of his life, without, however, changing the fervor of his spiritual life and his religious duty as he saw it," said Professor W.S. Simkins, a colleague at the University of Texas Law Department.[35] None of the Tarlton descendants today know what the professor was referring to with regard to the "domestic incident."

During law school, B.D. supported himself by teaching Latin and Greek at the Jesuit High School in New Orleans. One of the most famous students to attend the high school was Edward Douglass White, who had graduated from the school in 1865 and went on to become the ninth Chief Justice of the United States Supreme Court.

While B.D. may have been insulated from his parent's litigation while attending St. Charles College, this was not the case while in law school. The cases of *Allen v. Tarlton*[36] and *Smith v. McWaters*[37] were issued in June 1870 after B.D. had completed his first year in law school. He had to have known about the opinions, studied them, and looked for ways to help his father.

B.D.'s interest in real estate law, title disputes, boundary disputes, trial, and appellate litigation matched the type of law that his parents struggled through to save their plantations. B.D.'s interest in the law, particularly real estate law, could have been out of a sense of necessity to help his parents survive. He had no idea what else was in store for his father, a medical doctor who seemed to attract litigious real estate disputes into his life and would pave the way to resolve unique issues of law in the appellate courts in Louisiana and Texas.

Litigation Continues

In April 1868, the sheriff of St. Landry Parish sold Dr. Tarlton's St. Landry property (that had been purchased for $26,000 ten years earlier) for $7,000 at an execution sale.

On January 5, 1869, the property in St. Mary Parish purchased from Elizabeth McWilliams in 1857 for $75,000 was sold for $21,050. The original Tarlton property in St. Mary Parish, purchased from William C.C.C. Martin, and the Dr. R.B. McKay property were still secure, but there was more to come.

In November 1869, Elizabeth McWilliams filed suit to recover $3,300 that Dr. Tarlton owed based on one of the promissory notes for the purchase of her property in St. Mary Parish.[38] Dr. Tarlton admitted that he owed the debt, and judgment was entered for $4,000 plus interest on November 20, 1869.

Caller v. Tarlton

B.D. Tarlton had no idea how serious the litigation would become or that it would extend into his own family, involving a claim between husband and wife. The issue involved the validity of his release of his mother's dowry in the St. Mary property purchased from Elizabeth McWaters. Dr. Tarlton released his wife's dowry claim to the property as part of the acquisition of the property from McWaters. Recall that B.D.'s mother, Frances Caller, invested $7,400 of her dowry in 1848 to acquire the St. Mary property. A dowry is a sum of money or property brought into the marriage by the bride.

In *Cause No. 6642. McWilliams v. Dr. John Tarlton*, McWilliams alleged that Dr. Tarlton had renounced his wife's rights, claims and privileges in the property during the purchase. This meant that Francis Caller Tarlton's dowry rights had to be re-established as a lien on the property. To do that, Frances Caller Tarlton would have to sue her own husband, Dr. Tarlton, to establish a lien that would date back to 1848 when her dowry claim was established.

Francis Caller Tarlton filed suit against Dr. Tarlton in *Cause No. 12004, Francis Ann Caller v. John Tarlton* in St. Mary Parish to establish a dowry lien on the property that McWilliams was attempting to sell by her foreclosure of her vendor's lien. This suit appears to have been a legal strategy thought up by the attorneys for the Tarltons and perhaps Jane Toulmin Caller, the mother of Francis Ann Caller and mother-in-law of Dr. Tarlton.

The pleadings of the suit say that on December 14, 1869, Francis Caller sent Dr. Tarlton a demand letter to him requesting he pay her the $7,400 he owed her. The suit was filed as "Jane M. Caller"—clearly a mistake.[39] But the mistake shows that it was likely Jane Toulmin Caller who was leading this effort and met with the attorneys to have a suit filed in her daughter's name to establish a lien that would be prior in time to the lien of McWilliams. The attorneys prepared the suit and confused the two names. An amended pleading was filed that read: "Plaintiff in the above cause moves to amend her petition & alleges that the name of the plaintiff in this cause is not Jane H. Caller but Francis Ann Caller. The mistake was made by her attorney. She prays for costs and general relief."

The final judgment granted on July 16, 1870, in the amount of $7,400 with interest, granted a tacit mortgage on all the immovable property held and owned by Dr. Tarlton dating back to 1848, the date of the marriage between Dr. Tarlton and Frances Caller. Judge John E. King, 8th Judicial District of Louisiana, read the judgment on May 7, 1870.[40] Mrs. Francis Tarlton went on the offensive and filed suit, *Cause No. 6767, Mrs. Francis Caller, Wife v. Mrs. Elizabeth McWalters, Wife et al* against Elizabeth McWilliams for $1,000 in damages for seizing the St. Mary property, which she alleged was subject to her dowry and not subject to seizure by McWilliams.[41]

Allen v. Tarlton

In June 1870, the Supreme Court of Louisiana ruled in the case of *Allen v. Tarlton*[42] and affirmed in part the judgment against Dr. Tarlton and Elizabeth McWaters taken by Dr. Ethan Allen. Dr. Tarlton tried to prevent the foreclosure sale of the property by contending that he could not be sued in St. Mary Parish since he did not reside in that county, even though he appeared at the trial. The Louisiana Supreme Court disagreed:

> The position taken by John Tarlton to escape judgment *in rem*, is ingenious but not sound. His exception of domicile was not passed on prior to trial on the merits. It was considered only in the judgment on the merits. He was present and gave evidence at the trial, and it would be strange if the judge could not render executory the mortgage granted by him, on account of the exception of domicile which saved him from the consequences of a personal judgment also.

Smith v. McWaters

In June 1870, the Louisiana Supreme Court also issued its opinion in *Smith v. McWaters* and found that Arpha M. Smith, the widow of S. Smith, deceased, was entitled to judgment against the McWaters property for her indebtedness and with recognition of a mortgage upon the land purchased from him to secure the payment for $872.32 plus interest of eight percent. Recall that McWaters had conveyed the property to Dr. Tarlton, who was obligated on the debt

The court recited the factual background and found that Dr. Tarlton bought the plantation and twenty-six slaves from Mrs. Elizabeth McWaters at the price of $75,000, which was paid in $10,000 cash and the assumption of the outstanding liabilities of $40,000 and the execution of four promissory notes that were payable during the years 1858 through 1861. These notes were one for $5,000 and three others for $6666.66 with interest. Mrs. McWaters then purchased her own plantation from Homer Smith and endorsed the notes of Tarlton and one note of her own for $872.32. She subrogated Smith to her rights in the Tarlton notes.

Dr. Tarlton pled that the notes due in 1859 and 1860 were barred by the statute of limitations because the suit was filed in October 1865. The court agreed and found that the notes and accessory right of mortgage to be extinguished. The court found the note due in 1861 to be valid and that the plaintiff was entitled to judgment against McWaters for her individual note of $872.32 and the recognition of her mortgage on the land. The court however found that Dr. Tarlton's notes were given for both land and slaves and that:

> ...the payment of the one not prescribed can only be enforced to the extent to which the land mortgaged formed its consideration. We find no evidence in the record that enables us to fix the relative value of the land and slaves mortgaged and must therefore refer the case to the lower court for further proceedings for that purpose.

The high court affirmed the judgment against McWaters and remanded the case:

...with instructions to ascertain, by competent evidence, the relative value of the land and slaves sold by the defendant, Mrs. Elizabeth McWaters to John Tarlton, and mortgaged by him to the vendor by act before the aforesaid notary on the sixteenth of June, A. D. 1857, and to fix, ratably, the deduction to be made from the amount of the note herein before referred to as executed by said Tarlton, and which became due on the first of January 1861.

By September 1870, life for Dr. Tarlton must have been intense while facing the serious obligations due. In that month he penned a letter to *The Opelousas Courier* where he complained to the editor of the newspaper of its approval of the 15th Amendment to the United States Constitution. The 15th Amendment was the right to vote and was the last of the three civil rights amendments adopted after the Civil War. Dr. Tarlton wrote that, "I will have nothing to do with the foul thing—it is an unconstitutional fraud and lie, forced upon the country by corruption and the bayonet." He wanted the 1876 constitution of Louisiana restored. He believed that it was a "White Man's Government," of "Free Trade" and "Sovereignty of the States." Dr. Tarlton's rant to *The Opelousas Courier* in 1870 was unfortunate and does not represent the Tarlton legacy. Thus if Dr. John Tarlton had converted to Catholicism, his beliefs on slavery were incongruent with Catholicism that condemned slavery in 1839 by Pope Gregory XVI.

"You can't change the past," said George Farenthold, great-great grandson of Dr. Tarlton and second son of Sissy Farenthold. Like Sissy Farenthold and the other descendants of Dr. Tarlton, he was not aware of the 151-year-old letter to the editor, nor of any details of Dr. Tarlton until the research was conducted for this book. George Farenthold attended the University of Texas in the early 1970s and often campaigned for his mother and others on campus. What he remembers was an admonition engraved in stone, a quote from Jesus Christ as told by John 8:32, on the exterior wall of the undergraduate library next to the University of Texas Student Union building: "Ye Shall Know The Truth And The Truth Shall Set You Free."

"What we know for certain is that many of our relatives of this period failed the test of history and allegiance to the Constitution, let alone to the

Declaration of Independence that all men (sic) are created equal..." he said in July 2021.

McWilliams v. Tarlton

In February 1871, *in Cause No. 6706, Elizabeth McWilliams v. Dr. John Tarlton,* Elizabeth McWilliams filed a second lawsuit against Dr. John Tarlton to recover $5,000 and for the promissory notes in excess of $6,666 for sale of the "upper half measuring one mile" from the Bayou.[43]

One year later, in February 1872, the court issued a writ of execution to seize the St. Mary property to pay for the judgment of $3,300 plus interest. The sheriff advertised the property for sale on Saturday, April 1, 1872, but Dr. Tarlton secured an injunction to stop the sale.

Sometime in 1872, the Tarltons relocated to the St. Mary plantation because in April of that year, The *St. Landry Democrat* reported that Dr. Tarlton attended a meeting in Opelousas to secure delegates for the Democratic convention to be held that same month. The paper reported that Dr. Tarlton and others who were delegates were not residents of St. Landry parish.[44]

Graduation from Law School

In 1872, B.D. graduated with a Bachelor of Laws from the University of Louisiana. Louisiana law permitted B.D. to begin practicing law immediately because he had graduated from the University of Louisiana.[45] In that same year, St. Charles College conferred an honorary LLD degree on him. After graduation, B.D. studied law briefly under George Hudspeth, who was the District Attorney, Eighth Judicial District, in Opelousas, St. Landry Parish.

1872 Gubernatorial election

The November 1872 Louisiana gubernatorial election was the second election to take place since Louisiana adopted its Constitution in 1868.

Republican William Pitt Kellogg would face Democrat John McErnery in the race for Governor.

Kellogg grew up in Vermont and moved to Illinois when he was eighteen to become a schoolteacher. In Illinois he read law to become an attorney and began to practice law. He met Abraham Lincoln, who was a fellow lawyer, in Illinois. When Lincoln became president, he appointed Kellogg as the Chief Justice of the Supreme Court of the Nebraska Territory. Kellogg served in the Civil War in the 7th Regiment Illinois Volunteer Cavalry. By 1862 he had risen to the rank of colonel and served in a battle near Sikeston, Missouri. Kellogg resigned due to ill health in June 1862 and resumed his work as Chief Justice.

In 1865, near the end of the Civil War, Lincoln appointed Kellogg as a federal collector of customs for the port of New Orleans. In 1868, he was elected to the United States Senate from Louisiana, the same year that Louisiana was readmitted to the federal Union.[46] Kellogg was clearly trusted by Lincoln, and President Ulysses S. Grant also supported Kellogg's run for governor. But in Louisiana he was viewed by Democrats as a carpetbagger and his election was perceived as illegitimate.

John McEnery was a Louisiana Democratic politician and lawyer who served as a Lieutenant Colonel in the Confederate States Army. He was supported by a coalition of Democrats and anti-Grant Republicans, including Louisiana's sitting Governor, Henry Clay Warmoth, a Republican who supported McEnery and opposed the Republican Party faction loyal to President Grant.[47]

Kellogg was elected Governor of Louisiana, receiving 72,890 votes to 55,249 votes, or 56.88 percent of the vote, compared to Democrat John McEnery, who received 55,249 votes or 43.12 percent of the vote. The advantage of the Republican candidate was because the end of slavery made way for Black voters being eligible to vote. But McEnery disputed the election results. Both candidates claimed victory, and both held inaugural parties. McEnery claimed to be the 25th Govenor of Louisiana and began his service on January 13, 1873.

Louisiana Governor Henry Warmoth appointed a State Returning Board, which administered elections. A rival board endorsed Kellogg.

Violence ensued throughout Louisiana during 1873 over the disputed election and the taxes imposed by the Kellogg government which were considered to be illegal. Many attorneys in St. Landry Parish offered pro bono services to citizens to help fight what was considered to be illegal taxes.

At the beginning of the book *Gone With The Wind*, Margaret Mitchell includes a fictional scene of two twin brothers vying for the hand of Scarlett O'Hara. Mitchell named the twins Brent and Stuart Tarleton (spelled with an "e"). In real life, two Tarlton brothers, B.D. Tarlton and his older brother Toulmin Tarlton, began calling on the daughters of Isaac F. Littell[48] and Mary Eliza Haw,[49] who lived in Grand Coteau.

Isaac Littell was a planter in Grand Coteau and served as a state representative to the Lower House of the Louisiana Legislature from St. Landry Parish.[50] He and his wife Mary had five children. B.D. was interested in Susan Marie Littell, and Toulmin was interested in Constance Tarlton, the oldest daughter of the Littells. Isaac's sister was Mrs. Ann Eleanor Littell Millard, the wife of Dr. Edward Millard, who attended to Mary Wilson.

B.D.'s decision to practice law in Grand Coteau could have been influenced by his pursuit of Susan Littell, and because he liked living in Grand Coteau where he could practice law. He formed a law partnership with attorney John F. Smith, forming the firm of Smith & Tarlton. Their partnership began while the controversy over the Kellogg – McEnery governor's race was about to boil over.

On April 12, 1873, a meeting was called in St. Landry Parish. At that meeting Dr. John Tarlton was elected president and explained that the purpose of the meeting was to discuss resolutions challenging the taxes being imposed by the Kellogg government[51] which he considered illegal.

The meeting adopted resolutions that regarded "William Pitt Kellogg as an usurper with no right or title whatever to the office of Governor of this State…That we will not voluntarily give any aid and countenance to this illegal government, by the payment of any license or tax to its collectors; but we deem it the duty of the people of Louisiana and of our Parish to form an association of tax-payers to resist, by every legal means in their power, the collection of all taxes and licenses, they being levied without authority, and, to a great extent, for the purposes of a fraudulent, corrupt and illegal character."[52]

The next day, Easter Sunday April 13, 1873, in Colfax, Louisiana, in Grant Parish, a group of white Democrats armed with rifles and a cannon overpowered Republican freedmen and state militia (also Black) occupying the Grant Parish courthouse in Colfax.[53] This was the Colfax Massacre or Colfax riot.[54] Most of the freedmen (former slaves) were killed after surrendering; nearly 50 were killed later that night after being held as prisoners for several hours. Estimates of the number of dead ranged from 62 to 153; three white people died, but the number of Black victims was difficult to determine because many bodies were thrown into the Red River or removed for burial, possibly at mass graves. It was said to be the worst instance of racial violence during Reconstruction.[55]

On April 28, 1873, at the St. Landry courthouse in Opelousas, Dr. Tarlton, B.D. Tarlton, John Smith and State Representative E.D. Estilette spoke at an event, contending that the taxes imposed by the Louisiana government were unjust and illegal.[56]

Nine attorneys, including B.D. and Estillette, signed a letter to *The Opelousas Courier* offering free legal services to the taxpayers:

To Tax Resisters

In view of the grievous burdens of taxation illegally and unjustly imposed upon the people and the inability of a large majority of the taxpayers to procure legal advice, we the undersigned, members of the Bar at Opelousas, deeming it our duty as good citizens to come to their relief as far as practicable, do hereby tender our legal services, without compensation, to all taxpayers who may desire to resist the payment of taxes and licenses.[57]

Figure 15 B.D. Tarlton speaking about the perceived illegal taxes being collected by the Kellogg government at the courthouse steps in St. Landry Parish.

The Settlement

On October 23, 1873, Dr. Tarlton and Mrs. Tarlton settled all litigation with Elizabeth McWaters. Dr. Tarlton, on his own behalf and using a power of attorney for his wife, Frances Caller Tarlton, and as attorney in fact for B.D. Tarlton, transferred the title to 560 arpents of the St. Mary property to McWilliams, settling all their litigation. The suit filed in *Cause No. 6767 Frances Caller v. Elizabeth McWilliams* was settled for $500. McWilliams agreed to pay $82.50 to Dr. Tarlton for taxes against the property. B.D. renounced and abandoned his claim to the property from the purchase of the property at a tax sale.[58]

By 1873, the Tarltons lost their St. Landry property and part of their properties in St. Mary Parish. Without credit, the only mechanism to pay the debts was to convey the land back to McWilliams. There were no bankruptcy laws in effect in 1873 to assist the Tarltons. The Bankruptcy Act of 1898 was twenty-five years away. Today's Bankruptcy Code, under Title 11 of the United States Code enacted in 1978, would have been a perfect solution for Dr. Tarlton to stay the litigation against him and to provide a reorganization of debts by payment over a time pursuant to a plan of reorganization.

In December 1873, Dr. Tarlton and most of the Tarlton family made plans to leave Louisiana and head for Texas. They found a ten- acre tract for sale in the downtown Waxahachie area for sale. Louisiana was too violent and unstable after the Civil War. Dr. Tarlton left his oldest son, John B. Tarlton, in charge of the remaining property in St. Mary Parish.

G.D. Tarlton moved to Austin, Texas where he found a position with the Institute for the Deaf and Dumb. G.D. graduated in 1870 from Louisiana State University and received accolades as one of the most successful students in all the branches, earning a certificate in Latin, Greek, moral philosophy, engineering, and German.[59]

Dr. Toulmin Tarlton, who graduated from the Alabama Medical College in Mobile in 1871, set up a medical practice in St. Mary Parish but decided to close the practice and move to Texas with the family.

B.D. had no plans to leave Louisiana. He was establishing his law practice. In February 1874, the law firm of Smith & Tarlton took out an advertisement in the newspaper that read:

> LAW ASSOCIATION. The UNDER-signed having entered into an association for the practice of law, under the style of Smith & Tarlton, will practice law in the parish of St. Landry and neighboring parishes. Prompt and strict attention will be given to all business confided to them. Office at Grand Coteau.[60]

Race for Louisiana Legislature

For B.D. Tarlton to run for the state legislature he would have to become involved in local politics. This goes hand in hand with establishing a career as an attorney. But he would face a significant opponent: E.D. Estillette, the incumbent Democrat state representative for St. Landry Parish.

Estillette attended St. Charles College for six years and graduated from Yale College in 1857. He was admitted to the Louisiana bar in 1860. In 1865, he was appointed District Attorney of the Eighth Judicial District and served until 1868.[61] Estillette's law partner was John King, the same attorney who filed suit against B.D.'s parents to foreclose the mortgage on the St. Landry property. King represented the Estate of Hardyman in the case of *Hardyman v. Jane Caller and Dr. Tarlton*.[62]

The only way B.D. stood a chance to be elected would be to combine forces with other factions in the Democratic party to attract as many Democratic votes as possible. This meant combining with the Conservative and White League factions of the party.

In August 1874, B.D. Tarlton was one of thirty delegates nominated to serve as a delegate to the Democratic Convention as part of the "White League Club" in St. Landry's Parish. These groups were organizing across Louisiana seeking political clout in the Democratic party and to acquire delegate status at the Democratic convention. *The Opelousas Courier* reported that the term "White League" was meant "to offset the Black

Leagues,"[63] meaning to attract white voters to the Democratic party because the Republicans had an election advantage with freed slaves eligible to vote. This was shown in the Kellogg election to governor, where Kellogg had more than 17,000 more votes than McEnery.

The White League included many prominent attorneys and members of the public. B.D. was not alone; State Representative Isaac Littell, his future father-in-law, and E.D. Estillette, who would become Speaker of the Louisiana House, were named delegates from the White League.

B.D., Littell, Estillette, and others named as delegates were operating transparently and were interested in lawful political activity. Unfortunately, the Democratic party at that time included radical elements of the White League, former members of the Confederacy, who wanted to remove the Kellogg government and were determined to do so even by extralegal means. Some referred to the White League as "military arm of the Democratic Party"[64] or a paramilitary group. The ambiguous political agenda of the White League is shown by an article on August 22, 1874, in *The Opelousas Courier* that reported that at "a grand Mass Meeting of all the elements opposed to Republicanism in the Parish of Rapides, held at Alexandria recently, the following plain-spoken resolution was unanimously adopted:

> ***Resolved,*** That we regard the recent promulgation of the infamous Registration Law, by W.P. Kellogg, the Usurper, as an outrage upon our rights, and as an attempt on his part to deprive the honest people of the State of an opportunity to register and vote, while it is doubtless intended by him to afford a basis for carrying the coming election by fraud. We warn the Register of this Parish that any attempt to regulate or control the registration in this Parish as not to afford a full and fair opportunity for all to register, and any discrimination against the white citizens of his Parish, will not be tolerated for one moment, and will be resisted by us—'**Peaceably** if we can, **Forcibly**, if we must.' That we are in no humor to trifle with any attempt, either direct or indirect, to defraud us of any of our rights."[65]

The Opelousas Courier further announced:

From this date, the control of the editorial columns of the COURIER passes into the hands of the White League. The business department remains under my control.

—LEONCE SANDOZ
Opelousas, May 25th, 1874.

The newspaper publicly handed over its editorial page to the White League, a political faction within the Democratic Party. Violence in Louisiana worsened.

In August 1874, the White League threw out Republican officeholders in Coushatta, Red River Parish, assassinating six white people before they left the state, and killing five to 15 freedmen who were witnesses.[66]

On September 14, 1874, five thousand members of the White League descended on the Louisiana statehouse, armory, and downtown in an insurrection and *coup d'etat* of the Republican Kellogg government. The insurgents demanded Kellogg's resignation. Kellogg refused, and a battle was fought for three days, resulting in 100 casualties. Kellogg requested help from President Grant, who sent federal troops to forcibly return him to office. Once the troops arrived, Kellogg was restored to office. It was a remarkable event in United States and Louisiana history that is not commonly known.

Election of 1874

The Opelousas Courier endorsed B.D. Tarlton for the Louisiana Legislature during the November 1874 election.[67] There was no reference to the "White League" in the newspaper's endorsement:

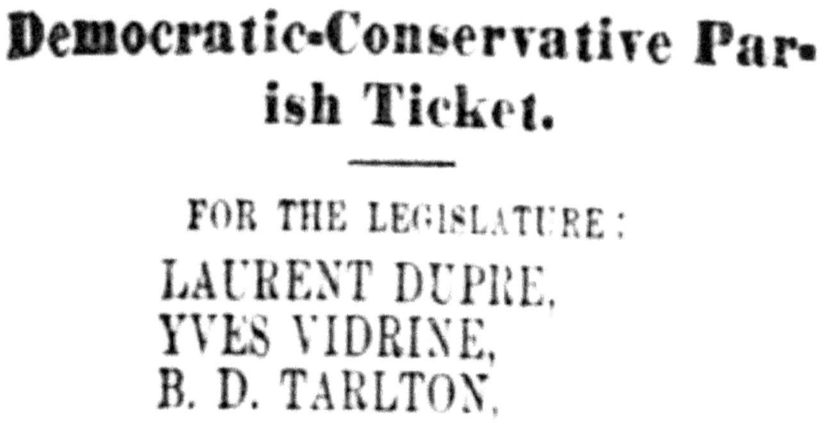

Democratic-Conservative Parish Ticket.

FOR THE LEGISLATURE:
LAURENT DUPRE,
YVES VIDRINE,
B. D. TARLTON,

Figure 16 News Clipping of endorsement.

Estillette won the election in November 1874 with 2,570 votes. B.D. came in sixth place with 1,811 votes.[68] B.D.'s foray into Louisiana politics, taking on the establishment at a young age, ended.

SEVEN

Waxahachie, Texas

WAXAHACHIE, TEXAS, IS A CITY organized on the banks of the Waxahachie Creek and whose name is derived from the Indian word "Buffalo Creek." The city serves as the seat of Ellis County, a county created by the Texas Legislature in 1849 and named after Richard Ellis, a noted jurist and president of the Constitutional Congress that declared the independence of Texas from Mexico.[69] Ellis never lived in the county and had no other connection to the county, but the Legislature decided his role in Texas history was so important that a county should be named after him.

Sissy Farenthold said that "Waxahachie and Hillsboro were the places that had political influence in those days. If you wanted to get a job with the government, that is where you went. I don't know why that was the case." Indeed, Ellis county's first county judge in 1850 was Oran M. Roberts, who became the governor of Texas and Chief Justice of the Texas Supreme Court.

Dr. Tarlton found a ten-acre property with a home for sale in the downtown Waxahachie area that was for sale by Dr. M.H. Oliver. If Dr. Tarlton thought his family could settle down peacefully in Waxahachie starting December 1873 shortly before Christmas, he was mistaken.

The title history shows that Daniel Daily owned the property and sold it in January 1862 to Mrs. Francis Ann Lacey, who lived on the property for the next eleven years. The property became known as the "Lacey Home."

Daily was known as "Colonel Daniel Daily" and was a resident of Lancaster, Texas. His name appears in litigation across the state, such as in a title dispute case in 1863 in Tyler, Texas, that went to the Texas Supreme Court in *Daily v. Starr*.[70] Daily served as a delegate to the Democratic State Convention from Dallas County in 1873[71] and was on the committee on Permanent organization and Credentials that recommended Colonel John M. Stemmons as Permanent Secretary.[72] He was involved in the case of *Watson v. Daily*, an appeal from Houston County[73] where he was accused of fraud. In 1877, the State of Texas recovered a judgment against Daily and others for $15,000 in the case of *The State of Texas v. James E. Barkley, et al* in the District Court of Travis County.[74] In 1880, the state advertised the judgment for purchase. Daily's connection to Mrs. Francis Lacey would go on for years as in 1886, she sued him in *Cause No. 2940 Lacey v. Daily* in Dallas County.[75]

Regardless of his colorful history, Daily held the first lien on the property dating back to 1862 when he sold the property to Mrs. Lacey. On March 3, 1873, Mrs. Lacey sold the property to M.H. Oliver.[76] The property needed renovation, and Oliver hired George W. Vaughn to work on the property, which he did on May 30, 1873.

Mrs. Frances Lacey was Frances Ann Howe Lacey, the daughter of William R. Howe, the founder of the Howe Settlement, the oldest settlement in Ellis County. Lacey was the wife of Benjamin Burton Lacey who died in 1872. The Lacey Home came from a 30-acre tract that had been subdivided.

Oliver was a medical doctor in Ennis, Texas, and a druggist with the firm of Oliver & Calhoun. His name shows up in newspapers as attending meetings of the Dallas Medical Society. He and his wife Lunette Oliver were investors who bought and sold properties from 1869 to 1875 in Ellis County, and they stood to make a small profit from the sale of the Lacey Home. But Oliver was possibly insolvent, and he failed to pay George Vaughn for the contracting work that he performed on the property after he purchased the home from Mrs. Lacey.

Vaughn procured a judgment against Oliver in the justice of the peace court on October 6, 1873, in the amount of $68.75, but Oliver appealed the judgment to the district court which meant that the judgment was not final but the lien still applied while the case was on appeal.

Vaughn had a constitutional mechanic's lien on the property that arose as a matter of law. He did not need to file any document of record to establish the lien. The lien would not be discovered by examining the title of the property in the deed records but by examining the civil court records. Those records do not appear in the deed records relating to the transfers of title.

The Closing

The closing of the sale from Oliver to Dr. Tarlton occurred on December 22, 1873. At the closing, Dr. Tarlton signed five promissory notes. The first note was for $812.50 and was payable to Mrs. Lacey and due on December 22, 1874. The second note was for $500 and due on January 15, 1874. The third note was for $400 and due on March 1, 1875. The fourth note was for $400 and due on January 1, 1876. The fifth note was for $587.89 and due on March 1, 1876. Oliver and his wife, Lunette Oliver, signed a deed to Dr. Tarlton that referenced the notes payable by Dr. Tarlton but made no reference to the judgment lien of Vaughn which was on appeal.

Witnessing the closing was a young twenty-five-year-old attorney named Anson Rainey, who worked briefly with Newton J. Nash, a prominent attorney in Waxahachie. Nash was a former prosecutor who practiced civil and criminal law. The local village of Nash, Texas, was named after him. Nash worked in the firm of Nash & Kemble. Rainey may have been sent by Newton J. Nash, who was representing Dr. Tarlton in the transaction, to witness the closing.

Figure 17 Anson Rainey, who would become Chief Justice of the Fifth Court of Appeals in Dallas.

In 1874, Rainey became associated with Justus Wesley Ferris to form the firm of Ferris & Rainey. Rainey was born in Arkansas and attended schools in Alabama. He served in the Confederate Army with Company A, Sixteenth, Arkansas Cavalry for two years and participated in the campaigns in Georgia, Alabama, and Mississippi. In April 1865, he was wounded at the battle of Fort Blakely. After the war, he worked in Texas and left for Louisiana, where he studied the law and practiced briefly in New Delhi, Louisiana, with an attorney named H.P. Wells. Rainey returned to Texas in 1873 and settled in Waxahachie after being admitted to the Louisiana bar in 1871. Over the next twenty years, Rainey's prominence would grow, and in 1893, Rainey was appointed associate justice of the Fifth District Court of Civil Appeals by Governor James S. Hogg. In 1900 he became chief justice of the court.

Justus Wesley Ferris was fifty-one years old and the former judge of the Sixteenth Judicial District. Ferris served one term as judge until the end of the Civil War. He became a member of the 1875 Constitutional Convention and served on the Committee on Railroads. Governor Richard Coke appointed him to serve as a commissioner to revise the statutes of Texas.[77] Ferris partnered with W.H. Getzendaner, and together they opened a bank that became known as the Citizens National Bank, still in existence today in 2021. In September 1874, Ferris handled the transfer of 100 acres from a family to trustees to establish a town and railway station. The community was named after him, and the city incorporated in 1882.

After the closing

Within a month after the closing, Dr. Tarlton refused to make his first payment of $500 note due to Oliver when it came due in January 1874, making the note default. Oliver had created a serious problem. It posed the question: was Dr. Tarlton entitled to a credit against the first note of $500 since his property was encumbered with the judgment of Vaughn? Or would that credit only be available to Dr. Tarlton if Vaughn executed on his judgment and sold Dr. Tarlton's property, resulting in a loss of title? Must the new owner suffer an actual loss or be ousted from their property in order to prove they were damaged by a valid lien on their property? If the seller is responsible for the judgment, why does the new owner have to suffer a loss of title to prove a loss before they can seek recourse against the seller? What if the owner wants to keep the property but cannot pay the debt secured by the property?

If Oliver sued Dr. Tarlton, then Dr. Tarlton would assert the Vaughn debt as a partial defense to the payment of the $500 note that was due in January 1874. The question then became: would Dr. Tarlton pay the subsequent note of $812.50 note due to Mrs. Lacey in December 1874? Would he pay the subsequent notes that would become due in 1875 and 1876? This left Daily, Lacey, and Oliver in doubt about the future of their investments. Daily was not going to wait around, and Oliver had another plan. On January 29, 1874, Oliver endorsed the $500 note to Daily and let Daily take up enforcing the debt against Dr. Tarlton.

Daily v. Tarlton

On April 14, 1874, Daniel Daily, as assignee, filed suit against Dr. Tarlton in *Cause No. 1025, Daily v. Tarlton, District Court, Ellis County, Texas,* to enforce payment of the $500 note to foreclose the property based on the default in the note. The case would be tried by the Honorable H. Barksdale, a young judge who resided in East Dallas. Barksdale was said to be "one of the ablest and best-known lawyers in Texas and stood in the front rank of Dallas practitioners."[78]

Daily hired R.S. Guy, an attorney in Lancaster, Texas, and a State Senator from the Thirteenth Senatorial District, to represent him and file suit against Dr. Tarlton. Guy advertised in the newspapers that he "will practice in all the courts of Dallas and the surrounding counties" and "all business entrusted to him will receive prompt and faithful attention."

Dr. Tarlton answered the suit and alleged that the Vaughn judgment was *"still in force and a lien upon the property for which said note was given"* and that the deed from Oliver to Dr. Tarlton was *"not a good and perfect title."* He contended that while Daily could enforce the $500 promissory note, he appeared to take subject to Dr. Tarlton's defense that the Vaughn judgment (which was on appeal) would attach to the property.

It was clear that Oliver did not convey a good and perfect title to Dr. Tarlton and had breached his warranty that all debts and liens against the property had been discharged. Oliver did not disclose, reserve, or except the mechanic's lien or judgment of Vaughn in his deed to Dr. Tarlton. Dr. Tarlton alleged that Daily was subject to his claims because he acquired the note after maturity and that Daily held *"the same subject to all the equities existing between the original maker and the payee of said note."*

Dr. Tarlton requested that no judgment be rendered *"greater than sufficient to pay & discharge the note and interest sued upon less the amount of the judgment, interest & costs in the case of Geo. W. Vaughn vs M.H. Oliver above specified amounting in all to the sum of one hundred dollars."* Dr. Tarlton's suit was answered by Nash & Kemble, but no specific attorney was mentioned in the pleading.

To make matters worse, in December 1874, Dr. Tarlton declined to pay the $812.50 note to Mrs. Lacey for the sale of the Waxahachie property. This set up a new dispute between Dr. Tarlton, Daily, and Lacey, who would have to decide whether to file a second lawsuit to enforce the $812.50 note and their vendor's lien against Dr. Tarlton.

At trial, Judge H. Barksdale excluded the Vaughn judgment against Oliver. He considered the Vaughn judgment to be disputed debt that was on appeal to his court, and since the validity of the debt would have to be tried again, he would give it no weight. This meant that Dr. Tarlton had no defense to the payment of the $500 note owed to Daily.

Dr. Tarlton appealed the ruling of Judge Barksdale, and on April 17, 1875, Dr. Tarlton's attorneys filed a writ of error to the Texas Supreme Court. At that time, the Texas Supreme Court was extremely busy with appeals coming from all over the state, and the court was in serious need of assistance with its appeals. The Texas Legislature would decide whether it was time to create a new court to assist the Texas Supreme Court or establish intermediary appellate courts across the state to handle the first round of appeals.

Dr. Tarlton stayed the enforcement of the Vaughn judgment by placing a $1,100 supersedeas bond with the court. This step would effectively tie up the dispute for years because the Texas Supreme Court did not have the resources to devote to the case.

The appeal of Vaughn v. Oliver

In the meantime, on May 6, 1875, the case of George W. Vaughn against Oliver over his mechanic's lien went to trial in the district court in Ellis County and was tried.

The jury found: "We the jury find for the Plaintiff $86.42 gold Principal & Interest $12.67 Gold aggregate $99.09, and the property described subject to the Mechanic's Lien. W.B. Anthony, foreman." The jury found that the work was performed on May 30, 1873, and the district court granted execution and foreclosure of Dr. Tarlton's property.

On June 12, 1875, the Sheriff of Ellis County conducted a sheriff's sale of Dr. Tarlton's property and sold the property at the courthouse steps to Dr. Tarlton, who paid $175.59 at the sale to satisfy the Vaughn judgment lien. Now Dr. Tarlton had proof that Oliver had breached his warranty of title in his deed to him because he had to pay to discharge the Vaughn debt. But there was a problem: the evidence of the sheriff's sale occurred in June 1975, after the trial of *Daily v. Tarlton,* which was on appeal to the Texas Supreme Court. The high court would never know that Dr. Tarlton had actually experienced a breach of warranty of his title and had to defend his own title by paying off the judgment lien at a sheriff's sale.

B.D. Tarlton moves to Texas

In March 1876, B.D. Tarlton closed his legal practice in Grand Coteau and moved to Waxahachie where he would start over and look for work. Had he moved to Texas in December 1873 with the rest of the family perhaps he could have prevented the *Daily v Tarlton* dispute by paying off the George Vaughn judgment lien and seeking recourse against Dr. Oliver.

EIGHT

Death in Waxahachie

On September 10, 1876, Frances Caller Tarlton, B.D.'s mother, died at the age of fifty-four from pneumonia. The death must have been a shock to Dr. Tarlton and the entire family and B.D. who had settled six months earlier looking for work. Now seventy-six years old, Dr. Tarlton, who seemed impervious to anything, found himself a widower again. Who would have expected that his young wife would die first? News of her death was reported in The *Opelousas Courier* in Louisiana:

> Died – At Waxahachie, Texas on Sunday, September 10, 1876, of pneumonia, Mrs. Frances Ann Caller, wife of Dr. John Tarlton, aged 54 years, 8 months and 7 days.

Frances Tarlton was buried in the Waxahachie City Cemetery in downtown Waxahachie. B.D. was twenty-seven at the time and had no clue of the significance of her cause of death; pneumonia was a dangerous illness.

Figure 18 Tombstone of Jane H. Toulmin Caller.

The inscription reads:

Frances A. Caller
Wife of John Tarlton
Born in Mobile Ala
Feb 2, 1824
Died in Waxahachie, Tex
Sept. 10, 1876

Figure 19 Tombstone of Frances Caller Tarlton.

Frances Caller Tarlton had married Dr. Tarlton, a man old enough to be her father. She bore him ten children and took care of two stepchildren. She left her home in Mobile, Alabama, and moved to St. Mary Parish to start a new family, investing her dowry in the family farm. She survived the Civil War, the violence in Louisiana, and the difficulties of a marriage and a business operation with enormous liabilities. She had to sue her husband to try to protect the plantation. She made the final trip to Waxahachie only to succumb to pneumonia two years later. The cause of her death would haunt the family afterwards.

Two months later, on November 2, 1876, Frances's mother, Jane Toulmin, died at the age of seventy-four. Being in a very different, new environment–along with the loss of her daughter at such an early age–must have been devastating. She was buried next to her daughter in the Waxahachie City Cemetery.[79]

The inscription reads:

Jane H. Toulmin
Wife of Green Duke Caller
Born in Lexington, Ky
Jan 15 1802
Died in Waxahachie, Tex
Nov 2, 1876

Dr. Tarlton must have felt totally alone at this point. The two women he had spent most of his life with, from 1838 to 1876, were gone.

The Waxahachie City Cemetery is in the downtown area of the quaint city, located thirty miles outside of Dallas. Ellis County has a typical courthouse square with the older courthouse on the square and a new courthouse one block away. The Waxahachie City Cemetery is on the northern part of downtown. As you enter, you will see a baseball stadium on the left. The entrance will take you to a cemetery road with roads on either side to travel to the other side of the cemetery.

NINE

Hillsboro, Texas

Abbott & Tarlton

BY 1875, JOSEPH ABBOTT MADE a name for himself as an able statesman of Central Texas, where he was an attorney, district judge, and United States Congressman from Hill County. Born on January 15, 1840, in Decatur, Alabama, Abbott was one of twelve children of William and Mary (McMillan) Abbott.

At age thirteen, his family moved to Freestone County, Texas, and he was educated by Professor George F. Allison, a local teacher. Abbott began reading the law in 1859 with Franklin L. Yoakum, a physician, minister, and the first president of Larissa College. He pursued his studies until the Civil War began. He enlisted in the Confederate Army in Company B, Twelfth Texas

Figure 20 Mentor to B.D. Tarlton, attorney, State Legislator, District Judge and U.S. Congressman Joseph Abbott (D-Texas).

Cavalry. After being commissioned a First Lieutenant, Abbott served in many engagements and was wounded at Yellow Bayou, Louisiana. He was disabled for a few months but rejoined his command until the end of the war.[80]

Abbott became licensed to practice law in 1866 in Springfield, Texas, and came to Hill County in 1867, where he taught school and resumed his legal practice in 1868. In 1869, he was elected to the Texas Legislature and married Rowena Sturgis, with whom he had five children. In 1871, the town of Abbott, a stop for the Missouri-Kansas-Texas Railroad, was named after him. This small town would be the future birthplace of Willie Nelson in 1933.

Tarlton and Abbott had much in common, being attorneys and having been involved in politics. Abbott needed an attorney to assist him and Tarlton needed a mentor in Texas. They formed the firm of Abbott & Tarlton.[81] Tarlton was a named law partner in Hillsboro with one of the most influential attorneys in Hill County.

Marriage to Susan Littell

While the Tarlton family left Grand Coteau for Texas, Grand Coteau never left them. On April 24, 1877, B.D. returned to the city to marry Susan Littell.[82] In February 1877, B.D. purchased a home in Hillsboro from A.L. Smith and wife Ann P. Smith. The price was $68 dollars in cash and a promissory note payable at $75 in monthly payments at ten percent interest and $145 dollars for twelve months.

Will Lowrance served on the Hillsboro Heritage League Board and said that the B.D. Tarlton home was recently purchased and saved from destruction. "We put on a new roof and painted and offered for sale. We determined not to take the façade back to its original style but kept the remodel from the 1920's and the house today is known as the Turk-Maier house and is home to State Farm Insurance and David Teel Realtors. Few in Hillsboro know this as the B. D. Tarlton house."

Figure 21 Current photo of the B.D. Tarlton home restored. The home was modernized in the 1920s and is now known as the Turk-Maier house and is occupied by State Farm Insurance and David Teel Realtors.

Daily, Lacey v. Tarlton II

On May 15, 1877, the case of *Daniel Daily and Francis Lacey v. John Tarlton*, to recover the sum of $812.50 that became due in December 1874 for the sale of the Lacey home came up for trial. The dispute over the large note due one year after the sale had been postponed for more than two and one-half years after the debt was due. Since the *Tarlton v. Daily* suit was pending in the Texas Supreme Court, and with the deaths in the Tarlton family, Daily and Lacey may have chosen not to push the subsequent cases for trial. The district court entered a judgment for $1,088.74 against Dr. Tarlton. The judgment referenced the note dated December 22, 1873 and secured by the "R.B. Lacey House & Lot." The court ordered the property sold by sheriff's sale. The case was not appealed.

B.D. and Susan Tarlton children

On April 5, 1878, Susan Tarlton gave birth to the couple's first child, Frances Ann Tarlton,[83] named after her grandmother. The couple had five children in all: Mary Eleanor,[84] born on November 26, 1879, and died April 1897; Elizabeth Millard,[85] born June 7, 1882, and died August 9, 1965.[86] B.D. Tarlton Jr., born on January 7, 1889, and died on April 22, 1956.

Figure 22 The only known image of Susan Marie Littell, B.D. Tarlton's wife, known as Miss Nannie Littell prior to her marriage to B.D.

Daily, Lacey v. Tarlton III

Under the terms of the December 1873 sale from Oliver to Dr. Tarlton, Dr. Tarlton owed $587.89 under a fifth note that was due on March 1, 1876. Daily and Lacey filed suit to recover the $587.89 due, and the case was heard on November 12, 1878, in *Cause No. 1219, Daniel Daily et al v. John Tarlton*, Ellis County, Texas.

At that trial, Dr. Tarlton withdrew his answer and said "Mrs. F.A. Lacy ought to recover against the said John Tarlton her damages by occasion of the premises." The court assessed damages of $587.89 payable in Gold Dollars with interest at the rate of ten percent.

This meant that Daily and Lacey had two judgments that they could execute on the Tarlton home, but even if they had done so, the property would still be clouded by reason of the pending appeal in the *Tarlton v. Daily* case that had been pending since 1875 in the Texas Supreme Court.

District Judge Jo Abbott

In February 1879, Governor Oran M. Roberts appointed Joseph Abbott as Judge of the 28th Judicial District court. Abbott would preside over cases in Hill, Johnson, and Bosque counties. After three years, B.D. lost his mentor and would now be appearing in his court. But it was good to know the local judge, and moreover, not many could say that they were former partners of the new judge.

Bullock & Tarlton

Without his influential mentor, thirty-nine-year-old B.D. Tarlton teamed with forty-nine-year-old John H. Bullock, a respected Hill County attorney, and formed the firm of Bullock & Tarlton.[87] Bullock was born in 1830 in Warren County, North Carolina, and was the son-in-law of Chief Justice R.M. Pearson of the Supreme Court of North Carolina. Bullock ran for County Judge of Hill County in 1878 but lost to J.S. Blanton by a vote of 1,370 for Blanton to Bullock's 1,313 votes.

Bullock had a daughter that married J.W. Perrill, an attorney who practiced law briefly in Hillsboro. The couple moved to Seymour, Texas, where Perrill was appointed by the governor as district judge of the 50th Judicial District in Baylor County, Texas. The marriage was troubled, and his wife would eventually leave the judge, who would have difficulty accepting the separation. A scandal would erupt in on front page news in 1892.

Texas State Legislature

Figure 23 State Representative B.D. Tarlton

In 1880 the United States Federal Census showed there to be eight people residing in the B.D. Tarlton home in Hillsboro, Texas. B.D. was thirty years old. His wife, Susan, was twenty-six. His father, Dr. John Tarlton, moved from Waxahachie to Hillsboro to live with B.D. and his family was 80 years old. Others in the were listed as: Sallie Littell, who was twenty-four; Richard Manning Tarlton, who was eighteen; Farmuba Tarlton, who was 15; M.E. Tarlton, who was seven; and Francis Tarlton, who was age 2.

In 1880, B.D. entered Texas politics, running for state representative, the same House legislative seat previously held by Jo Abbott. This time he won; it was his first race for public office in Texas. He was elected to the 17th Legislative Session representing the 56th District of Texas consisting of Hill County.

While in the Texas Legislature, B.D. served on six committees: Internal Improvements; Judiciary No. 2; Memorial for Hon. H.G. Bruce of Johnson

County; Quarters for State Departments, Select; Revenue and Taxation; and Senatorial and Representative Districts. He served on the Executive Committee of the Democratic Party of Texas during the 17th Legislative session.[88] As shown in Figure 23, his photo in the Texas Legislature, B.D. is hardly recognizable as the same man from his later photographs, where he looks more like a wealthy British barrister.

Tarlton v. Daily

In 1879, the Texas Legislature established the Texas Commission of Appeals to handle the numerous appeals being filed in the Texas Supreme Court. With the consent of the parties the commission could hear the appeals. To say that the Texas Supreme Court needed assistance is apparent by reason of the *Tarlton v. Daily* appeal, a case that involved a dispute of $500 and had been pending on the court's docket for four years with no decision.

On April 25, 1881, the Texas Commission of Appeals ruled in *Tarlton v. Daily*, affirming the judgment.[89] The short opinion does not describe the facts of the case with any degree of clarity, and unfortunately the subsequent history showing Dr. Tarlton purchasing his property at a sheriff's sale in 1875—proof of a breach of warranty of title—is not discussed in the opinion because the evidence was not before the trial court and therefore not before the court on appeal. While Dr. Tarlton had proof of an eviction, his defense at trial was premature because the eviction had not occurred at the time of the suit.

In May 2021, the Texas archives found the *Tarlton v. Daily* appeal, which consisted of the petition, briefs of the appellant and appellee and the opinion, all written on yellow paper. The file was so old that before they could be copied, the papers had to be humidified and flattened before they could be delivered.

The appellant's brief, being Dr. Tarlton's brief, was written by Mark Humble and the firm of Nash & Kemble. The appellee's brief, being Daniel Daily's brief, was written by Justus Wesley Ferris with Ferris & Rainey, except that Rainey's name was marked out in the petition. This could be because Rainey had a conflict in the case since he may have been working for the Nash & Kemble firm at that time of the closing of the sale to Dr. Tarlton. In other words, Rainey had represented Dr. Tarlton and was a witness to Dr. Tarlton's signature at the closing in 1873.

Dr. Tarlton's brief cited to the case of *Smith v. Kale*[90] as its only authority where the court held:

> The only question for the court in this case is: Does an appeal from a judgment rendered in the county court vacate the lien secured by the judgment creditor, on the real estate of the judgment debtor, situated in the county where judgment is rendered? We think not.

Dr. Tarlton argued that the lien of Vaughn still attached to his property even though the case was on appeal to the district court. But does a lien alone represent recoverable damages under the warranty of title?

Daily's brief by Justus Wesley Ferris charged that the defense that Dr. Tarlton raised in the trial court was frivolous and that the appeal was for delay. Ferris wrote: "The deed to Tarlton is an absolute deed, and there is no allegation in his answer that he was ignorant at the date of purchase of an outstanding lien. He argued that *Smith v. Kale* "can hardly be called authority" and cited to *Cooper v. Singleton*, 19 Tex. 260, 263 (1857) where the court held:

> But when the title has been passed and the deed executed, the purchaser cannot, according to the doctrine in England and in most of the states, resist the payment of the purchase money, on the ground merely of defect or failure in the title. Where there has been no fraudulent representations on the part of the vendor as to the title, the general rule is, that the vendee under a deed must pay the purchase money and rely upon the covenants in his warranty for redress; and if there be no fraud and no covenants, he is not entitled to any relief.

In other words, Ferris argued that Dr. Tarlton could not resist payment of the price for the property unless his seller (M.H. Oliver) had *no* title to convey. That was not the case. Oliver had title—an encumbered title—due to the lien of Vaughn. The court noted in its opinion that Dr. Tarlton's defense—that the judgment lien was an encumbrance on the land in the amount of one-hundred dollars at the time of the purchase and that Oliver would not be able to respond in damages if the lien encumbering the property should be foreclosed—were facts that were *"insignificant as a bar to the plaintiff's right to recover on the note sued on."*

The excluded evidence—being the Vaughn judgment—did not result in error that was material to the court's decision. The court recognized the issue of constructive notice of the existence of the judgment lien of record, but Dr. Tarlton's answer to the lawsuit did not plead that he was ignorant or had no knowledge of the lien.

In the early days of Texas litigation, the parties had to plead what they proved at trial. The court wrote:

> He does not pretend, or intimate in his answer, that his vendor was guilty of any fraud or misrepresentation, or in any wise improperly superinduced his want of knowledge, if he was, in fact, ignorant concerning the lien in question.

The court held that when a vendee (the purchaser) gives a promissory note for the purchase of the property and takes a general warranty deed and there is no fraud on the part of the vendor, nor ignorance on the part of the vendee as to the defect in the title, *"the vendee cannot successfully resist the payment of the note for the purchase money, unless he has been evicted. Proof of a paramount title outstanding in a third person is no defense."*

The court found that the exclusion of the evidence of the Vaughn judgment was *"merely abstract, and was one of which the defendant cannot complain as being to his injury."* The court adopted the arguments of Ferris who filed the more substantial brief.

What was the problem?

"There were many," said Roland Love, Vice President of Independence Title Company in Dallas, Texas, having practiced law for over forty-four years. Love is Board Certified in Commercial, Farm and Ranch, and Residential Real Estate Law by the Texas Board of Legal Specialization, Chair of the Legislative Committee of the Texas Land Title Association and has been recognized as one of the Best Lawyers in America.

"The court is all over the board in the opinion discussing the impact of the exclusion of the evidence of the judgment against Oliver," he said. "There were many reasons touched by the court, commonly accepted today such as bona fide purchaser status and the efficacy of an appealed justice court judgment, that might be meaningful, but the court never chose to apply any of these theories. Ultimately the failure to properly plead specific defenses did him in.

"Dr. Tarlton had many potential defenses he could have raised, such as Daily acquiring the note after default or he was a bona fide purchaser, but his pleadings did not set out how Oliver was in default and that there was a partial failure of consideration. The court found that Dr. Tarlton had not lost possession of the property. Another issue is that the judgment he obtained against Oliver was not final and on appeal. I'm not even sure from the opinion whether the judgment against Oliver was actually recorded, based on the opinion because it references that where a vendor sells part of the same property to another person that the other deed has been recorded. If Dr. Tarlton's purpose was to offset the judgment he obtained against Oliver as against Daily, he didn't plead offset and the court never got into that issue.

"The court didn't need to decide which reason they relied on to exclude the evidence of Dr. Tarlton's judgment against Oliver. I believe they were correct in their holding under the pleading requirements for that time. There was no proof of eviction of Dr. Tarlton and no loss of title. More important, possibly, was Dr. Tarlton's attempt to use a much smaller unrelated money judgment that had not been enforced in any way to avoid paying a larger amount he clearly owed for the property he enjoyed.

"This case shows the court developing some of the most fundamental principles that are commonly accepted today in the land title industry regarding when a loss of title occurs—abstracts of judgment, bona fide purchaser status, finality of judgments, and breach of warranty."

No title insurance in 1873

The *Tarlton v. Daily* case was rendered years before title insurance came to Texas to offer indemnity in case of a loss of title in a real estate transaction by a purchaser. Title insurance would not be invented until 1876 in Philadelphia when a title insurance company was formed to insure purchasers of real estate and mortgages against losses from defective title, liens, and encumbrances.

In the days of *Tarlton v. Daily* it was up to the real estate attorneys in the counties to examine the title by finding the relevant documents pertaining to the real estate being sold in the county courthouse. This is termed "abstracting" the property. The next process is reviewing the documents. What do they mean? This is termed the "examination" of the title. In today's world, records are now computerized, and an examination is performed on a computer screen showing digital images of the deeds and relevant documents. Title insurance is offered as part of the sale in case of a loss by a seller. The title examination today is conducted for the benefit of the title insurance carrier to determine whether it will insure the title.

In Dr. Tarlton's day it was old-fashioned shoe leather title examination in the courthouse, sometimes called a "stand—up" title examination because the attorney literally stands up in the courthouse to examine the real estate documents, usually in the basement of the courthouse in bound volumes of records. One well known oil and gas attorney, William David, former managing partner of Cantey Hanger LLP in Fort Worth, said that attorneys in the early days of title examination of oil and gas interests, "examined title, delivered a title opinion and then prayed for a dry hole."

But here, an examination of the title in the deed records would not have disclosed the mechanic's lien of George W. Vaughn. Vaughn who was an original contractor who held a constitutional mechanic's lien that arose as a matter of law and required no documentation. It would have taken a physical inspection of the property or an inquiry from the seller to have discovered the lien.

Dr. Tarlton must have known about the lien before he purchased the property because he did not raise the bona fide purchaser defense which would have defeated the lien.

Death of Dr. Tarlton

Dr. Tarlton lived another six years after the death of his young wife, Francis Caller Tarlton. He died on March 2, 1882, in Hillsboro. His body was returned to Waxahachie to be buried next to his wife and mother-in-law in the Waxahachie City Cemetery.[91]

Figure 24 Grave marker for Dr. John Tarlton (1800 – 1882) in the Waxahachie City Cemetery.

Dr. Tarlton, at eighty-two years of age, had lived a long life and fathered fifteen children. He could only be judged by the standards in which he lived. He did not always win, but he went out a fighter until the end. A Tarlton family genealogy book says that Dr. John Tarlton was a man of strong character and prominence in his profession and a disciple of John C. Calhoun.

Upon Dr. Tarlton's death, John Belser Tarlton inherited the remaining property in St. Mary Parish, and he continued to operate it as a sugar farm until 1890, when he sold the property to Borue O'Brien, a descendent of one of the first families to settle in the Morgan City area.[92]

Recall that Sissy Farenthold said that Dr. Tarlton *"courted the mother but married the daughter."* Perhaps Jane Toulmin Caller wanted to marry Dr. Tarlton, but she was married to Green Duke Caller. If she wanted security, then having her daughter marry the older and established southern gentlemen would provide that safety, as well as a family, for her daughter. It is possible that had Jane Toulmin Caller not arranged for the marriage of her daughter, then none of the subsequent history in this book would have happened in the same way. The future of the Second Court of Appeals in Fort Worth, Texas, would have been entirely different but for one woman's instinct, that of Jane H. Toulmin Caller, who decided that her daughter would marry a medical doctor in Mobile, Alabama.

To reach the Tarlton-Caller graves, take the Andrews Highway, which is a one-car paved road that will extend to the back of the cemetery; it circles around to another road that leads out of the cemetery. As you follow the road, the land slowly elevates, and you will see a tall cedar tree with sprawling limbs stretching to the left and right. To the right of the tree is a modern-day monument with the name "Tarlton—Caller." The three graves are side by side in front of the monument. It is a peaceful setting and fitting that all three, who lived through an incredible period of U.S. history, are buried together.

Death of John Bullock

B.D.'s law partner, John Bullock, met a sudden death on January 12, 1883, when he was involved in a driving accident from the railroad depot to the residence of one Dr. Kennedy, which caused a skull fracture. Bullock died at the age of fifty-two and was buried in the Hillsboro City Cemetery. The newspaper reported: "Our whole community regrets his death, as he was a friend to everyone and did not have an enemy in the world. His burial will take place tomorrow under the auspices of the Hill County Bar."[93]

Reelection to the State Legislature

In 1884, B.D. was re-elected to the 19th Legislative session to his seat for State Representative, 39th District, with 3,243 votes. He ran unopposed. He represented Ellis, Hill, Johnson, and Navarro counties from January 13, 1885, to January 19, 1887.[94] He served on the Finance, Judiciary No. 2 (Chair) and Privileges and Elections committees.

During his two terms in the legislature, he was known as a "splendid speaker, cool and liberal in his judgments, fearless in support of all just measures and a man well fitted to lead in legislative halls."[95] He was regarded as one of the active leaders of his party, and his services have been recognized and appreciated for their sound judgment and practical ability.[96] While serving in the Texas Legislature, Tarlton befriended Jim Hogg, who served as the Wood County Attorney from 1880 to 1884.[97]

Tarlton & Tarlton

After the death of John Bullock, B.D. reached out to his brother G.D., to join with him in his firm.[98] G.D. had moved to Austin where he taught school and became superintendent of the Texas Institute of Learning for the Blind for six years.

In 1880, G.D. married Sarah "Sallie" Elizabeth Scott, who was blind and said to be musically talented.[99] They had five children. The first child, Guy Duke Tarlton was born in Austin, Texas in 1880. By 1881 the G.D. Tarlton family had moved to Waxahachie and then settled in Hillsboro, Texas. The other children, Huldah Tarlton, Sarah Elizabeth Tarlton, Richard Toulmin Tarlton and Helen Collier Tarlton were born in Hillsboro, Texas.

Tarlton, Jordan & Tarlton

In 1881, B.D. and G.D. were joined by George I. Jordan, becoming Tarlton, Jordan & Tarlton. George I. Jordan was born in Noxubee County, Mississippi, in 1854 and went to boarding school in Woodlawn, Mississippi, after which he attended Bloomfield College for two years. For the next three years he traveled from place to place with no established business. In 1869 he moved to Covington in Hill County and farmed for three years before moving to Mansfield, Texas, for two years to work on a bachelor's degree under Professor John Collier.

Figure 25 A younger G.D. Tarlton.

In 1876, Jordan returned to Hill County and was appointed Deputy Tax Collector and returned to Mansfield, Texas, to complete his degree, graduating in 1879. After graduation he ran a gin in Itasca, working eighteen hours a day.

In January 1880, he moved to Hillsboro and read law under Tarlton & Bullock for four months, then served as the Deputy County Clerk. He returned to resume his law studies under Tarlton & Bullock and obtained his license to practice law in 1881.

Retired District Judge Frank B. "Bob" McGregor Jr. of Hillsboro, Texas, served in the Sixty-Sixth District Court from 1993 to 2015. He is also the Chair of the Hill County Historical Commission. McGregor located the application of George Jordan to practice law and the report of the examination committee in Hill County. The examination committee consisted of attorneys Abbott, Ivy, Upshaw, and McKinnon.

"The Report of Committee on file is dated April 29, 1881. These documents were badly damaged in the courthouse fire, January 1, 1993," said Judge McGregor.

TEN

District Judge Abbott

Now appearing before Judge Jo Abbott, his former law partner, B.D. did not always win. He appealed two of Judge Abbott's decisions, reversing him in one of the cases.

Jones v. Fancher

In *Jones v. Fancher*,[100] B.D. tried a "trespass to try title" case before Judge Abbott. The reference to "trespass to try title" is sometimes called a "TTT" (triple T case) and is the exclusive legal mechanism in Texas to decide who owns title to real property and to oust the unlawful party in possession.

Jones sued Fancher because he believed that Fancher did not have title to the property described in his deed. The property had been surveyed into an area referred to as "metes and bounds," (measures and boundaries) but the property was later platted and subdivided into lot and block and then sold with the lot and block property description thirty years earlier by the chief justice of Hill County. The county could not locate the court order approving the sale by the chief justice, and Jones argued that the property described in his deed by metes and bounds was not the same property located in the lot and block of Fancher. These were two valid arguments. Fancher needed to prove that Hill County had valid title, a valid court order, and he needed to prove that the same property described by metes and bounds was within the lot and block of the subdivision. Judge Abbott ruled in favor of Fancher, giving him the title.

Tarlton appealed the decision to the Texas Supreme Court. Associate Justice John William Stayton wrote that after such a lapse of time, it would be presumed that the chief justice made a valid sale of the property to vest title in the purchaser. But he disagreed that there was proof in the record that the property was owned by Hill County. The court reversed the case for a new trial. This meant that at a new trial, Fancher would have to prove that Hill County had title to the property. To do that there would need to be testimony to prove that the same property described in the metes and bounds description was the same property described on the ground by lot and block.[101] This case shows the importance of survey evidence that could come from a professional surveyor in real estate disputes.

Rosenthal, Meyer & Co. v. Middlebrook

In 1884, B.D. handled *Rosenthal, Meyer & Co. v. Middlebrook*,[102] which involved a prejudgment writ of attachment to attach the defendant's property prior to the court hearing the case. It is a rare process and allows the sheriff to temporarily seize a defendant's property while a lawsuit is pending. The prejudgment writ allows the property to be seized and allows the court to decide who has the valid claim to the property.

The questions before the court were: does title to personal property pass based on payment of the debt? Is a witness's "belief" that the title passes at the point of payment relevant in the dispute?

Judge Abbott excluded the witness from testifying as to his *belief* of the ownership of the property as a consequence of payment. The Texas Supreme Court held that the exclusion of the witness's belief was not harmful.

The case stands for the proposition that with well-defined exceptions, witnesses must state facts and not opinions, and cannot state conclusions or their legal effect. In this case, the witness was simply stating his opinion, which was not supported by the facts. It was not relevant what the witness believed. The court could have permitted the testimony and given the jury a limiting instruction on its effect, but it was not harmful to have excluded the testimony altogether.

ELEVEN

District Judge J. M. Hall

JOSEPH MARION HALL WAS BORN on October 15, 1828, in Greene County, Alabama, and grew up in Eutaw, Alabama, where he attended country schools and an academy. In September 1857, he entered Cumberland School of Law in Lebanon, Tennessee. Hall was licensed to practice law by July 1858 and began his practice in Grove Hill, Tennessee, with James Dickerson.[103]

When the Civil War broke out, Hall was opposed to secession, but he joined the Confederacy and was commissioned a captain by Alabama Governor A.J. Moore. Hall raised a company and left for Fort Morgan under governor's orders until the Confederacy was established. He was mustered out of state service, and the company was ordered to Montgomery, Alabama, where they became part of the Fifth Alabama. The regiment contained one company of artillery and was ordered to Pensacola, Florida. His regiment reinforced Richmond and Manassas in June 1861.

In February 1862, Hall was ordered home as a recruiting officer for his old company. He returned to his company with 163 recruits and under Joe Johnston he was ordered to Yorktown and promoted to lieutenant-colonel. He engaged in battle in Seven Pines, Redoubt No. 7. During this battle Hall was shot in the left hand and was sent home. While absent he was promoted to colonel.

Hall returned to his regiment after the Battle of Antietam and participated in the battles of Fredericksburg and Chancellorsville, where he commanded a brigade.[104] At Gettysburg, Colonel Hall lost 175 out of

400 men. He participated in the Mine Run Campaign, Wilderness, and Spotsylvania, where he lost his right arm by a minié ball, which was a hollow-based bullet used during the war. After receiving poor treatment and suffering from blood poisoning, Hall returned home and found that his mother had died of grief on account of his loss.

In November 1864, Hall resigned from service and married Miss Lida Hamill, and left for Marshall, Texas, to practice law. In July 1876, Hall left for Cleburne in Johnson County and formed a partnership with James W. Brown for two years.

Race for District Judge

In 1880, Hall challenged incumbent District Judge Jo Abbott for the district bench. But Abbott defeated him with 1,579 votes to Hall's 1,216 votes. Another account says that Hall lost by only eight votes out of 10,000.[105]

Figure 26 J.M. Hall, District Judge, Eighteenth Judicial District.

Hall was not finished. In 1884, Hall decided to run a second time for the bench. This time Abbott chose not to seek reelection, and his decision set up a three-way race for the open seat between S.C. Upshaw, S.H. Lumpkin, and Hall. Hall won the race with 1,983 votes to Upshaw's 1,922 votes and S.H. Lumpkin's 82 votes.

Hall's decision to challenge Abbott resulted in Abbott moving to a higher calling: in 1886, Abbott was elected to the U.S. House of Representatives and served for ten years, from March 4, 1887, through March 3, 1897.

TWELVE

Private Practice

By 1884, the Tarlton firm was successful and reported to have been lucrative. The Hillsboro and Hill County Directory in 1884 included a page for the Tarlton, Jordan & Tarlton law firm:

> **Tarlton, Jordan & Tarlton**
> **LAWYERS**
> AND
> LAND AGENTS
> HILLSBORO, TEXAS.

Have a complete Abstract of Title to every survey of land in Hill county, compiled from the records of the General Land Office, and from the records of Robertson, Navarro and Hill counties.

Special attention given to buying and selling lands, perfecting titles, rendering land for non-residents, redeeming lands from tax-sales, to writing deed, powers-of-attorney, leases, mortgages, trust-deeds, contracts, and to LAND LITIGATION. Claims, accounts, and notes collected, abstracts furnished, titles examined, opinions given. A general civil and criminal law business conducted. In fact, every character of business pertaining to Law and Land will meet prompt attention to our hands. We represent, and offer for sale about 40,000 acres of land in Hill county. We have an extensive correspondence. We are ready, willing and anxious to serve you, and invite you to call on us at our offices, over Abbott's brick building, southeast corner of square, Hillsboro, Texas.

With his reputation growing, his activities were often reported in the newspapers around the state. In those days it was common for hotels to release the names of guests visiting in the town. This was a sign of status.

In April 1885, The *Times-Picayune* in New Orleans reported that B.D. and his wife, his older brother Dr. Toulmin Tarlton and wife of Grand Coteau, and his law partner George Jordan and wife from Hillsboro were visiting New Orleans and were aboard the steamboat John W. Cannon.[106]

In 1887, the firm advertised their services in The *Dallas Morning News*:

TARLTON, JORDAN & TARLTON, Attorneys at Law and Land Agents, have a complete abstract of titles to all lands in Hill county, including town lots. Special attention given to commercial and land litigation. Abstracts furnished on short notice. Hillsboro, Hill Co., Tex.[107]

G.D. Tarlton, in his later years, became a large landowner of investment property in Hill County. Perhaps the Tarlton interest in real estate came from their upbringing in Louisiana where the family saw their parents acquire large holdings in St. Mary and St. Landry parishes in Louisiana.

Tarlton v. Kirkpatrick

One example of the Tarltons acquiring property for investment is shown in the case of *Tarlton v. Kirkpatrick* that lasted fifteen years. The case was tried two times and appealed two times with opinions from the Fort Worth and Dallas courts of civil appeals before it was resolved in 1902. In that case the Tarlton firm acquired property that was subject to numerous title claims from owners who relied upon their possession and titles from the firm of McKinnon & McCall, a competing law firm in Hill County.

The backstory of the case shows Tarlton, Tarlton & Jordan and McKinnon & McCall claimed title to the same 178-acre tract in Hill County. The Tarlton firm traced the title to October 14, 1860, based on a certificate containing 682 acres issued to the heirs of Shackelford. The McKinnon & McCall established title as of April 1883 to 139 4/5 of the 178 acres from G.Y. Tarver. The case did not explain how Tarver acquired his interest in the property.

The property had been surveyed multiple times, but there was a problem with the survey in the General Land Office that the McKinnon & Call law firm based its title upon. In Texas, a title examiner's opinion of who has valid title to real property is based upon the entire chain of title, being the successive conveyances beginning with the severance from the sovereign (Texas) down to and including the conveyance to the present holder. But the severance from the sovereign (Texas) occurs on the *date of the survey* of the property for severance purposes, not on the date of the patent, which will come after the patent.[108]

If the survey that the McKinnon & McCall firm relied upon for their title was invalid, then their conveyances would be invalid. This meant that a party had to establish title by possession, termed "adverse possession" except that the concept does not apply as against the state of Texas. Title could be proved by either ten years of possession cultivating and enjoying the property or a shorter five-year adverse possession statute by relying upon "color of title" by a registered deed to the property, paying taxes and possessing the property at the same time. With the title being valid in the name of the Tarlton, Tarlton & Joran firm, this meant that they had to evict the occupants from the property.

The diagram below was set out by the court and shows W.A. Kirkpatrick with a claim to 112 acres, Z.T. Huff with two properties claiming 27 3/5 acres and 19 4/5 acres, and J.P. Allen claiming 25 4/5 acres. However, Allen had bigger plans: he planned on claiming title to the 80 acres above the property depicted below:

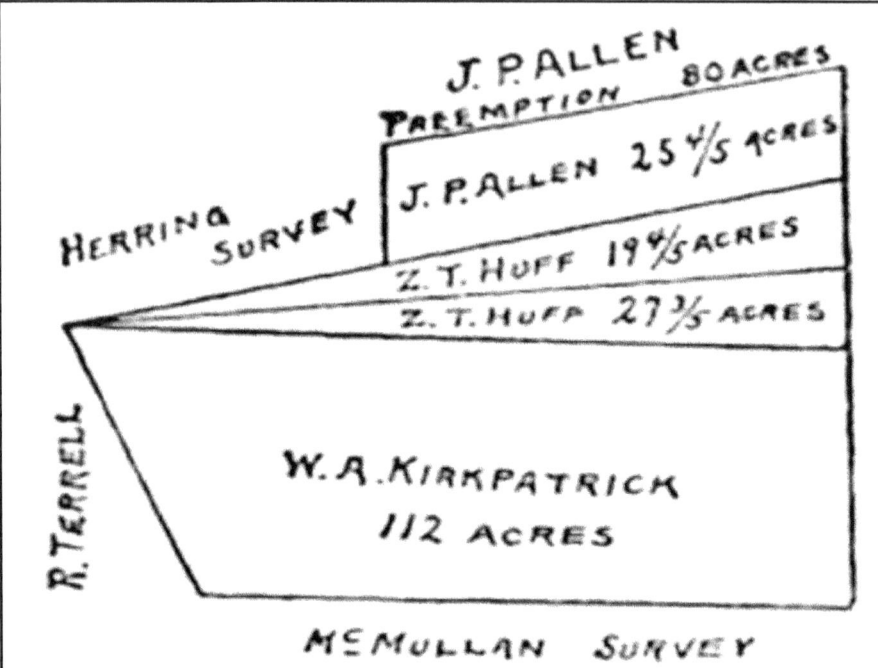

Figure 27 This illustration was provided by the court in its opinion in Tarlton v. Kirkpatrick I and shows the property in dispute. The Tarlton firm would have to recover possession of the property from Kirkpatrick, Huff, and Allen, who claimed title by deeds from the McKinnon & McCall law firm and possession of the property and adding to their time in possession by including the time in possession of their predecessors, McKinnon & McCall, and G.Y. Tarver.

The McKinnon & Call firm transferred title to the property days after receiving deeds, and this step set up the ability of Kirkpatrick, Huff, and Allen to claim title under the five-year adverse possession statute.

The Tarlton firm was in luck. The General Land Office reissued the certificate excluding the land that the McKinnon & McCall firm relied upon to convey title. This meant that McKinnon & McCall conveyed nothing to Kirkpatrick, Huff, and Allen.

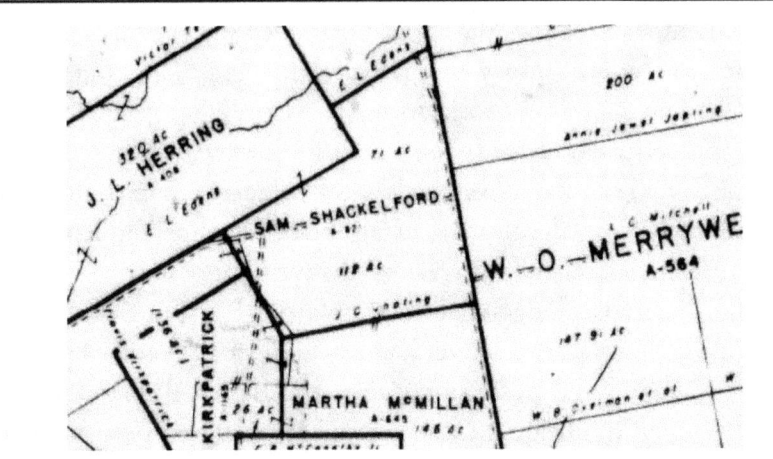

Figure 28 This is another map showing the Sam Shackelford survey showing the location of the disputed property.

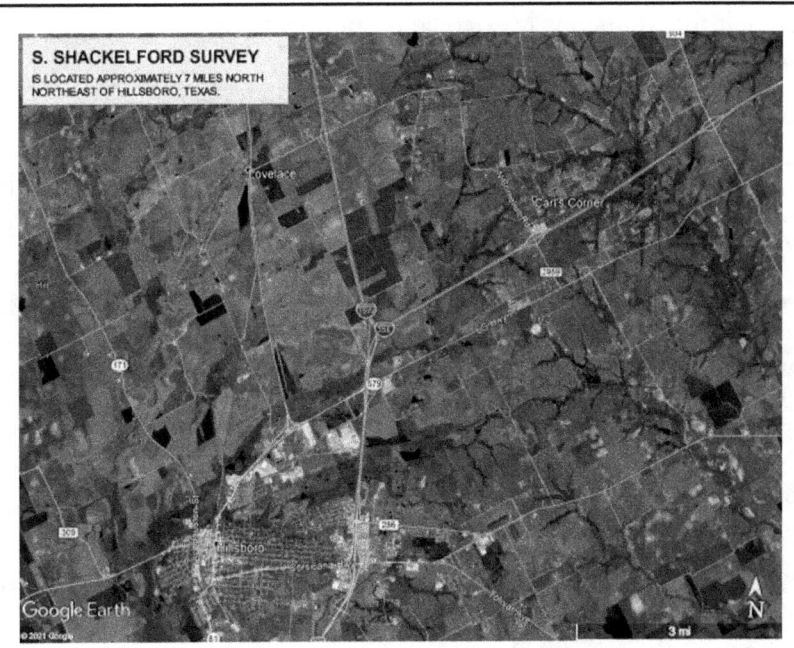

Figure 29 Aerial photograph showing the disputed property in Tarlton v. Kirkpatrick in relation to Hillsboro, Texas.

On September 27, 1887, the Tarlton firm filed suit to adjudicate the title in their name and to remove Kirkpatrick, Huff, and Allen from the property. The firm filed a trespass to try title action in Hill County, the county where the property was located. The purpose of a trespass to try title suit is to determine who has the superior claim to title to the land. The Tarlton firm could now prove the superior chain of title leaving the Kirkpatrick, Huff, and Allen, defendants with claims of adverse possession.

In a non-jury trial, Judge Hall ruled in favor of Kirkpatrick, Huff, and Allen. Judge Hall found that Tarver had adversely possessed the land under the five-year year adverse possession claim. The Tarlton firm appealed.

In December 1888, Jordan experienced ill health and was advised to spend time in southwestern Texas. He might have had enough of the litigation. He settled his affairs and conveyed his interests in numerous properties in Hill County to the Tarlton firm, including his rights in the *Tarlton v. Kirkpatrick* litigation. The firm of Tarlton, Jordan & Tarlton dissolved. Jordan left for Monterey, Mexico, and Southwest Texas.

Tarlton, Tarlton & Morrow

Figure 30 Wright Chalfont Morrow.

After Jordan left, Wright Chalfont Morrow joined the firm. He married B.D.'s sister, Fanietta Tarlton, on January 8, 1884. Morrow was born October 12, 1858, in Elizabethtown, Kentucky. In 1870, at the age of seventeen, he left home for Fort Worth, Texas, where he worked briefly before moving to Whitney, Texas.[109] Morrow was educated at private schools and summer lectures at the University of Virginia. Morrow may have met G.D. Tarlton at the University of Virginia while the two studied law at the school and may have decided to move to Texas as a result. The firm became known as Tarlton, Tarlton & Morrow.[110]

The firm was now an entirely family-run law firm, and Morrow would go on to become an important judicial figure in law in Texas. In 1916, he was elected to the Texas Court of Criminal Appeals. In 1921, he was appointed as the presiding judge of the court and served until he retired on October 15, 1939.[111] He died on October 6, 1942 and was buried in the Hillsboro City Cemetery.

Race for District Court against Judge Hall

In 1888, B.D. decided to run against incumbent District Judge J.M. Hall for the Eighteenth Judicial District Court. It is not known what prompted Tarlton to run against Hall. Perhaps Tarlton was troubled over Hall's decision in the *Tarlton v. Kirkpatrick* case.

It is serious business for any attorney to run against an incumbent judge: it is a signal that there is something wrong with the rulings from the court. Hall was from Johnson County, and perhaps B.D. believed that Hill County attorneys were not being treated fairly. There must have been a tug of war over whose county resident would occupy the court. Such a challenge comes with a price. The challenger will face severe criticism if they lose and will become an enemy of the incumbent judge.

Tarlton was heading into familiar territory taking on Hall. Recall his race against E.D. Estillette in Louisiana, the incumbent state legislator. Had he not learned his lesson in 1874 when he ran against Estillette? But Tarlton was now older, and with political clout as a former member of the Texas House of Representatives, he stood a chance of ousting Hall. He would have the Hill County vote behind him.

Not even B.D.'s influence could defeat Hall, who won the race with 2,657 votes to B.D.'s 2,162 votes. B.D. lost by 495 votes, losing his second race for public office. He had not learned from his prior race against Estillette. Jo Abbott won his race for re-election to Congress with 3,096 votes to Sam Evans' 1,517 votes.

Figure 31 A young B.D. Tarlton appearing before District Judge J.M. Hall. B.D.'s race against Hall and loss turned him into a skilled appellate attorney, which ultimately led to his appointment to the Texas Commission of Appeals and to the Second Court of Civil Appeals.

Master of Arts Degree

On July 27, 1889, B.D. traveled to St. Charles College for the graduation ceremonies at the Jesuit College. The degree of Master of Arts was conferred on B.D. Tarlton and his brother, Toulmin Tarlton. The College Band opened the ceremonies, followed by a debate: "Should Capital Punishment be Abolished?" The play *The Nervous Man* met "with approbation of the auditors," followed by the College Glee Club and a rendition of *Norma* by an orchestra.

The newspaper reported the event:

> Hon. B.D. Tarlton was asked to address the graduates. He spoke in glowing terms of the brave and noble sons of St. Ignatius, at whose hands he received paternal care, good counsel and complete instruction. Indeed St. Charles has reason to be proud of such a scholar, one who will always prove to be a true man and true Christian. Glorious America may well be proud of such men, who will cherish love for their God and love for their country. The band concluded the entertainment with Home Sweet Home, and the faces of many were illumined with smiles, which indicated that the exhibition was a treat which will long be remembered.[112]

Judge Hall's court

For six years, from 1885 through 1891, B.D. appeared before Judge Hall as a trial attorney handling civil and criminal cases. In the six-year period he appealed Hall eleven times and reversed him nine times. Seven of the nine reversals on appeal were civil appeals, and both criminal appeals were reversed. There was a reason for B.D.'s loss. Judge Hall's rulings turned him into a skilled appellate attorney and gave him the credentials to be appointed to the Texas Commission of Appeals in 1891, which then led to his appointment as Chief Justice of the Fort Worth Court of Civil Appeals in 1892. Had B.D. not run against Hall and lost, he may never have become an appellate justice and the first Chief Justice of the Fort Worth Court of Civil Appeals.

Retired District Judge Frank B. "Bob" McGregor Jr. researched Judge

Hall and located his biography and a photo of him for this book. Hall served when the district judge served Hill, Johnson, and Bosque counties. Today the counties of Hill and Johnson are no longer in the same judicial district.

Judge McGregor said that "Hall is remembered as the tough, one-armed judge, that brought a colorful and determined brand of judicial service to us."

Appeals of Judge J.M. Hall

Here are some of the interesting cases that B.D. Tarlton appealed from Judge Hall's court:

Crumley v. McKinney

The case of *Crumley v. McKinney*,[113] shows that Hall made things difficult for Tarlton. In that case, Tarlton represented Crumley, the district clerk of Hill County. McKinney had an interest in land that was the subject of a judgment lien and was being sold by the sheriff to satisfy the judgment. McKinney was not responsible for payment of the judgment, but he didn't want to see his property sold by the sheriff and wanted to stop the sheriff's sale. To do that, he was required to put up double the amount of the judgment plus interest and costs based on a judgment owed by someone else. He could not afford the supersedeas bond to stop the sheriff's sale.

The underlying judgment was between John R. Nunn Sr. as plaintiff and against William M. Nunn Sr. as defendant for $7,140.66 and foreclosure of a lien on 175 acres of land to secure payment. McKinney put up a bond for $1,500 with the clerk of the court. This amount was not enough to stop the sheriff's sale. This amount would cover the costs of the appeal but had nothing to do with stopping the sheriff's sale.

After the bond was posted, Nunn, as plaintiff, recognized that this bond would not stay the sheriff's sale, so he requested an order to direct the sheriff to sell the property. McKinney sued Crumley, the clerk of the district court in Hill County, to issue a writ of supersedeas to the sheriff to stop the sale while his suit was on appeal.

Judge Hall conducted an ex parte hearing in his chambers and directed the clerk to issue the writ of supersedeas to stop the sale by the sheriff. An ex parte hearing is one conducted without the presence of all parties entitled to notice. Judge Hall issued his order without notice to Crumley, the district clerk, or Nunn, who owned the judgment and had a right to have the property sold to pay for his judgment. Perhaps Judge Hall's days as a Civil War officer allowed him to issue orders to subordinates, and they were not to be questioned. But this was not the military, and in the civilian world a subordinate can easily topple the civilian leader by going public with the actions of their superior.

Tarlton appeared for Crumley and answered the suit. He asked Judge Hall to set aside its order because the bond was not a supersedeas bond, and the court appeared to have issued mandamus relief without notice or opportunity of a hearing. Tarlton offered documents showing where Judge Hall directed the clerk to accept the bond. Judge Hall overruled Tarlton and excluded the evidence of the ex parte order. Tarlton filed a bill of exception offering the evidence of Judge Hall's prior action. In other words, Tarlton presented in court the documents showing Judge Hall's prior actions, which he could show to the higher court that Hall's actions were invalid.

Tarlton appealed the case to the Texas Supreme Court, who ruled that the judge should have received the evidence. The court found that the bond was not a supersedeas bond because it was not double the amount of the judgment, interest, and costs. The higher court set aside all of the orders of Judge Hall that restrained the execution of the judgment and found that this was a matter for the Legislature:

> To require a bond so large from one who is made a party to an action only in order to establish and foreclose a lien on property claimed by him, he not being personally the debtor, may appear in many cases, to operate a hardship, and if this be the effect of such a requirement, the legislature would no doubt provide a different rule for such cases, if attention was called to the subject. The legislature, however, has the power to prescribe the terms on which an appellant may have the execution of a judgment suspended during an appeal, and, having so prescribed, the courts have no power to refuse to give effect to such a law.

Farrar v. State

B.D. Tarlton showed that his expertise extended to criminal law when he represented a defendant named Farrar in Judge J.M. Hall's court in *Farrar v. State*[114], a case that advanced to the Texas Court of Appeals. Farrar, a tenant sharecropper of J.R. Corry, had been found guilty of assault with intent to kill Corry but was freed on appeal.

The dispute arose after Farrar gathered his share of the crop in the field and left his rent crop there for Corry to gather. Farrar allegedly threatened Corry with a gun. Farrar said Corry assaulted him. Farrar surrendered in Hillsboro after the incident.

At trial Corry and Farrar told markedly different stories.

Corry's testimony: Both men were at church the night before the incident, and Corry told Farrar that his religion should make him help gather the corn.

[Farrar would testify that he went to the field once to help and waited half a day. "You did not come," Farrar told Corry, "and now you can gather it yourself." Upon reflection, Farrar thought it right to help Corry gather the corn.]

The next day Corry was in the field and saw Farrar talking to a man named William Truitt.

Farrar, on horseback, came over to Corry and said, "So you think my religion ought to make me help gather this corn?"

"I do. I told you that before."

"Well, I think my religion will make me do that," Farrar said.

Farrar then cursed Corry and took out a pistol from his saddle pocket. Corry called for Truitt two times in a loud voice. No answer.

Corry said to Farrar: "You have a pistol, and I am going to town and have you arrested."

"You won't get to town," Farrar replied.

As Corry walked toward his house, Farrar followed, still cursing and holding his pistol. When Corry crossed a small road that traversed his field, Farrar told him to stop. Corry did so and turned to face Farrar.

Farrar got within 20 feet of Corry, looked around for possible witnesses, and said, "I am going to shoot you." Farrar fired and missed.

Corry threw up his hands and said, "You are a coward to shoot me when I am unarmed and have nothing with which to defend myself."

Figure 32 Corry faces Farrar.

Farrar rode closer and shot Corry in the back of the left shoulder.

When Farrar snapped his pistol two more times but it didn't fire, he proceeded to examine it. Corry rushed Farrar, but Farrar hit him on the head with the pistol.

Corry ran home, and Farrar rode off toward Hillsboro.

Corry did not have a pistol or a knife on him, he never acted in a hostile manner with Farrar, never threw a stone at him, never cursed him or called him a son of a bitch. Corry's shoulder wound was superficial.

Farrar's testimony: Corry told Farrar the night before the incident that he thought Farrar's religion should make him help gather the corn in the field. After leaving Truitt the morning of the incident, Farrar, on horseback, went to Corry in the field and said:

"Mr. Corry, you think my religion should make me help gather this corn. I think so, too."

Corry then began to curse Farrar and said: "You have come here for a row, and if you will get down [from the horse] you will get it."

"I have not come here for a row," Farrar said, "but if nothing but a row will do you, I guess I can accommodate you."

Farrar dismounted, and he and Corry approached each other, Corry with an open knife in his hand. Seeing the knife, Farrar stepped back to his horse and put his hand in the saddle pocket.

"You have a pistol. I will go to town and have this corn gathered by law," Corry said, and he started up the cornrows going away from his house.

Farrar followed, talking with Corry, until Corry became angry and picked up a stone. Corry turned around and started going toward his house. Farrar still followed until they reached the turn row near a small branch. Corry crossed the branch, and Farrar started up the turn row toward his brother Jim's house.

Corry stopped.

"You damned cowardly son of a bitch," he said, "I thought you would run off."

Farrar turned to Corry.

"That is too hard to take," he said, "and you must take it back." Corry cursed Farrar and said he would retract nothing.

Farrar started to get off his horse when Corry began throwing stones at him. A stone as large as a man's fist struck Farrar on the left elbow, deadening the arm and producing a soreness that lasted two or three days.

Farrar drew his pistol and fired two shots at Corry, who raised his hands and asked Farrar not to shoot again. Farrar said he would shoot no more, but Corry walked up to Farrar's right and tried to cut his throat, inflicting a small scratch.

Farrar struck Corry over the head with his pistol, then rode directly to Hillsboro and surrendered to George Patterson, the deputy marshal.

The incident occurred on ground covered with stones, and Farrar considered himself in danger, which is why he drew his pistol and fired. He made no effort to fire again; four shots remained in his pistol, and he easily could have fired them at Corry.

Deputy Marshal Patterson testified for the defense that the defendant surrendered to him on the day of the incident. Farrar noted a scratch on the right side of his throat.

In addition to B.D. Tarlton, Farrar also was represented by R.P. Hadge and W.C. Wear. William Clayton Wear was a well-known trial lawyer in Hillsboro.[115] Assistant Attorney General Davidson represented the state.

At trial Farrar testified that Truitt advised him to go help Corry gather the corn and that he was acting on this advice and therefore had no intent to commit murder. The state objected, calling the evidence immaterial, and Judge Hall sustained the objection.

Farrar was found guilty and sentenced to two years in prison.

His counsel filed a "bill of exception" to preserve the exclusion of Truitt's testimony and objected to Judge Hall's failure to submit an instruction on self-defense.

The prosecuting attorney objected to the bill of exception being defective, arguing that it did not show the relevancy and materiality of Truitt's testimony.

Judge J. Willson of the Texas Court of Appeals ruled in *Farrar v. State*[116] that it was material error to reject Truitt's testimony "in view of the evidence upon which the conviction is based."

The court found that the "the bill is sufficiently explicit and full, stating all the facts essential to enable this court to revise the said ruling. We think the bill shows that the offered testimony was relevant, material to the defendant, and admissible for the purpose of showing that defendant went to where Corry was with innocent intent and for a lawful purpose. It was testimony explanatory of defendant's act of going to where Corry was gathering corn. It was *res gestæ* of that act and tended to show that said act was innocent and lawful."

The court found no error in the failure to submit the instruction requested by the defendant, saying the instruction was substantially contained in the charge to the jury.

THIRTEEN

1890

In 1890, B.D. Tarlton remained politically active and publicly prominent. He appeared at local and statewide events across the state and as a delegate from Hill County. Tarlton was vocal with his support for Jim Hogg in his race for governor. Hogg was popular for his support for a commission that would reign in the railroads.

One crowded event occurred on June 7, 1890, at the Hill County courthouse that included prominent citizens of Hillsboro and Hill County who assembled to organize a "Hogg and commission Democratic Club."[117] The Hillsboro cornet band played for the event and entertained the audience. B.D. Tarlton called the meeting to order, and the club elected J.R. Thompson as president, Capt. W.A. Fields of the *Reflector* and L.J. Thomson of the *Mirror* as vice-presidents, and Dave Derden, Esquire, as secretary. Derden was a Hillsboro attorney who teamed up with Tarlton on appellate cases.

Figure 33 Governor Jim Hogg appointed B.D. Tarlton to the Texas Commission of Appeals and as Chief Justice to the Second Court of Civil Appeals.

The club was unanimously named "The Hogg and Commission Democratic Club."[118] The club adopted resolutions to use every honest and honorable effort to bring about the nomination of Hogg for Governor. "Hons. B.D. Fulton and T.S. Smith being loudly called for speeches, responded in a graceful manner, and their utterances were heartily cheered by all."[119]

On July 4, 1890, buggies and wagons rolled into Hillsboro, bearing loads of people on the hot day that amounted to between 3,000 to 5,000 people to honor the ex-Confederate soldiers of Hill County. The day was the reunion of the ex-Confederate soldiers of the county and the laying of the cornerstone for the new courthouse by the Masonic lodge of the city. "Very early in the morning, yes, the night before, buggies and wagons began to roll into town bearing loads of people anticipating a grand time," reported the Hillsboro *Mirror*.[120]

The Masons marched from their hall, preceded by the Hillsboro cornet band, to the northeast corner of the new building, where corn, oil, coins, letters, papers, and mementoes were placed in the stone. "Although it was intensely hot the vast crowd stood and watched the ceremonies with eager interest."[121] The crowd left for Abbott's grove, "a cool and shady retreat just suitable for such occasions. Before the crowd had assembled a rain came on, putting a 'damper' on the enthusiasm of many and frightening them home, especially those living in town. In an hour or two the rain cloud disappeared, and the crowd reassembled."[122]

Dr. A.M. Douglas, President of the Ex-Confederate Encampment, addressed the crowd followed by Captain A.P. McKinnon, who delivered the address of welcome, and Dave Derden made a speech. A recess was taken for dinner, for which eleven beeves had been barbequed and an abundance of bread ordered; but the rain so "demoralized" the event that the dinner was not a "success." Many people who had prepared baskets did not bring them on the ground.[123]

After dinner B.D. Tarlton and Judge Hall addressed the veterans, and the rest of the afternoon was spent in social reunion until the roll was called.[124]

On August 8, 1890, Tarlton attended the Texas Bar Convention held in Galveston and was appointed to the committee on publications. Other members were B.G. Bidwell of Weatherford, T.F. Harwood of Gonzales, Henry Sayles of Abilene, and James B. Stubbs of Galveston.

On August 14, 1890, Tarlton served as the temporary chairman of the Democratic Convention in San Antonio, where Attorney General Jim Hogg was nominated for governor. Delegate Smith of Hill County placed Tarlton's name in nomination for temporary chairman, and he was elected by acclamation. Tarlton was escorted to the chair while a band played a musical number.[125] His job was to give the permanent chairmanship to J.C. Hutcheson.[126] Tarlton spoke to the convention to nominate Web Finley, who was seeking a second term as chairman of the state executive committee. *The Austin Weekly Statesman* reported Tarlton's speech:

> The next remarkable achievement of this remarkable body was the election of Web Finley to a second term as chairman of the state executive committee. It was without precedent, but so was nearly everything else done by the remarkable body. Mr. Tarlton explained that Finley needed vindication and that he must have it in the shape of another term as chairman and forthwith Mr. Finley got it, made a speech and the convention of 1890 passed into history.[127]

Hogg won election as governor in 1890 by seventy-six percent against W. Flanagan, the Republican opponent, by twenty-two percent. Hogg had served as Attorney General since 1886. Through legal means, Hogg forced out-of-state corporations operating the railroads to establish operating offices in Texas and pushed for the creation of the Railroad Commission. He sued the railroads in 1888 for attempting to create a monopoly. Hogg had the support of farmers, ranchers, and small merchants.

Figure 34 Governor Lawrence Sullivan Ross, 19th Texas Governor.

Hogg succeeded Governor Lawrence Sullivan Ross who served two terms. Ross served as a Confederate States Army general during the Civil War. On November 26, 1890, Governor Ross appointed B.D. Tarlton as a delegate to the Interstate Immigration convention to be held in Asheville, North Carolina.[128]

On December 18, 1890, Tarlton represented the Twenty-first district in Hill County, urging the governor and legislature of the state of Texas to make an appropriation of $1,000,000 to be used to defray the expenses of the World Columbian exposition "as a creditable exhibit of the resources and productions of the whole of Texas."[129]

FOURTEEN

Eastland County

WHILE B.D. TARLTON PURSUED HIS political and legal career in Hillsboro, Truman Holman Conner was pursuing a similar successful practice in Eastland County. Conner was born in Peru, Indiana. His parents were Samuel S. Conner and Margaretta (Holman) Conner. His mother was the daughter of U.S. Congressman W.S. Holman, of Dearborn, Indiana, who served in sixteen congresses during 1859 to 1897. Samuel Conner and Margaretta Lucinda Conner had six children:

Figure 35 Samuel and Lucinda Conner with a young Truman Conner.

Truman Holman Conner, born December 5, 1849; Mary Maude Coleman, born November 10, 1853; Ella Nora Parsons, born May 1, 1856; Claude Leon Conner, born November 11, 1869; William Earl Conner, born December 2, 1872; and Jennie LaRue Calhoun, born January 1, 1865.

Conner's family immigrated to Texas in 1853. A rugged looking character in his later years, Conner understood hard work and was determined to be well-educated and to become a lawyer. Conner attended Marion College in Ellis County in 1873 and 1874 and received legal training at Trinity University at Tehuacana, Texas, where he graduated in the spring of 1876. Conner was sworn into practice law before Judge H. Barksdale of Dallas, the same judge who tried the *Daily v. Tarlton* case.

Some of Conner's biographical information reports that he worked with Wesley Justus Ferris and Anson Rainey while in Waxahachie. Ferris would have been a mentor and Rainey would have been a young colleague with Conner. It is not clear if Conner met or knew B.D. Tarlton who arrived in Waxahachie in March 1876. Thus, for a brief period there were three future chief justices of the courts of appeals working as practicing attorneys in Waxahachie at the same time: Anson Rainey, B.D. Tarlton, and Truman Conner.

Eastland County

In August 1876, Conner's father, Samuel Conner, sold the family's 160-acre tract in Ellis County, and the family departed for Eastland County. The Conner family arrived in Eastland County when the new county was undergoing a migration and boom after it was organized in 1873. At that time the county was still considered to be a wild frontier. One source says there were eighty-eight persons living in the county in 1870. By 1872, the population of the county was estimated to be ninety-nine inhabitants from over twenty families who settled in the county. Game was plentiful: bear, wolf, deer, turkey, buffalo, wild horses, cattle, a few panther cats, wild cat, catamount, fox, opossum, and skunk. The county still had the appearance of Indians in search of plunder with the last Indian raid occurring in 1874.[130]

Eastland was known as the county where Josiah Gordon "Doc" Scurlock, an American gunfighter, settled down to live a respectable life. Scurlock was a founding member of the Regulators, who fought in the Lincoln County War in New Mexico. He fought alongside Billy the Kid and worked as a line rider for John Chisum to prevent cattle rustling.[131]

In August 1875, a vote was taken to move the county seat from Merriman to Eastland. The vote was seventy-seven for Eastland to nine for Merriman and a few other scattered votes. There were 123 votes in Eastland.

By 1880, the population of the county was 4,855.[132] The Texas and Pacific Railway Company rolled through the town after lots were offered in the downtown area to the company. A new courthouse and jail were built, and the town grew from a one-roomed cabin in the woods to a substantial town. It was one of the best counties in the state, touting an excellent public-school system with an enrollment of three hundred pupils.

By 1883, the estimate was 8,500 but still considered to be sparsely settled.[133] Unimproved land could be purchased from 75 cents to $3 per acre. By 1883, there were forty-two schools organized for 992 pupils. There was plenty of opportunity, and some of the most wealthy and prosperous citizens came to the county with nothing.[134]

The county had a home, and soon offices and lawyers began to locate to the city, including J.R. Fleming, (who became the District Judge), J.M. Moore, son of Chief Justice William Folsom Moore of the Texas Supreme Court, Judge E.T. Hilliard, J.E. Thomas (of Dallas) who served as County Attorney; G.W. Perryman; A. Lawrence (who became County Attorney and Judge); R.B. Truly (District Clerk), and B.F. Collins. J.R. Fleming and J.M. Moore formed the firm of Fleming & Moore and handled one of the first appellate cases heard by the Fort Worth Court of Civil Appeals, *Texas Central Railway Company v. Stewart*,[135] which began operations in October 1892.

Truman Conner: Private Practice

Truman Conner engaged in the private practice of civil and criminal law in Eastland County from 1876 to 1888. Conner practiced law with ex-Senators John Henry Calhoun of Eastland County and Jouett Harbert "John" Davenport, a former senator from Bell County.

Conner represented the Texas Pacific & Railway Company in a claim made against the railroad in the case of *Tex. & Pac. R'y Co. v. McCumsey*,[136] where McCumsey recovered a judgment against the railroad in the justice court. The appeal was dismissed when the bond described the judgment rendered as against "The Texas Pacific Railway Company" instead of "The

Texas and Pacific Railway Company." The word "and" was omitted in the name of the defendant railway company. The Court of Appeals of Texas reversed the case, finding that the omission was a clerical error and not substantial and did not affect the validity of the bond.

In the case of *A.M. Price and Others v. The State*,[137] Conner had to testify as a fact witness over his partial preparation of an appeal bond that unwittingly caused his client to be released from jail without signing the bond. Conner represented Marion Tanzy, who was under indictment for horse-theft. Conner filled out the defendant's name "Marion Tanzy as Principal" on the bond and gave it to the sheriff, who then released Tanzy from jail without securing Tanzy's signature. The sureties subsequently signed their names to the bond.

After Tanzy did not appear for trial, a dispute arose over the liability of the sureties. At the bond hearing, the sheriff, H.S. Schmick, testified that Conner procured the signatures of some of the sureties and that they also appeared at his office to sign the bail-bond. The court rendered a judgment against the sureties who appealed, contending that the bond was invalid since Tanzy did not sign the bond. The state argued that since Conner, as attorney for Tanzy, prepared the bond and the bond contained Tanzy's name, these facts constituted his signature. The Texas Supreme Court found the bond to be void since Tanzy did not sign his name to the bond for purposes of giving authenticity to the bond.

Conner married the Sallie Jones, and from 1886 through 1900 the family would have eight children.

District Judge

Conner's real success occurred when he became a district judge. Once he took the bench, he remained a jurist the rest of his life. In 1888, Governor Lawrence S. Ross appointed Conner as Judge of the 42nd Judicial District Court. The court had civil and criminal jurisdiction in cases originating in Eastland, Jones, Callahan, Comanche, Taylor, and Stephens counties.[138]

From 1887 to 1892, the appeals from the district court went directly to the Texas Supreme Court for civil appeals or the Court of Appeals for criminal cases. During the period of 1888 to 1892, thirty-one cases from Conner's court were appealed. Eighteen of those cases were criminal appeals, and thirteen cases were civil appeals. Fourteen of the eighteen criminal appeals were reversed. Seven of the reversals were due to insufficient evidence to support the conviction. The other reasons for reversal were due to exceptions to the indictment not being sustained, errors in instructions to the jury, or failing to instruct the jury of limitations on the evidence. Of the thirteen civil cases appealed, eight appeals were affirmed, four appeals were reversed, and one judgment modified.

Figure 36 Truman Conner.

In the case of *Warren v. Mayberry*,[139] Conner dismissed an appeal from the justice court because he found that the appeal bond failed to describe or misdescribed the judgment being appealed from by failing to describe it as being rendered against the sureties. The Supreme Court reversed the case, finding that the bond correctly stated the number, style, and the court of the case. The cases of *Warren v. Marberry* and *Tex. & Pac. Rey Co. v. McCumsey*, which involved defective appeals bonds, show that the Texas Supreme Court refused to allow litigants to lose their day in court because of technical errors caused by the clerk or their attorneys.

Once the courts of appeals were established in 1892, Conner's appeals would be assigned to the Second Court of Civil Appeals in Fort Worth.

FIFTEEN

Texas Commission of Appeals

IN 1891, THE APPEALS COURTS in Texas included the Texas Supreme Court, established in 1846, and the Texas Court of Criminal Appeals, established in 1841. In 1879, the Texas Commission of Appeals was established to assist with appeals to the Texas Supreme Court. The new commission could hear appeals with consent of the parties. In 1881, the law changed, allowing the commission to hear cases without the need for the consent of the parties. If the Texas Supreme Court adopted the opinion of the commission, then the decision would have the force of law in the state. The Texas Commission of Appeals consisted of two panels, A and B, with three justices.

Appointment

In May 1891, Governor Hogg, impressed with Tarlton, nominated him to Section B of the Texas Commission of Appeals. Tarlton was forty-two years old and had been in the state for sixteen years. He would now serve on one of the highest courts in Texas as shown by the newspaper clipping below.

News spread of the appointment:

AUSTIN, TEX., May 12. The new Judges of the Commission of Appeals met yesterday and selected Hon. C.C. Garrett as presiding Judge. This will be known as Section B, and is composed of C.C. Garrett, Presiding Judge and B.D. Tarlton and H.C. Fisher,

Associate Judges. This new section of the court has gone to work in earnest, and it is hoped that the long and stale docket will be reduced.[140]

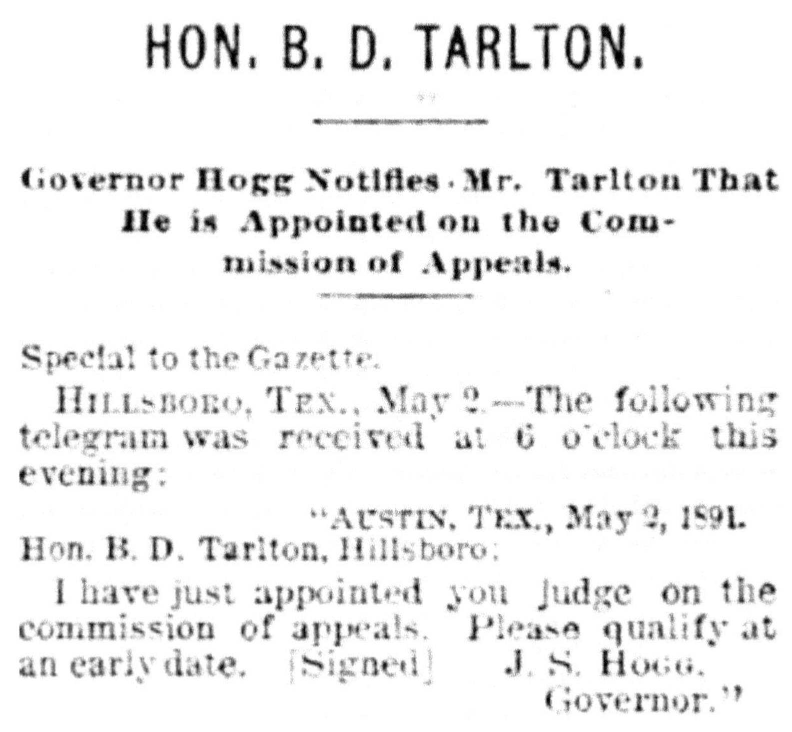

> ## HON. B. D. TARLTON.
>
> **Governor Hogg Notifies Mr. Tarlton That He is Appointed on the Commission of Appeals.**
>
> Special to the Gazette.
>
> HILLSBORO, TEX., May 2.—The following telegram was received at 6 o'clock this evening:
>
> "AUSTIN, TEX., May 2, 1891.
> Hon. B. D. Tarlton, Hillsboro:
>
> I have just appointed you Judge on the commission of appeals. Please qualify at an early date. [Signed]   J. S. HOGG.
>   Governor."

Figure 37 The Fort Worth Daily Gazette, May 3, 1891.

A large ceremony was held in Hillsboro following the announcement of the appointment. Leading citizens of Hillsboro assembled at the opera house to ratify the appointment of Tarlton to the Texas Commission of Appeals.

The Fort Worth Daily Gazette reported that Jo Abbott "in a feeling and appropriate address introduced Judge Tarlton, who in an eloquent and feeling address returned his thanks for the honor done him by his friends … the stage was beautifully decorated with a magnificent profusion of rare and costly flowers. The most pleasing feature of the evening was the presentation to Judge Tarlton by the ladies of Hillsboro of a number of magnificent bouquets."[141]

HON. B. D. TARLTON.

His Friends at Hillsboro Rejoice Over His Appointment to the Commission of Appeals.

Figure 38 *The Fort Worth Daily Gazette, May 5, 1891.*

Significant Decisions

The following are important opinions written by Justice Tarlton while on the Texas Commission of Appeals:

Authority in powers of attorney
In *Frost v. Erath Cattle Co.*,[142] Tarlton wrote what is still considered the bedrock instruction in how to interpret the powers in a power of attorney document that contains general and specific powers. In this case, the power of attorney document gave the power to *sell* property and administer assets, but it did not give the authority to *settle litigation by discharging and conveying land in exchange, or to partition land*. Tarlton wrote that the general expressions in a power of attorney are to be referred to specific acts elsewhere specified in the agreement.

Allan Howeth, former managing partner of Cantey Hanger LLP in Fort Worth with over fifty years of experience in probate, estate, and wills, commented that the *Frost v. Erath Cattle Co* decision "has been favorably cited many times." Howeth said that "the decision is frequently cited for the holding that powers of attorney, unlike deeds and wills, are to be strictly construed, and authority delegated is limited to the meaning of the terms in which it is expressed."[143] Howeth explained how the powers of attorney remains an ongoing issue in todays' legal practice:

> Today, the legal issues involving powers of attorney continue to come up in office practice and in litigation, since the volume of powers of attorney, mostly all now Durable Powers of Attorney which continue notwithstanding the later incapacity of the principal, has increased because when most attorneys prepare wills for client, they almost always strongly urge clients to utilize Durable Powers of Attorney, and Medical Powers of Attorney.
>
> The enactment of statutory durable powers of attorney into Texas law, which are only examples, not mandatory, has introduced a great degree of uniformity in the terms of the documents.
>
> Unfortunately, Powers of Attorney still do not infrequently meet objections from banks, brokerage firms, and title companies, which are many times not well founded. Some banks insist on use by their customers of a nationwide standard Durable Power of Attorney created by their bank, which sometimes causes unjustified delays and roadblocks, especially in instances in which the principal may have become incapacitated.
>
> By statute, third parties accepting a power of attorney are protected from their good faith acceptance and reliance on the validity of a power of attorney, but still refusals to deal with an attorney in fact are frequently encountered. The basic principles of old but wise jurisprudence authored by great legal minds like Justice Tarleton continue to guide us.

Another interesting aspect of the *Frost v. Erath Cattle Co.* case is that it defined the meaning of the term "sale" of real property. Tarlton wrote: "A sale is defined to be an agreement by which one of two contracting parties, called the seller, gives the thing, and passes the title to it for a certain price in current money." Tarlton looked to Iowa law in the case of *Hampton v.*

Morhead, 62 Iowa, 93, 17 N.W. Rep. 20 (1883) to support the definition. The Texas Supreme Court adopted this opinion as Texas law.

Damages in shortage of area limited to the pleadings
The case of *Cregg v. Hill*[144] shows how important it is for attorneys to make sure that their pleadings match the relief that they seek based on the facts of the case. In that case, the court dealt with a case where the seller agreed to convey 2,420.49 acres, but due to conflicts in the surveys ended up conveying 313.3 acres less than what was agreed. Due to the shortage in the survey, the court credited the appellant with $4.50 per acre, but since the pleadings alleged a deficiency of 299.40 acres, the court limited the shortage at that number pled at $4.50 per acre.

More recent surveys that find corners, bearing trees, well-defined lines, or objects prevail over older surveys that generally overrun the quantity called for.
Sometimes when property is purchased a boundary dispute occurs between adjoining landowners. These can be extremely complicated cases to sort out. In some cases, the issue of where the line is can be well established, but in other cases the jury may have to sort out the evidence based on conflicting surveys. The case of *Blum v. Watson*[145] involved a boundary dispute where the court interpreted five different surveys ranging from 1833 to 1852 that had conflicting evidence. The court found that "old surveys generally overrun the quantity called for." The court held that the more recent surveys would prevail over the prior surveys.

Permissible to reverse the calls and trace lines to harmonize the objects of a grant.
Swenson v. Willsford[146] is a survey case that involved locating the property on the ground in a way that made sense of the conveyance. In locating the property on the ground, the rule is to "follow the footsteps of the original surveyor." In boundary disputes, once the boundary line is created in the field notes or on paper and identified on the ground it cannot be changed. In other words, the original surveyor's actions have the force of law and it

will be presumed that the surveyor did his duty and that he actually traced and marked the lines of the survey.[147]

What if locating the property as described in the legal description creates a nonsensical result? The courts permit the "calls" to be reversed in order to harmonize what was intended. In other words, accurately locating the property on the ground may require reversing the calls to trace the lines in a different way from that indicated in the field notes in order to harmonize the objects of the grant. This holding is described in 2 Tex. Jur. 3d *Adjoining Landowners* § 34 as follows:

> A survey may be constructed from any well-established point or corner found on the ground.[1] The initial corner is of no greater dignity or importance than any other point or corner that is as well established and identified.[2] Indeed, all corners found are of equal importance.[3] A beginning call, however, as well as an intermediate one, may be controlling when viewed in the light of the surrounding facts and circumstances.[4]
>
> ***Illustration:***
>
> If a grant is identified in no other way than by the beginning corner marked and established on the ground, a survey may be constructed from it by the calls for course and distance.[5]
>
> In relocating a survey, the calls are ordinarily followed in the order in which they are set forth in the field notes or other instrument into which they have been copied.[6] However, the order of calls may be reversed if a survey may be more definitely and satisfactorily located by this method.[7] Thus, reversal of the order of calls should occur if a more accurate result can be obtained,[8] or whenever by doing so the land embraced most nearly harmonizes all the objects of the grant.[9]

Tarlton recognized the earlier decisions from the Texas Supreme Court and wrote that under such conditions "we deem it permissible to 'reverse the calls and trace the lines a different way from that indicated in the field notes,' in order to harmonize the objects of the grant."

Kent McMillan, a Professional Registered Land Surveyor in San Marcos, Texas, said that "the *Swenson* case prevents inequitable results from occurring."

Jointly owned property subject to a mechanic's lien
In *C.B. Carter Lumber Co. v. Simpson*,[148] individuals agreed to jointly contract for the erection of one building on their property. Tarlton reversed the dismissal of the suit, holding that the parties could treat their property as their joint estate.

Purchaser from Naked Trespasser
In Texas, a person who acquires property in good faith, for value and without notice of a third-party claim or interes is a bona fide purchaser. But this concept does not mean that a party can take a good title from a vendor who has no title to the property. In *Armstrong v. Oppenheimer*,[149] Tarlton held that a purchaser from a naked trespasser cannot invoke the doctrine of good faith purchaser because a slight inquiry would have disclosed the absence of title in his vendor. A purchaser in good faith should have some reason for the faith that is in him.

Renewal of a lease frees it of fraud
Tarlton wrote in *Hunter v. Lanius*[150] that if a party renews an obligation that is known to be fraudulent or without consideration, then they have freed the transaction from the fraud or want of consideration. The Texas Supreme Court in 1965 reaffirmed this holding in *Gaylord Container Div. of Crown Zellerbach Corp. v. H. Rouw Co.*[151]

Duplicate is regarded as an original
The case of *Missouri Pac. Ry. Co. v. Heidenheimer*[152] involved a bill of lading that was placed as collateral security for a loan. The question before the court was whether an instrument stamped "duplicate" of the bill of lading possesses the same validity as the one stamped "original." The court found

that if the instrument was executed in duplicate, or triplicate, or more parts, the loss of all the parts must be proved, to let in secondary evidence of its contents; thus, indicating that all the parts are upon the same plane—each is to be regarded as an original.

The rationale of this holding is now found in Rule 1003 of the Texas Rules of Evidence that provides that "A duplicate is admissible to the same extent as an original unless (1) a question is raised as to the authenticity of the original or (2) in the circumstances it would be unfair to admit the duplicate in lieu of the original."

No right of subrogation when payment is voluntary

In *Missouri Pac. Ry. Co. v. International Marine Ins. Co.,*[153] Tarlton found that "The payment was made without obligation, either moral or legal, resting upon the insurance company, and no right of subrogation could spring therefrom."

Loss of time damages require proof

The case of *International & G.N.R. Co. v. Simcock*[154] involved a suit for personal injuries in which the plaintiff recovered $2,750 in damages. The court instructed the jury to consider the loss of time up to the filing of suit in estimating damages. Tarlton found that the evidence of loss of time was vague and an indefinite manner, and there was a failure to detect any evidence whatever of the value of the time lost, or of any amount whatever of damages incident thereto. The court found that where the law implies damages such as necessarily result from a wrongful act complained of, proof is required to show the extent and amount of damages. "The proposition is too well established to require elaboration that the charge of the court must comport with the evidence and be supported by it."

Special damages in libel suit cannot be remote

The case of *Democrat Pub. Co. v. Jones*[155] involved a libel suit by Jones against the Democrat Publishing Company for publishing a story that Jones had left with a buggy and not returned. The article read, "He Didn't

Come Back" and suggested that Jones had committed a crime. Jones lost his job and sued for $15,000. The jury found damages of $591.75.

Tarlton wrote:

> The words of a publication might be literally true; yet, if the sense of the publication is to import a crime, it will be deemed libelous. Language is often more significant in suggestion than in expression. Truth half told is frequently more hurtful than blatant falsehood. It is not less venomous, and is more insidious.

Tarlton found that the special damages were too remote because Jones worked a few more months before being discharged. The court found that "Special damages must be pleaded and proved by the plaintiff. They must be such as naturally and reasonably result from the libel complained of, or such as can be shown to have been in the defendant's contemplation at the time."

Aggs v. Shackelford County

The case of *Aggs v. Shackelford County*[156] involved the condemnation of property for a public road that was burdened with a deed of trust lien on the property. A deed of trust is a lien on property that secures repayment of a debt. It is a non-possessory interest in the land. If the debt goes into default, then the lender can foreclose the property and sell it and apply the proceeds of sale against the debt. In the *Aggs* case, the lienholder was not notified of the condemnation proceeding, and there was no proof in the record whether the debt was not being paid. If the land is condemned, how are the proceeds split? In this case, title to the property was not being taken, but the land would depreciate in value since it would be burdened by a public road. The owner would still own the title underneath the road.

Theodore Mack, an attorney in Fort Worth, represented Thomas Aggs, the owner of the mortgage (mortgagee) and filed suit to prevent the opening of the public road and claimed damages of $1,000 due to the depreciation of the land. In trial court, Judge Truman Conner dismissed the suit, finding no valid cause of action. Aggs appealed the case. Justice Tarlton

Figure 39 Fort Worth attorney Theodore Mack who would later help B.D. Tarlton in his reelection bid in 1898.

affirmed the ruling. While he found that a mortgagee should be a party to the condemnation proceeding and would be entitled to damages if its property were impaired, the mortgagee was not bound by the condemnation proceeding since he was not a party to the suit. Tarlton pointed out that the petition did not state if the mortgage was in default or had matured. He reasoned that if an award of damages was claimed against the county, a stranger to the debt, before the mortgagee could sue on the debt, and was not applied against the debt then "he would be thus permitted to put in his pocket an amount of money, without reference to the value of the land at the date of the foreclosure to be had in the future. This would be inequitable." The suit was prematurely brought because the mortgagee had not established that he was damaged by the condemnation proceeding.

Other Activities

In July 1891, at the Tenth State Bar Convention in Galveston, Texas, Tarlton was named to the Committee on Legal Administration and Admission.[157]

In January 1892, Tarlton traveled home to Hillsboro to host an event with local attorneys. *The Dallas Morning News* covered the event and wrote that "The affair proved to be of more than usual brilliance and a magnificent, prepared spread formed a decidedly pleasant feature of the evening. The entire bar of the city, including local newspaper men, were present."[158]

That same month, Tarlton attended an oyster roast for the judges of the Texas Supreme Court, Commission of Appeals, and Court of Appeals in Galveston. The event was held at Woollam's Lake. The judges were the guest of General L.M. Oppenheimer, the head of the Texas Volunteer

Guard. Oppenheimer chartered an electric car to drive the judges to the lake. While their car passed another car, someone inquired who the fine-looking excursionists were. The conductor replied, "They are the delegates to the liquor dealers' convention, going to fill up on oysters." The judges laughed at the quip.[159]

In February, a reporter from The *Dallas Morning News* covering Hill County traveled to Hillsboro to test the public sentiments of the race for governor between Jim Hogg and George Clark. Hogg was running for reelection.

"Who is your choice for governor of Texas in the campaign of this year?" the reporter inquired. Many in the group said they were for George Clark and others for Hogg. A few in the group, W. Reavis, A.W. Young, and L.F. Malone, said they were for Judge Tarlton from the Commission of Appeals.[160] The paper reported:

> Judge B.D. Tarlton has long been prominent in the county and also has many friends in the county, a large number of whom are supporting Hogg for the reason that, among other things, the governor elevated that gentleman to the commission of appeals. Now it is pretty generally understood, although no such intimation has come from the gentleman himself, that he will stand for one of the judgeships of the court of civil appeals soon to be established by the legislature in called session. Now there is hardly a democrat to be found in Hill county who will for a moment consider that the democracy of the estate will award to such desirable positions on the ticket to Hill County, and thus it is to be seen that a local complication of a very serious character is likely to arise just here which would inevitably have no little bearing on the gubernatorial preference of the county in the way of instruction, to say the least.[161]

On May 13, The *Dallas Morning News* reported:

> The friends of Judge B.D. Tarlton of the commission of appeals are daily receiving assurances of support all over the second supreme

judicial district in his race for presiding judge of this court. Already a number of bar associations have indorsed his candidacy. Judge Tarlton has the unanimous support of both Clark and Hogg, men in this section for the position.[162]

Tarlton served on the Texas Commission of Appeals from May 1891 to September 1892. His term was short-lived because the Texas Legislature ended the Texas Commission of Appeals in 1892 in favor of three intermediary courts of civil appeals to serve the entire state's 254 counties. The Texas Legislature established the First Court of Civil Appeals in Galveston, the Second Court of Civil Appeals in Fort Worth, and the Third Court of Civil Appeals in Austin.

For his term on the Texas Commission of Appeals, the state biography reported that Judge Tarlton was a highly successful practitioner. He was not only a fine advocate, but also possessed a rare judicial mind and was well fitted to grace the bench. His selection, like all others made by Governor Hogg, was peculiarly fortunate and in the interest of a thorough and intelligent administration of the state government.[163]

SIXTEEN

Second Court of Civil Appeals

ONE OF THE REASONS THE Texas Legislature selected Fort Worth to establish one of the new courts of civil appeals was its access to railway transportation. In 1873, B.B. Paddock, the editor of The *Fort Worth Democrat,* predicted that Fort Worth would one day be a railroad hub.[164] Paddock drew his vision on a map that resembled a spider and was dubbed as Paddock's *Tarantula Map.* Fort Worth entered the railroad age when the first locomotive passed through downtown at 11:23 am on July 19, 1876, providing the first leg of the Tarantula Map. By 1881, there were five legs to the map, and two years later, a vision that had eleven legs. The railroads changed the way of life and connected everyone to every place. By the late nineteenth century, people in Fort Worth could board a train downtown and connect to other railroads and go almost anywhere. They could travel to New York City and the steamship lines of the Atlantic Ocean. A train could travel from Fort Worth to New York in fifty-six hours.[165] The railroads made Cowtown "cowsmopolitan."[166]

Lawyers could travel from all parts of the state to Fort Worth to argue cases at the court and could stay in reputable lodging at Ginocchio's Hotel, located next to the T&P train depot at the south end of downtown. The Grand Hotel was located on the corner of Weatherford and Rusk (now Commerce Street) and cost from $1.50 to $2 per day. The Hotel Pickwick at the corner of Main and Fourth streets cost $2.50 per day. The Mansion Hotel on 4th Street cost $2.00 to $2.50 per day. Street cars to and from the train depot passed the door of the hotels.

Figure 40 This depiction in 1888 from The Fort Worth Daily Gazette shows how Fort Worth served as the "hub" for the railroads and why the Texas Legislature chose Fort Worth as the site of the Second Court of Civil Appeals.

By 1892, the population of Fort Worth was 42,000, and it had eighty-nine lawyers.[167] As the county seat for Tarrant County, it was the prime spot for one of the new courts of appeals because it was a central point for mass transit across the state and the nation.

For travelers coming west to the city, it did not make sense for them to have to depart Fort Worth to take another train to Dallas to complete their trip. This was the argument put forward by Fort Worth attorney Ben Ayers, who traveled to Austin in March 1892 to pitch Fort Worth as the prime location for the new court.

Figure 41 The third Tarrant County Courthouse in 1878.

Ayers was the senior member of the law firm of Benjamin P. and Jefferson D. Ayers.[168] He received his college education at Adrian College in Hood County in 1878 and read law with the firm of Hanna & Hogsell for two years before being admitted to the Texas bar in 1880. In 1888 he was elected county attorney for Tarrant County and served until his term ended in 1890.

Ayers was well known in Fort Worth. In 1887, The *Fort Worth Daily Gazette* described him as a "popular Fort Worth attorney" who was "alive and fatter than ever."[169] The *Gazette* reported his trip to Austin as part of the "log-rolling for Fort Worth in the matter of securing one of the courts of appeal." A reporter for the *Gazette* questioned him after his trip on the chances of the city securing the court.[170] Ayers responded:

Figure 42 Fort Worth attorney Ben Ayers talks to a Gazette reporter about the new court of civil appeals to be established in Fort Worth after his trip to Austin, Texas. Behind Ayers is the third Tarrant County courthouse built in 1866. The two prior courthouses were built in Birdville, Texas. This courthouse was demolished, and the current courthouse was dedicated in 1895.

Our chances, I will say, are exceedingly good, and I think Fort Worth will secure what she wants. The representatives from the Northwestern part of the state are inclined to respect the interests of Fort Worth and consider her the most convenient point at which to establish the court of appeals. Dallas wishes the court established there for the convenience of three or four counties in that part of the state. The people from the northwest living on the Fort Worth and Denver, and those living on the Fort Worth and Rio Grande to get to Dallas would have to suffer the inconvenience of changing cars at Fort Worth, which is very annoying; and then the number of people who would be convenienced if the court were established at Dallas is small compared to those who live on the Fort Worth and Denver and the Fort Worth and Rio Grande. In the country tributary to the former road there are 300,000 people and in that through which the latter runs there are over 100,000.

Figure 43 Downtown Fort Worth from Main Street in the late 1880s.

Conner Rising

By 1892, District Judge Truman Conner's reputation was growing statewide. It is unusual for a state judicial district judge to have political ambitions outside of the judicial bench. But Conner appeared to want more than what Eastland could provide.

On March 31, 1892, The *Fort Worth Daily Gazette* included a large drawing of Conner, touting him as a potential candidate for governor. The

Figure 44 A younger District Judge Truman Conner.

article reported that "Judge Conner has been unanimously indorsed by the bar of West Texas for a seat on the new civil court of appeals and has never sought or held political office."

The article could have been a signal to the Governor to appoint Conner to the new court and remove one less potential rival against him at the next election. Hogg was not swayed. He would appoint B.D. Tarlton as chief justice to the new court of civil appeals to be established in Fort Worth. If Conner wanted the nomination, he would have to fight for it at the convention.

The Judicial Convention in Dallas

In July 1892, B.D. Tarlton and V.W. Hale, candidates for chief justice of the Second Court of Civil Appeals, arrived in Dallas to attend the Judicial Convention of the Second Judicial District. The convention would nominate three judges to the new court.[171] Tarlton and Hale checked into the Windsor Hotel as their headquarters during the convention.[172]

Edward Gray, the state Democrat chairman, called the convention to order: "Who are the candidates?" Gray asked.

"For chief justice, B.D. Tarlton of Hillsboro and V.W. Hale of Paris, with the possibility of some one of the other candidates entering the fight for the office. The candidates for associate justice are Charles T. Todd of Texarkana, J.A.B. Putman of Sulphur Springs, H.O. Head of Sherman, W.O. Davis of Gainesville, L.W. Stephen of Parker County, and Dallas County candidate H.G. Robertson."

The convention nominated Tarlton as chief justice, with Isaac W. Stephens and Henry O. Head as associate justices. Governor Hogg appointed all three to the court on September 1, 1892.

The Dallas Morning News reported the story:

> Politically speaking Hill County is strictly in it this year. Judge B.D. Tarlton, nominee for chief justice of the Supreme Court for the Second Supreme Judicial District, is an honored citizen of Hill County.
>
> Judge Jo Abbott, who was re-nominated to congress from the Sixth Texas District at Waxahachie for his fourth term, has long been a citizen of this city, than whom none stands higher.[173]

Figure 45 B.D. Tarlton.

Isaac W. Stephens

Isaac Weatherstone Stephens was born in Bledsoe County, Tennessee, in 1850. In 1872, he received his A.B. degree from Washington & Lee, a private liberal arts university in Lexington, Virginia. Stephens attended school when Robert E. Lee served as president of the university until his death in 1870.[174] The college was named Washington & Lee after his death.

A few years later, Stephens came to Texas and passed through Fort Worth in a stagecoach. He decided to live in Weatherford, where he taught school while studying law. In 1874, he was admitted to the Texas bar and began his practice of law. In 1876, he was appointed Parker County Attorney in Weatherford, Texas, and was re-elected two years later. He returned to private practice in Weatherford with attorneys H.M. Chapman, S.W.T. Lanham and A.J. Hood. In 1882 Stephens' name was mentioned in the newspapers as one of the attorneys being appointed to representing Eli McConnell in a murder criminal case.[175] After his appointment to the

Second Court of Civil Appeals in 1892, Stephens remained in Weatherford for a few years and moved to Fort Worth, but in 1896 he moved back to Parker County.

Stephens was a noted orator whose skills dated back to his college days when he received the debater's medal in the Washington Literary Society. In 1897 he delivered an address to the University Literary Exercises. *The Austin American-Statesman* reported his entire speech, calling it a "brilliant oration" attentively listened to by a large audience.[176] On stage with Stephens was former governor Jim Hogg.

In 1907, Stephens moved to Fort Worth to prepare for his retirement from the court and to practice law. He retired in 1908 with five years remaining on his term and formed the firm of Stephens & Miller.[177] He sent his resignation letter to Governor Campbell to take effect May 1, 1908. *The Fort Worth Star-Telegram* reported Stephens' resignation and wrote that "As a jurist and lawyer Judge Stephens is considered one of the ablest in the state, and his opinions from the bench here have always carried with them authority on points of law that leaves but little room to question."[178]

Figure 46 Justice Isaac Weatherstone Stephens.

Stephens and his wife purchased a large, elegant mansion at 800 8th Avenue in Fort Worth, and he practiced law for another twenty-two years before retiring in 1930. He and his wife were known to take daily strolls in the neighborhood and to leave their home weekly to drive to their 2,000-acre ranch near Godley to look after their cattle. They would ride horseback at the ranch. Stephens died in 1945 at the age of 94. His wife died in 1961. In 1962 their home burned and was torn down. Today the Medical Plaza Professional Building sits on the site of his former home.

Henry Oswald Head

Henry Oswald Head was born in Sumner County, Tennessee, on March 17, 1851. He received his law degree in 1871 from Cumberland University, then moved to Sherman, Texas, and opened a law practice in the offices of Joseph Bledsoe and Silas Hare. From 1886 to 1889, he served as Judge of the 15th District Court, covering Grayson and Collin Counties.[179] Head chose to step down from the court after three years to return to private practice and to form the firm of Head, Dillard, Maxey, Freeman, McReynolds, and Hay.

Justice Head was famous for his excellent memory and his ability to refer accurately to relevant cases without notes.[180] Justice Head died at his home in Sherman April 24, 1929. A memorial written to Justice Head in the Texas Law Review, states:

Figure 47 Justice Henry Oswald Head who retired from the court after three years in 1895.

> But beyond any accomplishments of Judge Head as a lawyer or a judge—great as those were—his higher excellence was as a man. He was quick to see the right of any issue, prompt in aligning himself with that right and tenacious in holding to it. Quiet and modest and not self-assertive, he was courageous in the expression of his views and firm in abiding by them. He was a true friend and loyal citizen, taking an active part in everything that tended to advance the good and prosperity of his fellow citizen, his city, his county and his State.[181]

W.L. Huff

On September 5, 1892, the three justices traveled to Fort Worth for a conference to select a clerk of the new court. The court had numerous applications that included George W. Blair of Bonham, Walker Moore of Jack

County, and E.A. Thomas of Sherman.[182] The court selected W.L. Huff as the first clerk. The salaries for the new justices were $3,500;[183] Each justice would have a stenographer who was provided a salary of $20 per month.[184]

Tarlton purchased a home in Fort Worth at 408 Henderson Street in the area known as the Jennings South Addition, Betts Subdivision. The Henderson address was a direct route to the old Tarrant County Courthouse, built during 1876 and 1877.

Office Quarters

The October 3, 1892, edition of The *Fort Worth Daily Gazette* contained an extensive description of the new courthouse and its offices:

> Nearest the elevator is the room of Clerk W. L. Huff, fitted with desks for his use and for the use of his assistants. Next on the west is the receiving and filing room, fitted with cases to hold the transcripts of cases sent up for adjudication. Below those cases are lockers, all provided with ample shelving. In the center of the room is a long double desk for the use of the clerks and for the use of attorneys when looking over transcripts.
>
> Westward of this is the court room, about 40x20. Next the western wall is a platform on which is the desk of the judges, a beautiful piece of work made by Lowe, here in Fort Worth, and of a finish that would do credit to any cabinet maker in the country. It is so solid and massive it looks as if it would last for centuries, and yet it is of good design, in no sense cumbersome looking.
>
> In front of the Judge's stand will be the bar; tables giving ample room for the books and papers to be used in arguing the cases.
>
> Northward of this room and extending eastward are the library rooms, with shelving to a convenient height extending around the sides of the rooms. There are 135 feet of sets of bookshelves, with room for thousands of books. Five cases of books for the library are already unpacked and the books on the shelves, a set of great value, being a digest of the statutes of all the states in the union. The

shelving is of native pine with oil finish and is the work of Maxwell, and a very neat job he has made of it. All these rooms are covered with cocoa matting.

Figure 48 Location of the Second Court of Civil Appeals in Fort Worth in 1890 in the Powell Building.

Across the corridor are the three private rooms of the judges, Tarlton, Head and Stephens. These look out on Main street and are uniform in size, in convenience and in furnishing. All the furniture of the court is antique oak, and that of the judges' rooms is of the same style. Each room is provided with cabinet desks, easy chairs upholstered in leather, folding beds, ordinary chairs, desk chairs, washstands, etc. The carpets are very heavy and of good pattern. Each room is provided with a fireplace and all are steam heated.

The lighting of the entire court is to be by electric light, though gas is provided in all the rooms, for use in an emergency.

The arrangement of the court rooms is very good, and the committee in charge of the work has well discharged the by no means easy task imposed upon it.[185]

According to Quentin McGown IV, Associate Judge of the Tarrant County Probate Court Number 1, noted Fort Worth historian, and author of *Historic Photos of Fort Worth*[186] and *Remembering Fort Worth,*[187] the Powell Building "stood about mid-block on the west side between 1st and 2d streets and was demolished after 1937 when Stripling's built a new store. With the nice arched windows, I can see why the Court liked the building."

Judge Perrill Incident

While Chief Justice Tarlton was settling in his new office, his name appeared in newspapers across the state days before the court's first oral arguments. The sensational article reported an incident involving John Bullock's daughter who who was married to Judge W.M. Perrill, the District Judge in Baylor County. The newspaper reported that Mrs. Perrill was "a lady of the highest culture and refinement" and who said that her father had been the partner of Judge Tarlton.

The newspaper did not report the first name of Mrs. Perrill, but the article went into details of how her troubled marriage led her to leave Judge Perrill for Fort Worth and then to Rockwall. When Perrill came home and found his home empty, he went searching for her and found her in Rockwall, where he shot her and then surrendered. He was found in great agony saying, "My God, My God."

Mrs. Perrill said that his actions were due to his dissipated habits. "I do hope so, as I do not want him punished too severely, as I believe the judge was crazy with drink and morphine, and can't believe that any man would shoot down his wife in cold blood … Oh, won't he be sorry when he realized what he has done? I feel sorry for him," she said.[188]

SEVENTEEN

The Court Officially Opens

AT 10:00 AM ON OCTOBER 3, 1892, Chief Justice Tarlton and associate justices Head and Stephens entered the courtroom. Chief Justice Tarlton called the court to order for the first time:

> "Be it remembered that on this the third day of October A.D. 1892, at 10 O' Clock A.M. the Court of Civil Appeals for the Second Supreme Judicial District of the State of Texas met in the City of Fort Worth in the County Tarrant in accordance with General Laws of the State of Texas passed at the first Called Session of the 22nd Legislature. Present Hon. B.D. Tarlton, Chief Justice; Hon. H.O. Head and Hon. I.W. Stephens, Associate Justices, W.L. Huff, Clerk."[189]

The court announced that it would hear the following cases for oral arguments on October 11, 1982:

- *Sanger Bros, et al v. R. M. Henderson*[190] originating in Taylor County. District Judge presiding: Truman Conner.
- *Texas Central Railway Company v. Stewart*[191] originating in Eastland County. District Judge presiding: J.M. Moore as a Special Judge.
- *W.C. Robinson vs Moore*,[192] originating in Collin County. District Judge presiding: Henry O. Head (now Associate Justice on the Second Court of Civil Appeals).

- *Gulf, Colorado and Santa Fee v. M.S. Johnson*,[193] originating in Johnson County. District Judge presiding: J.M. Hall.

That same day, Texas Governor Jim Hogg arrived in Fort Worth for the day for a campaign stop to address the citizens. The governor had spoken in Denton on the same day and was traveling across the state campaigning against George Clark. *The Dallas Morning News* reported that "Governor Hogg arrived here to-day from Denton on his way to Austin. He has remained at the hotel all day, and has been surrounded by Jim Swayne, Bob Higgs and Judge Randolph.[194] The newspaper reported Capt. W.C. Walsh, a Democrat candidate for commissioner of the General Land Office, arrived in Fort Worth after a ten-day campaign in East Texas. Walsh favored George Clark for governor and was convinced that "the days of Hoggism are numbered."[195]

Meanwhile, in the Tarrant County courthouse, the criminal trial of Mrs. Zarelda Stafford was being sent to the jury. Stafford was being tried for negligent homicide in the death of her husband, whom she had shot and killed. Her husband was referred to as the famous "one-armed Bob" who had often cruelly beaten her.[196] After a few moments of deliberation, the jury returned a verdict of negligent homicide, with a fine of one dollar. A lady coming to her rescue paid the fine. Mrs. Stafford walked out of the court a free woman.

That evening in the courthouse in the 17th District Court was a meeting of the friends of Judge Clark that included local clubs termed "Clark Clubs," who adjourned to hear speakers such as E.A. McDowell, a candidate for attorney general, and Major J.J. Jarvis, a candidate for the legislature.[197] The Robert E. Lee Camp of the Confederate Veterans held its monthly meeting that evening in the Tarrant County Courthouse.

The First Oral Arguments: October 11, 1892

The first day of oral arguments in the Second Court of Civil Appeals occurred on Tuesday, October 11, 1892. The courtroom was most likely ice cold with tension as the best and brightest attorneys traveled from all parts of the state to participate in the first oral arguments in the new court.

Sanger Bros. v. Henderson

The first case on the docket, *Sanger v. Henderson*,[198] originated in Abilene in Taylor County and was tried by District Judge Truman Conner. It was the oldest case before the new court and had been in litigation for over eight years. It had been tried two times, with the first trial being a mistrial. The case inovlved a significant money damages judgment against judgment creditors based on wrongful execution. The jury even found that the sheriff of Taylor County was involved in a civil conspiracy along with the judgment creditors.

In the *Sanger* case, the firm of Donovan & Wylie was insolvent and had three judgment creditors with court orders that allowed for the sale of the assets of the company. Sanger Brothers held a judgment against Donovan & Wyle for $838.17. The second judgment creditor was Middleton & Daugherty for an unstated amount. The third judgment creditor was Martin & Brown in the amount of $3,574.27.

Donovan & Wylie held property consisting of clothing and other property in storage that was valued at $23,714.73. Donovan & Wylie were indebted to Fechheimer & Co., and J.W. Carter in an amount in excess of the value of the property in storage, but they had not reduced their debts to judgments.

On July 26, 1884, Donovan & Wylie decided to prefer Fechheimer & Co and J.W. Carter ahead of the judgment creditors so they conveyed the assets to Henderson in trust for their benefit by using a "deed of trust" to convey the property to Henderson. A deed of trust is an instrument used when conveying real estate and a lender takes back a lien on the property as security for payment of the loan to buy the property. It is not used to secure personal property.

When Sanger Brothers learned of the property in storage in Abilene, their attorneys in Fort Worth reached out to Taylor County Sheriff Northington to levy on the property pursuant to the order of sale issued by the court where they obtained their judgment. The levy and order of sale authorized the sheriff to seize the property and to sell it by a public auction.

Figure 49 An appellate attorney argues his case on the first day of oral arguments on October 11, 1892, in the new Fort Worth Court of Civil Appeals before Chief Justice B.D. Tarlton, Associate Justice Head and Associate Justice Stephens.

The attorneys for Sanger Brothers accompanied the sheriff to see Henderson, and upon meeting him, Sheriff Northington demanded Henderson give him the keys to the storehouse. Henderson complied, and the sheriff seized clothing valued at $3,250 to cover the levy on the Sanger Brothers judgment, and then he seized the remaining property in storage to cover the levy on the Middleton & Daugherty judgment. The sheriff and the judgment lien creditors were not aware that Henderson held the property in trust. After seizure, the Middleton & Daugherty company was dismissed from the suit. On July 27, 1885, the sheriff executed on the third levy pursuant to the judgment of Martin & Brown.

Sheriff Northington left office and was replaced by Sheriff Cunningham, who eventually conducted the sheriff's sale based on the third levy and order of sale in favor of Martin & Brown Company. Then he remitted the proceeds to the attorneys for Sanger Brothers in Fort Worth to pay off the first judgment and to the Martin & Brown Company. In other words, the sheriff paid off the first judgment but did not conduct a sheriff's sale pursuant to the first judgment.

Henderson sued Sanger Brothers, Martin & Brown Company, and Sheriff Northington on his own behalf and on behalf of Fechheimer & Co. and J.W. Carter as beneficiaries of the trust deed for conversion and conspiracy. Henderson sued for the value of the goods seized in the amount of $23,714.73 and his commission and for a recovery for the benefit of Fechheimer & Co. and J.W. Carter.

Prior to trial the defendants challenged the lawsuit by special exception, contending that Henderson had no right to bring suit without joining the beneficiaries, and they alleged that the deed of trust to Henderson was fraudulent because Carter did not agree to it. District Judge Truman Conner overruled the special exceptions and held that Henderson could not recover on his own behalf, but only on behalf of his beneficiaries, and he apportioned the damages to the amount of their debts.

At trial after the jury was selected. Henderson's attorney introduced the deed of trust. The creditors' attorneys objected to the document being introduced because it was at variance with Henderson's pleadings in the case. Henderson's attorney asked Judge Conner if he could withdraw his announcement of ready so that he could cure the issue with the deed of trust. District Judge Truman Conner agreed and dismissed the jury. The court granted a mistrial and allowed the plaintiff to start over. The creditors' attorneys vigorously objected to the jury's dismissal and contended that the case had been tried again.

At the second jury trial, Henderson sought damages of $23,714.73, and the jury found against the defendants. The court granted judgment of $15,146.22 for the conversion. This was quite a large sum of money in 1892. By today's standards in 2021 it would amount to a sum in excess of $400,000, when the Sanger Brothers judgment was for less than $1,000. Now they had a sizable damage judgment to overturn on appeal. Their attorneys must have been shaking in their boots over the potential loss during the years of litigation.

The opinion

(1 Tex. Civ. App. 412.)
SANGER et al. v. HENDERSON.[1]
(Court of Civil Appeals of Texas. Oct. 18, 1892.)

ASSIGNMENT FOR BENEFIT OF CREDITORS—ACTION BY TRUSTEE—CONVERSION—DAMAGES—TRIAL.

1. A trustee for the benefit of creditors need not join the creditors mentioned in the deed of trust as beneficiaries in an action at law brought by him for the conversion of the assigned stock of goods by other creditors, who caused the goods to be taken from the trustee's possession, and sold, under attachments issued by them.

Justice Stephens wrote the first opinion from the new court, reversing the judgment in *Sanger v. Henderson*. Stephens ruled that an attaching creditor who causes property held in pledge to be seized and taken from the possession of the pledgee is a trespasser and that the measure of damages is the full value of the goods, without reference to the amount of debt secured by the pledge. The court declined to reach the issue of whether the trust agreement was vitiated by fraud, and the court held that Henderson was entitled to maintain his suit and to recover the full value of the stock of goods, without reference to the amount of the debts secured.

Justice Stephens held that the trial court erred in submitting a jury issue on the conspiracy claim because there was no evidence that the appellants caused the order of sale under which the goods were sold based on an understanding and agreement between them at the time that they would participate in and together share the benefits of such sale. To show joint liability, the court held there should have been evidence of the alleged concert of action. The court wrote that:

> It seems to us that the sale by Sheriff Cunningham of the entire stock of goods in bulk, under the order issued upon the judgment in favor of the Martin Brown Company, and the distribution of the proceeds of said sale among the several attaching creditors, including Sanger Bros., in the absence of any proof as to why he pursued this course, should be deemed a mere irregularity on his part, and not proof tending to show an agreement or understanding between appellants.

The court found no abuse of discretion by Judge Conner in allowing Henderson to withdraw his announcement of ready after introducing testimony and discharging the jury. The court remanded the case for a new trial. The case stands for the holding that a person in possession of property under a pledge agreement has sufficient title to recover damages against the creditor who wrongfully seizes the property by writ of attachment.[199] In other words, even though Henderson did not own the property, he had the right to bring suit for damages in his capacity as trustee as holding the property for the benefit of others. The case was appealed to the Texas Supreme Court, but the application was dismissed.

In 2021, Steve Hayes of Fort Worth, Texas, former Chair of the Texas Appellate Council with over forty years of experience, analyzed the *Sanger* opinion and offered the following comments: "Interestingly, *Sanger* was cited eight times in the roughly half-decade following its issuance—most often for the proposition that a pledgee (or trustee) has sufficient rights to recover damages for, or defend against the seizure of, the pledged property. After a three-decade hibernation, *Sanger*'s final citation as authority also provided support for that general proposition.

"It also was cited as authority—both by the majority of the Fort Worth Court, and by Justice Stephens (citing himself) in dissent—for the proposition that it is reversible error for the trial court to submit a material issue in the jury charge upon which no evidence was introduced.

"But most interesting to me is the fact that this first opinion of the Fort Worth Court invoked the concept of error preservation to dispatch (in part) the motion for rehearing in *Sanger*. On rehearing, Henderson (the trustee) tried to get the court of appeals to allow him to "remit and dismiss" as to the sheriff 'to whose prejudice the error was committed in the trial below,' and to 'have the judgment affirmed as to the other appellant.'

"In other words, Henderson would have been happy to keep just his judgment against the execution creditors and cut the sheriff loose. The court of appeals wouldn't have it-at least, not at that late date. 'Under the practice adopted by the Supreme Court, which we feel bound to follow, such an offer comes too late in a motion for rehearing," primarily because it deprived the trial judge of the opportunity to fix the problem in the first place:

> If appellee had suggested such a course before the judgment of this court was entered, the judgment below might have been affirmed as to the Martin Brown Company, upon his entering a dismissal as to Sanger Bros. . . .

"Interestingly, a Fort Worth Court opinion by Justice Stephens allowed such a remittitur in a subsequent, unrelated personal injury case (*Higby*), but a later case, in an opinion by Chief Justice Tarleton, followed *Sanger*'s error preservation holding that "remittitur comes too late on motion for rehearing." *Martin-Brown Co. v. Pool*, at 822. Even at that early stage of Texas jurisprudence, and certainly the early stages of the jurisprudence of the Fort Worth Court, the Fort Worth justices were disinclined to allow parties to raise a complaint on appeal they had not preserved in the trial court."

In 1894, the Second Court of Appeals revisited the case in *Martin-Brown Co. v. Henderson*[200] after the case was tried after remand. On appeal the second time, the court affirmed the jury verdict.

Appellate counsel

The attorneys handling the appeal in *Sanger* were from Abilene, Dallas, and Fort Worth. M.A. Sprouts came from Abilene, Texas. Charles I. Evans came from Dallas, Texas, and Frank B. Stanley from Fort Worth.

Sprouts and Stanley represented Sanger Brothers, Martin Brown Co., and the sheriff of Taylor County, who were found liable to Henderson. Sprouts was a prominent attorney from Abilene who handled litigation across the state.[201] His name appeared frequently in the newspapers in Austin as checking in the Driskell Hotel and cited as attending the State Bar Convention. He was politically prominent and noted in the newspaper as a supporter of George Clark for governor in 1892.[202]

Frank B. Stanley began his law practice in Eastland and moved to Fort Worth, where he became a distinguished attorney[203] handling trial and appellate law.[204] Stanley was interested in local, state, and national politics. Active in local politics in Fort Worth, Stanley urged the city to relieve companies from taxation for a period of time to induce the manufacturers, producers, and wage earners. Stanley donated $250 towards the goal of raising $113,000 to build a grand hotel in downtown Fort Worth and to buy six lots at Houston and Main streets for a new hotel. Stanley was unusual for his day: he was a well-known Republican in Fort Worth.

In 1900, Stanley ran for Associate Justice of the Texas Supreme Court. In 1904, he ran for Governor of Texas. In 1906, he ran for the Texas Supreme Court. He helped form the Roosevelt Central Republican Club in Fort Worth.

Charles I. Evans with Evans & Gooch, with offices in Dallas and Austin, represented Henderson. Charles I. Evans advertised his appellate practice in the Texas Supreme Court, Federal courts at Austin and the courts in Travis and surrounding counties. Evans served as a major in the Confederacy until the end of the Civil War. Evans wrote about the Battle of Corinth for Yoakum's History of Texas.[205] After the Houston and Texas Central Railway established a railway to the Dallas in 1872, Evans began to practice in multiple cities, including Abilene.

Politically active, in 1886 Evans changed his allegiance from the Democratic party to the Republican party. On February 1, 1887, The *Dallas Daily Herald* reported that Charles I. Evans, a prominent lawyer of Abilene, is in the city prospecting with a view to locating here to practice his profession."[206]

In 1896, Evans spoke in Austin and said that he had never voted for a Republican but intended to vote the whole ticket.[207] He spoke at other places, including Fort Worth, where he denounced the Democrat Party. The talk was picked up by The *Houston Post, which* commented: "It was a pitiable spectacle that General Claiborne and Charles I. Evans made of themselves at Fort Worth when they denounced their old party and lifelong associates and slobbered over Cuney and Ferguson and Grant. They must have been fearfully disappointed in their aspirations elsewhere."[208]

In September 1896, Evans tried to organize a group to visit President William McKinley. A newspaper reported the effort: "Charles I. Evans who was a Confederate soldier, a former Democrat, but who is now a Republican, is trying to get up an excursion of 500 ex-Confederate soldiers to visit McKinley on Oct 10."[209]

Texas Central Railway Company v. Stewart

The second case argued was *Texas Central Railway Company v. Stewart*,[210] which originated in Eastland County before Special Judge J.M. Moore. The case involved personal injuries involving a minor child. Sallie Stewart, a minor child at age three at the time of the accident, was awarded $5,000 in damages after an accident on the train when the locomotive stopped and detached and coupled again in a negligent manner. The minor child received a cut over one of her eyes of considerable length, and also a concussion of her back. The suit was filed by A.J. Stewart as "next friend" of Stewart, the minor child.

The Opinion

Writing for the court, Justice Head found no contributory negligence on the part of the mother or her daughter and affirmed the judgment and reformed it to reflect the recovery was for the sole use of the minor and would remain in court until the minor reaches her majority. The final judgment did not mention A.J. Stewart as next friend. The court found that the judgment was final and reformed the final judgment.

(1 Tex. Civ. App. 642.)
TEXAS CENT. RY. CO. v. STEWART.[1]
(*Court of Civil Appeals of Texas.* Oct. 18, 1892.)

CARRIERS—INJURIES TO PASSENGERS — CONTRIBUTORY NEGLIGENCE — PLEADING—INSTRUCTIONS—VERDICT—MISCONDUCT OF JURY—NEW TRIAL.

1. In an action for personal injuries against a railroad company, it appeared that, on the day of the accident, plaintiff, who was three years old, with her mother and younger sister, were passengers on a passenger train of defendant; that, when the engine was coupled to the train, it was done with such force as to throw plaintiff from her seat, and against the stove in the car. At the time of the collision, plaintiff and her mother were sitting on a seat immediately fronting the stove. The plaintiff

[1] Writ of error denied by supreme court.

The appellate counsel

L.W. Alexander, an attorney in Dallas, represented the Texas Central Railway Company. Alexander raised numerous errors to overturn the judgment, including allegations that the mother and daughter were contributorily negligent.

J.R. Fleming with Fleming & Moore in Eastland, Texas, represented Stewart. Fleming was no stranger to the appellate courts. He frequently teamed with Theodore Mack in Fort Worth to handle appellate cases to the Texas Commission of Appeals. Between May 1891 to June 1892, he handled the cases of *Seay v. Diller*[211] and *Maloney v. Earheart*,[212] which were appeals from District Judge Conner's court while sitting in Shackelford County, and *Harris v. Monroe Cattle Co.*[213] and *Aggs v. Shackelford County*, in the Texas Commission of Appeals where Justice Tarlton wrote the decision.

Robinson v. Moore

The third case, *Robinson v. Moore*,[214] was an action to quiet a title that originated in Collin County. It was no surprise that Chief Justice Tarlton would select this case to write his first opinion on the court.

The Opinion
Chief Justice Tarlton found error in the case because the trial court awarded title to parties who were not heirs. The court reformed the judgment and remanded the case for a new trial regarding the claim of improvements to the property.

(1 Tex. Civ. App. 93.)

ROBINSON v. MOORE *et al.*

(*Court of Civil Appeals of Texas.* Oct. 18, 1892.)

QUIETING TITLE—VERDICT—AMENDMENT OF JUDGMENT ON APPEAL—IMPROVEMENT OF COMMUNITY PROPERTY.

The appellate counsel
Two Collin County law firms handled the appeal. Jenkins & Pearson and H.A. Finch handled the case for Robinson. The firm of Garnett & Muse handled the case for Moore. Tarlton was familiar with both law firms as he had ruled in the case of *Foote v. Seawall*[215] while on the Texas Commission of Appeals, and both law firms were involved in that appeal. In an interesting turn of events, the *Foote* case was tried by District Judge Henry O. Head, now an associate justice on the court. Tarlton mentioned District Judge Head in his opinion in and referred to him as the "learned judge who tried this cause" in affirming the decision.

M.H. Garnett with the Garnett & Muse firm handled civil and criminal appeals across the state. Garnett would become the Judge of the 59th District Court in Grayson County, Texas.

Gulf, C. & S.F. Ry. Co. v. Johnson

The fourth case was *Gulf, C. & S.F. Ry. Co. v. Johnson*,[216] which was tried in Johnson County before District Judge J.M. Hall. The case involved the death of A.D. Johnson, an employee of the railway company who was killed on the job when the train derailed between Cleburne and Alvarado. Johnson was twenty-nine years old when he died, with a life expectancy of 36.03 years. He had been working since eighteen and accumulated no property. He worked in different capacities for the Gulf, C. & S.F. Railway Company for four years, earning between $60 to $65 dollars per month as a brakeman, passenger conductor, and baggage master. He had been married eight years to M.S. Johnson and had one child, who was two years old at the time of his death. The jury awarded $18,000 in damages based on ordinary negligence.

By today's standards, the sum of $18,000 is not much in value for a life that would have continued to work for another thirty years. By assuming an inflation rate of three percent, the sum of $18,000 in 2021 dollars would be $530,180—quite a large sum that would be divided equally between the mother and son.

This was a straight up death case that would determine what was the value of someone's life. There was no question that damages would be awarded, but what sum of damages is proper when life is cut short?

The Opinion

(1 Tex. Civ. App. 103.)

GULF, C. & S. F. RY. Co. v. JOHNSON *et al.*

(*Court of Civil Appeals of Texas.* Oct. 25, 1892.)

DEATH BY WRONGFUL ACT — EXCESSIVE DAMAGES — MASTER'S DUTY.

1. While the jury, in an action for wrongful death, have a right to compensate deceased's wife and child for the value of such incidental services as a husband and father usually performs, in addition to the actual money which he furnishes for their support, a verdict of $18,000 in favor of a surviving wife and child, for the death of a brakeman, 29 years old, earning between $60 and $65 per month, not shown to have been possessed of any special qualifications to make his promotion rapid, or his incidental services more than ordinarily valuable, is excessive.

2. The duty of exercising ordinary care to keep its roadbeds and track in proper condition for its employes rests on the master as a personal obligation, for which it is responsible, though such duty was in fact performed by other employes.

Appeal from district court, Johnson county; J. M. HALL, Judge.

Justice Head wrote the opinion in the appeal. After discussing the contribution the deceased would have made outside of his job during his marriage, the court found that the "sum of money which at the current rate of interest would annually yield a sum considerably in excess of the total wages deceased was earning at the time of his death." The court's third opinion and Justice Head's second opinion held that the verdict of $18,000 was excessive.

The appellate counsel

The firm of Poindexter & Padelford handled the case for Johnson. The railroad sent J.W. Terry of Galveston, who regularly defended the railroads in litigation across the state and before the Texas Railroad Commission. Terry was a prominent attorney with a combative style. He was rebuked by the court of appeals in a motion for a rehearing being struck by the Court of Appeals two years earlier in 1890 in the case of *Gulf, C. & S.F.R. Co. v. Vaughn*,[217] where the court found that a great portion of the motion served no useful purpose and that the matter in which the motion was presented was offensive, indecent and the "spirit of it malicious" and that "whether they be rights of life and liberty or right of property. But the line of demarkation which separates the right to speak in open court the truth as counsel sees it, and the unbridled license of the mob orator, is clear, distinct, and known of all men."

Trial of E.P. Thorne

Oral arguments were concluded for the day, but that was not the end of the day in Tarrant County. Later, in the main courthouse in Tarrant County, the press covered the trial against E.P. Thorne, charged with administering poison to Mary West, a single lady, with intent to kill. Thorne, a married man, was married and having an affair with West. After purchasing morphine, Thorne and West went to an inn in Arlington and planned to attempt suicide. Thorne said he administered the morphine to West. When the hotel managers decided something was wrong and asked both to leave and ordered their buggy from the stable, Thorne asked for more time, and West became wild and excited. A doctor administered aid and told the manager not to let them go back to sleep.

As the trial of Thorne continued, the brother of West stood on a window ledge looking into the courtroom with a pistol, attempting to get a view of Thorne, but someone from the district clerk's office drove him away. West's father, Captain West, sat with a pistol in hand behind attorney Jim Davis, who represented Thorne. Sheriff Richardson placed both the father and son under arrest for having pistols. Davis told The *Dallas Morning News* that Captain West was seized by the sheriff as he was about to draw a pistol on Davis.[218]

That evening, the play *The Colonel* was performed at the Worth Opera House, located at 3rd and Rusk streets (now Commerce Street) east of the Knights of Pythias Lodge Hall. The opera house was built in 1883 for $55,000 and intended to transform cowboys into culture. It would be equivalent to present day Bass Hall in downtown Fort Worth.

The next morning, on October 12, 1892, *The Gazette: Fort Worth, Texas* reported that a good-sized audience appeared that evening to watch the play. "The Colonel is new and fresh, and as a comedy is entitled to rank among the best ... The dialogues are bright and witty and in the hands of a competent company proved most entertaining to a good-sized audience last night. The humor of the piece is of the sparkling, effervescent kind which pleases without palling." The play featured sixty people, a carload of scenery, a superb orchestra and forty "pretty chorus girls."

The Gazette endorsed Tarlton, Head and Stephens for Judges of the Civil Court of Appeals. The newspaper endorsed Grover Cleveland for president, Adlai E. Stevenson for vice-president, and George Clark of McLennan over Governor Jim Hogg.

The newspaper advised the voters: "Do not forget that unless you register and preserve your certificate of registration that you cannot vote."

The Second Oral Arguments: October 14, 1892

On Friday, October 14, 1892, the court heard oral arguments in *Roberts v. Helms*,[219] a case that involved a dispute over a strip of land in Eastland County. Roberts filed suit to recover a strip of land 330 varas in width and 2,736 varas in length. A *varas* was a Spanish measurement based on the length of a pole, used both in Texas and in Latin America. It measures roughly 33½ inches (846.67 mm) or more accurately at 32.909 inches. This amounted to 904.99 feet in width and 7,503 feet in length. Roberts claimed that a vacancy existed–an area that was not covered by a survey and not subject to ownership except to the party possessing it. Roberts also claimed that the county surveyor did not actually conduct a survey on the ground

The case was tried before District Judge Truman Conner who had to sort out an unusual set of facts with the existing law at the time. If the surveyor did not actually survey the land on the ground then it would be up to the jury to decide the boundary line. The case had a curious set of facts since the court found that the patent from the State of Texas showed calls for natural monuments and courses and distances. This meant that a surveyor had to have surveyed some or all of the land. The accusation that the surveyor did not actually survey the property on the ground is a deep insult to the reputation of a surveyor and this accusation was being lodged against the county surveyor.

The law existing at the time of the *Roberts v Helms* case comes from *Urquart v Burleson*,[220] where the Texas Supreme Court examined a case where a surveyor made the survey on the ground and noted artificial monuments with sufficient notariety but there were mistakes in the surveyor's field notes of the survey. The court held that calls for natural or artifical monuments are to be given precedent over both inconsistent course and distance calls in the surveyor's field notes.

A "call" in a deed is a phrase in the written description of the location of a parcel of land. When there is a conflict in ascertaining the boundaries in instruments then the courts examine the "dignity of calls" which consist of (1) natural objects, (2) artificial objects, (3) course and distance, and (4) area and quantity. When there is a conflict in the instruments, the calls are ranked in accordance with priority. It is easy to see why: a natural or articial object will be present and noticeable but a surveyor could easily make a mistake in courses and distances and the area and quantity of land.

In 1867 the Texas Supreme Court decided the case of *Stafford v King*,[221] and held that the actual identification of the survey on the ground is performed by following the footsteps of the original surveyor. If the footsteps of the original surveyor can be identified and followed, they will control location or the line or boundary in question even though they may not be in harmony with the field notes of the surveyor. Thus, once the surveyor has made the survey on the ground, this line cannot be changed, even by a jury.

But when there is an allegation that the surveyor did not survey the land on the ground and there are calls for natural and artificial monuments, and courses and distances then it is become becomes quite complex in how to draft a charge to a jury to instruct them on what to do. Judge Conner had quite a responsibility on his hands in crafting the correct jury charge in this case.

With the background of law to work with and two divergent story lines in the case, Judge Conner gave two instructions: one that instructed the jury to find for Roberts if they found that no vacancy existed and a second instruction, that if no survey was actually made by the county surveyor, then the jury was to fix the east boundary line, and if the line "thus fixed was west of the land claimed by defendant, they would find for the defendant." The second jury instruction was in essence instructing the jury as a matter of law where the boundary line was fixed. The jury found in favor of Helms which meant that they followed the second instruction.

The opinion

(1 Tex. Civ. App. 100.)

ROBERTS v. HELMS.

(*Court of Civil Appeals of Texas.* Oct. 26, 1892.)

BOUNDARIES—COURSE AND DISTANCE—MONUMENTS.

The facts that land granted by the state had been simply platted on paper without an actual survey being made, and that the second corner called for was 300 varas further distant from the beginning corner than the distance specified in the patent, will not warrant an instruction that the jury should locate the grant by course and distance alone, when there are other calls in the patent for well-established monuments which would also have to be disregarded, as the rule is that all the calls of the patent should be looked to in determining what was the particular land intended to be conveyed.

Chief Justice Tarlton, with his real estate background had a case that he would relish. No doubt he couldn't wait to delve into a complicated boundary dispute case involving conflicting surveys, an allegation that the county surveyor did not survey the property on the ground, and sorting out the calls with well-established monuments. Only a jury could sort out this messy boundary dispute case. Tarlton would be on top of it.

Tarlton examined the jury instruction to see if the two alternative paths influenced the verdict. In his second opinion from the court, Tarlton ruled that the second instruction was error because it influenced the jury. The second instruction actually decided the boundary line based on the jury finding that the county surveyor did not make a survey on the ground. This was error because if the jury found that the surveyor did not survey the property then the jury would fix the boundary line. The second instruction was error because Tarlton found that the southwest corner of one of the surveys was "…well established. Could it be stated, should be identified by reference alone to course and distance? We think not." The jury could not disregard the corner as a matter of law. The jury could only determine the boundary line by examining *all* of the calls rather than subordinating the calls to the reference of course and distance. The court reversed the *Roberts v Helm* decision.

Houston appellate attorney JoAnn Storey summed up Tarlton's analysis in the *Roberts v. Helm* opinion:

> The Court's (i.e., Tarlton's) analysis of the facts involved an appreciation of higher math and geography ("To reach a stake on the *north* line of the Bradley, the course of the north line of the McGrew would be seriously deflected to the north, and the distance traversed in reaching the west line of the Bradley would be 1990 varas, instead of 1650 varas, as called for in the McGrew field notes").
>
> The legal analysis is pretty straightforward. A trial court cannot instruct a verdict when there are disputed facts for the jury to consider. All of us nerds agree with that concept.

The appellate counsel

J.H. Davenport and B.F. Cotton, attorneys in Eastland County, handled the case for Roberts. Davenport was one of the nominees for Congress for the 13th Congressional District in August 1892 in Decatur and had many supporters. He lost the nomination to Judge Joe Cockrell.[222] B.F. Cotton was a supporter of George Clark for governor and was secretary of the Eastland Clark Club.[223]

R.M. Black and D.G. Hunt handled the case for Helms. D.G. Hunt was an attorney in Eastland, Texas, and partners with J.R. Frost. He served in the military with the title of colonel and was a member of the Kings of Pythias lodge in Eastland.[224]

In less than a month of operation, the new court reversed three of the four cases before it. Chief Justice Tarlton picked two real estate cases for his first opinions, finding error in both of them. The reversals for new trials in *Sanger v. Henderson* and *Roberts v. Helms*[225] would not go unnoticed: both decisions came from District Judge Conner's court. Two other appeals from Judge Conner's court, *Minor v. Kirkland*[226] and *Robertson v. Mooney*,[227] were affirmed by opinions written by Justice Stephens.

EIGHTEEN

The 1892 Election

In November of 1892, Justices Tarlton, Head, and Stephens were elected to the Second Court of Civil Appeals in the general election. Governor Hogg won reelection by defeating George Clark. Hogg received 190,486 votes, over 43.74 percent, to Clark's 30.63 percent.

The Texas Railroad Commission

On December 4, 1892, a humorous article appeared in The *Dallas Morning News* that involved a meeting of the Texas Railroad Commission in Fort Worth at the Tarrant County Courthouse. They were to hear from numerous witnesses who were subpoenaed for the hearing that would take most of the day. No witnesses appeared. The article read:

> Fort Worth, Tex., Dec. 3—Getting testimony in the commission case may be all-fired easy business in some towns, but Fort Worth is not one of them. Yesterday the commission adjourned until 9:30 o'clock this morning when it was expected that the remaining eight witness subpoenaed would be on hand to give their evidence. Promptly at 9:30 Commissioners Foster and McLean and Attorney Simkins were on hand at the courthouse, and soon after Messr. Terry and Freeman, railroad counsel, were present. The commissioner stenographers and reporter were ready for business, and promises were good for business and plenty of it.[228]

All that was lacking was the batch of witnesses.

After a wait of twenty minutes a deputy sheriff was called and dispatched after the derelict witness, and pending the return of the officer and his game Judge Terry broke the silence by telling a chestnut. It was an old one, and though entitled to abject reverence on account of its age, the reporters joined the commission in laughing at it. Commissioner Foster, intent upon showing that Judge Terry had not delved deeper into the recesses of antiquity than he, produced one that Columbus had brought over centuries ago when this hemisphere was discovered, and Judge Terry joined the other lawyers in the convulsions that followed.

Later Judge Terry announced that an invitation had been extended to visit the brewery in Fort Worth:

This played the merry dickens with the morning session, for under the guidance of Capt. Tom West the entire party, with the exception of Judge McLean, took a bee line for the brewery. At the brewery beer rates were discussed for a while and then the secrets of brewing beer were studied. At the sampling counter, Mr. Cetti produced material evidence that Mr. Busch was in error when he said that good beer could not be made in Texas. The party took kindly to the evidence and accepted it. Col. Simkins was one exception. He looked on, while his mouth watered as he saw the others taking in the testimony. Mr. Freeman said he desired no actual test because it made him bilious.

An hour or so spent in the brewery, and there were half a dozen men ready to argue with Mr. Busch as to the quality of beer to be made in Texas.

After dinner the witnesses still failed to make their appearances, and it became evidence that they were hiding out. Then Cap. West, in order to show the strangers, the hospitality of the town, escorted the party to the rooms of the court of appeals. Arrived there Mr.

Terry said to Chief Justice Tarlton: "Judge, Capt. West is kindly showing us through the brewery and has brought us here because, next to that, the court of appeals is the institution Fort Worth is most proud of."

The judge smiled at this and invited the crowd to take seats, which were declined. Another visit to the county courthouse developed the fact that the witnesses had crawled into a hole and pulled the hole in after them and the investigation in Fort Worth came to an end. Capt. West, Martin Casey, Zane Cetti, J.J. Gannon, and Charles Scheuber left nothing undone to entertain the distinguished visitors and the visitors demonstrated that they had an appreciation for hospitality. And so it was. The evening train bore the commissioners and attorneys to their homes to spend the sabbath and on Monday morning the investigation will be resumed in Austin.[229]

NINETEEN

1893

IN 1893, FIVE APPEALS FROM Judge Conner's court were taken to the Second Court of Civil Appeals. The court reversed three[230] and affirmed two of the decisions.[231] However, one of the decisions affirmed by Justice Stephens was reversed by the Texas Supreme Court. Chief Justice Tarlton reversed Judge Conner's ruling in *Strickland v. Hardwicke*,[232] a suit to set aside a sheriff's sale of real property.

Andrew Johnson, an attorney with Thompson, Coe, Cousins & Irons, L.L.P. in Houston, Texas, analyzed Chief Justice Tarlton's decision in the *Strickland suit*[233] and gave his comments:

> In *Strickland v. Hardwicke,* the plaintiff filed suit to set aside a sheriff's deed regarding real property purchased at an execution sale, arguing the sale was fraudulent and that defendant paid a grossly inadequate price. As a defense, the defendant asserted that outstanding title was in a third party as established by a deed from plaintiff to the third party. Plaintiff responded that the third party did not pay consideration for the deed but held title as a naked trustee and the beneficial interest remained in the plaintiff. The third party appeared in the lawsuit as a co-plaintiff and admitted all of the plaintiff's allegations regarding the character of her interest in the property. Trial Judge Conner nonetheless held that outstanding title was in the third party, which defeated plaintiff's claim.

On appeal, Chief Justice Tarlton reversed and remanded, concluding that defendant's outstanding title defense should have been rejected. Chief Justice Tarlton reasoned that if the third party had before trial executed a "deed of relinquishment of reconveyance" of the property to plaintiff, the deed would defeat the outstanding title defense, so "We do not think that the solemn repudiation by [third party], made in open court by her unquestioned authority, in effect disclaiming all title or interest in the land, should be less binding or effective than would be such a relinquishment."

Johnson noted how the court accepted a conveyance that occurred during the lawsuit:

I think it is interesting that Chief Justice Tarlton took law stating that a conveyance occurring during suit can be used to rebut an outstanding title defense and applied it to the present case where the third party did not give a deed to plaintiff but instead simply agreed with plaintiff's characterization of the transaction between them which contradicted the plain face of the actual deed between them—and did so in such short order.

Chief Justice Tarlton wrote the opinion in *Savoy v. Brewton*,[234] reversing Judge Conner. The *Savoy* case involved the foreclosure of a vendor's lien on real property. A vendor's lien is a lien that the seller of property retains until receiving payment of the entire purchase price. The lien is placed on the property to secure repayment of the amount due. The word "vendor" comes from the Anglo-French word "vendur," which means "to sell." If the purchaser fails to pay the seller in full, then the seller can collect on the remaining debt by seeking a judgment in court and an order authorizing the sheriff to sell the property to pay the judgment.

The *Savoy* case occurred during the time period in which property could be acquired from the state of Texas for homesteading. If the owners resided on the property for three years, then they could acquire title to the property. In this case, Julia Savoy entered into a contract to sell her 160 acres to C.B. Brewton, but she had not yet resided on the property for the requisite three years. She conveyed title to the property to Brewton by quitclaim deed. In Texas, a quitclaim deed does not purport to convey a good title; it prevents the party conveying their interest by quitclaim deed from later claiming that they own the title.

Savoy sued Brewton to recover on the debt and to foreclose her vendor's lien. Savoy conveying title by quitclaim was a red flag that she likely knew that she had not resided on the property long enough to finalize her homestead claim. Brewton defended the suit by contending that there was a "failure of consideration" because Savoy had not resided on the property for the requisite three-year period. In other words, Brewton argued that Savoy could not deliver good title to him because she had not yet finalized her homestead claim to the property.

Handling appellate matters for nearly twenty-five years and rated since 2005 as one of "The Best Lawyers in Dallas," appellate attorney Chad Ruback is no stranger to examining jury charges. Ruback analyzed how the jury was instructed in the *Savoy* case and noted that Judge Conner's jury instruction placed a higher burden on the Plaintiff, Savoy, in the trial than Texas law allowed.

"In the jury charge, trial court Judge Truman H. Conner instructed the jury that if Savoy and owners of the property prior to Savoy had failed to occupy the property for the requisite three-year period of time, and if Brewton purchased the property without knowledge of this, the consideration (by Savoy) for Brewton's promissory notes would fail.

"In a unanimous opinion by Chief Justice Tarlton, the Court of Civil Appeals held that this jury instruction constituted reversible error.

"Specifically, Chief Justice Tarlton's opinion held that, even if the property had not yet been occupied for the requisite period of time, there would not necessarily be a failure of consideration.

"The opinion reasoned that, regardless of whether Brewton would be able to immediately obtain title to the property, Brewton was (1) entitled to immediate possession of the property and the improvements thereon; and (2) entitled to "tack" the two years of occupancy which had already taken place (and, as such, Brewton would need only one additional year of occupancy to satisfy the three-year prerequisite to obtaining title). The opinion indicated there these factors might constitute some consideration for Brewton's consideration, contrary to Judge Conner's jury instruction.

"Chief Justice Tarlton emphasized that, even if a trial court judge handles all other aspects of a case correctly, providing a jury instruction which mis-states the legal standard will require the entire trial to be redone.

"Chief Justice Tarlton indicated that Judge Conner provided the jury with an instruction that made the plaintiff's burden higher than Texas law actually requires.

"The opinion highlights the importance of a jury instruction strictly tracking Texas law. And the opinion provides guidance to Judge Conner as to how he should instruct the jury in the retrial of the case. Moreover, the opinion provides direction to other trial court judges those who might be faced with a similar situation in future cases. Although Chief Justice Tarlton's opinion reversed Judge Conner, there is no doubt that Conner learned from the experience, and after a few more years as a trial court judge, Conner proved himself to be a worthy successor to Tarlton as the chief justice of the court of civil appeals.

"Chief Justice Tarlton's opinion concluded that, because the jury charge wholly failed to recognize the significance of whether Savoy had made the fraudulent representation claimed by Brewton, the jury charge was fatally defective, requiring a reversal of the trial court's judgment."

TWENTY

1894

In 1894, the old Tarrant County Courthouse was torn down to make room for a larger courthouse. The Tarrant County Commissioners contracted with Frederick C. Gunn with the firm of Gunn & Curtiss in Chicago, Illinois, to construct a new courthouse at a cost of $408,840 that would take two years to complete. When the courthouse was finished, it was an architectural masterpiece and so expensive that the voters rejected the county commissioners at the 1894 elections.

On July 21, 1894, Tarlton traveled to Galveston, Texas, to deliver the annual address at the Texas Bar Association. His speech was "Some Reflections on the Relations of Capital and Labor."

During the year, the court handled ten appeals from Judge Conner's court, reversing five[235] and affirming five of the appeals.[236] Chief Justice Tarlton wrote two of the opinions reversing Judge Conner in the *Watson v. Texas & P. Ry. Co.*[237] and *Swink v. League.*[238]

The case of *Watson v. Texas & P. Ry. Co.*[239] involved personal injuries and property damages involving a carload of horses transported by train from Ranger, Texas, to Texarkana, Texas. While in transit through Fort Worth, the car carrying the horses wrecked and injured the horses and also Watson. Watson first sued the railroad and recovered a judgment for damages for the horses. Watson filed a subsequent lawsuit to recover damages for his own personal injury.

The railroad pled that since they paid the prior judgment, Watson could not sue for his personal injuries. The court disagreed and held that the suit for injuries inflicted on the horses was not the same as injuries to the person. Tarlton, relying on authority, held damage to goods and injuries to the person, although caused by one and the same wrongful act, are infringements of different rights, and give rise to distinct causes of action, and therefore the recovery of compensation for the damage to the goods is no bar to an action subsequently commenced for the personal injury.

Steve Hayes, the appellate attorney in Fort Worth who earlier commented on the *Sanger v. Henderson* decision, comments on the *Watson* decision:

> *Watson v. Texas & P. Ry. Co.* is another example of Chief Justice Tarlton, and the Court, referring to accepted treatises to establish the early jurisprudence of the District. Relying on "Black, Judgm. § 740," Chief Justice Tarlton noted that bringing separate suits for injuries to different properties "springing from the same source. . .would be considered as an attempt on the part of the plaintiff to split his demand, —a practice which, especially in our system, is reprobated."[240]
>
> "But," the Chief Justice continued, quoting *Black*, "'the recovery of compensation for the damage to the goods [caused by one accident] is no bar to an action subsequently commenced for the personal injury [caused by the same accident].'"[241]
>
> The Court therefore held that the "learned trial judge erred in sustaining the defendant's plea in bar," and dismissed the case.
>
> In the case at bar, the plaintiff sought damages for personal injuries arising out of the same accident which injured his horses. He had already recovered a judgment for the injuries to his horses in a prior lawsuit.[242]
>
> Whether a more extensive discussion of the concept of *res judicata* might have produced a different result here, we don't know. *See, e.g.*, Barr v. Resolution Trust Corp., 837 S.W.2d 627, 628 (Tex. 1992). But in 1894, the Chief and his Court apparently did not feel pressured by the size of their docket to explore ways to limit the number of future lawsuits.

The case of *Swink v. League*[243] involved a trespass to try title suit that centered on whether a document in the chain of title conveyed property to Caroline Schwartz as separate or community property. Judge Conner ruled the deed to be a gift and conveyed the property to Schwartz as separate property. Chief Justice Tarlton held this to be error and ruled that:

> The court evidently regarded the recitals in the deed as importing a gift to the wife. When, during coverture, a conveyance is executed to either of the spouses—whether in the name of the husband or of the wife—it is presumed to vest the title in the community ... The fact that the consideration named in the deed is nominal only is not sufficient to rebut the presumption ... We think that this presumption should obtain, unless the deed expressly, or by necessary implication, limits the title conveyed to the separate use of one of the spouses. In this instrument we find no recital expressing or indicating such a limitation. We are thus constrained to reverse the judgment and remand the cause, and so order.

Appellate attorney Jerry Bullard, 2021 Chair of the State Bar of Texas Appellate Council and partner with the firm of Adams, Lynch & Loftin, P.C. in Grapevine, Texas, commented on the *Swink* ruling:

> Chief Justice Tarlton's opinion is a perfect example of what an effective judicial opinion should look like. It is precise, simple, and concise. It briefly states the law upon which the court's decision turned and succinctly applies the law to fact. And, most importantly, the opinion is crafted in a way that makes it readable and understandable for those who may not be familiar with judicial decisions.
>
> *Swink v. League* continues to stand the test of time. Although the case has been cited only a handful of times since it was issued in 1894, the principles of law addressed in the opinion remain unchanged.

TWENTY-ONE

1895

In 1895, the Second Court of Civil Appeals handled eleven appeals from Judge Conner's court, affirming six appeals[244] and reversing five appeals.[245] Chief Justice Tarlton wrote two opinions reversing Judge Conner in *Brown v. Henderson*[246] and *Reeves v. Texas & P. Ry. Co.*[247]

In *Brown v. Henderson*,[248] Chief Justice Tarlton found that the jury was erroneously instructed that the filing of a document in the General Land Office was constructive notice of title. Corpus Christi appellate attorney William Chriss commented on the *Brown* decision:

> From the days of the republic well into the twentieth century, unclear or conflicting land titles vexed, bothered, and bewildered Texas legislatures, governors, courts, and even constitutional conventions. *Brown v. Henderson* is just one of a legion of examples of litigation over the subject. Courts grew ever more anxious to settle and secure the ownership of lands and the bona fide purchaser doctrine was one preferred method of doing so. This doctrine cut off the claims of those who should have known better than to try to buy a piece of land when someone other than the seller was on record as the owner in the local clerk's office. In *Brown*, the trial court expanded this doctrine to include records of title on file at the state land office in Austin, an innovation that Justice Tarlton's opinion on appeal rejected and overturned. In those days even before carbon paper. telephones, and typewriters, it was one thing

to charge an ordinary purchaser with knowledge of records at the local courthouse; something else again to expect a farmer, rancher, or mechanic to find out what might be on file hundreds of miles away in Austin.

The case of *Reeves v. Texas & P. Ry. Co.*[249] involved a claim of negligence against a railroad line after damage occurred to horses during their shipment from Abilene, Texas, to Aiken, South Carolina. Injuries occurred during transit from Abilene to New Orleans. The contract of shipment provided that no suit or action could be made unless it was filed forty days after the damage occurred and that after the expiration of the period, the lapse of time shall be taken and deemed conclusive evidence against the validity of the contract. District Judge Truman Conner instructed the jury that the forty-day clause was binding on them as this was an interstate contract and that the jury should find for the defendant.

Tarlton found the instruction to be error based on a Texas statute enacted in 1891 and in force when the shipment occurred forbidding contracts from limiting the time in which to sue to a shorter period than two years. He found that the act was binding in interstate and domestic shipments. He said that the Texas legislature had the power to adopt without infringing on the federal constitution and it was not an attempt to regulate interstate commerce.

Former Associate Justice Jason Boatright of the Fifth Court of Appeals in Dallas studied the *Reeves* decision and had three comments:

1. It didn't quote the text of the act and apply the facts to that text; it jumped straight to a series of conclusory statements about the legal effect of the act;
2. It didn't explain why the 3rd court opinion was both on point and right; again, it simply jumped to a legal conclusion;
3. It has a breezy and confident style that is a refreshing contrast from the ponderous opinions of its day. It's also unusually easy to understand. That's no small thing.

Associate Justice Henry Head Steps Down

In 1895, Justice Henry Head decided to leave the court and return to private practice in Sherman, Texas. His resignation left a vacancy to be filled by Governor Charles Allen Culberson, the twenty-first governor of Texas who served from 1895 to 1899 and later as a United States Senator from Texas from 1899 to 1923. The governor considered candidates from across the district, which had been divided into three sections. District Judge Truman Conner was a nominee.

Justice Sam J. Hunter

On November 28, 1895, Governor Culberson chose Sam J. Hunter from Fort Worth to fill the seat vacated by Justice Head. Seeds of discontent began to grow over the appointment, which was seen as Fort Worth having exerted influence to select its own candidate rather than to allow a representative from the outlying districts. By now, Chief Justice Tarlton was seen as being a resident of Fort Worth. Justice Stephens, while being a resident of Parker County, was seen as being too close to Fort Worth. The appointment left the impression that the justices were mostly from Fort Worth, and that if Fort Worth had not intervened, District Judge Truman Conner would have been appointed to the court.[250]

Figure 50 Justice Sam J. Hunter.

State v City of Cisco

If Conner was disappointed over not being selected by the Governor, two days later he would face another bitter pill. On November 30, 1895, Justice Stephens wrote a three-paragraph opinion in the case of *State v City of Cisco*,[251] reversing and remanding the judgment of Judge Conner where he was disqualified to hear the case.

In *City of Cisco*, the State of Texas filed suit to annul the corporation of the City of Cisco and to remove its officers. After trying the case and issuing judgment, Judge Conner discovered that he owned unimproved real estate, of little value, within the corporate limits of Cisco. Judge Conner said that he had paid all of the taxes, but declined to recuse himself, and set aside the judgment entered.

On appeal, Justice Stephens reversed the judgment finding that the Texas Supreme Court settled this issue in the case of *Nalle v City of Austin*,[252] where the court found that a judge of a court who owns taxable property in the city to be "interested" in an action against the city of cancel the bonds issued within the meaning of Tex. Const. art. V, § 11 that prohibits judges from hearing cases where they may be interested.

Justice Stephens pointed to the court's decision in *Wetsel v State ex rel. Holland*,[253] where Justice Head ruled that any holder of property within the city limits of taxation had a pecuniary interest in the result and therefore this would disqualify the district judge from hearing the case. There was no question that Judge Conner was disqualified from hearing the case and this case was ongoing while Judge Conner was pursuing an appointment to the Second Court of Civil Appeals. No doubt the justices on the Second Court of Appeals or the Governor, if he was made aware of the case, would have questioned whether Conner was the correct appointment to the court.

H.P. Brelsford with Scott & Brelsford in Eastland, Texas represented the City of Cisco in *State v City of Cisco*. This decision would not play well in Judge Conner's court or with Brelsford. It is possible that Conner and Brelsford viewed the decision in *City of Cisco* as a stinging rebuke of Conner's judgment.

TWENTY-TWO

1896

In 1896, the Second Court of Civil Appeals handled nine appeals from Judge Conner's court, affirming two[254] and reversing seven[255] of the decisions. However, *Texas & P. Ry. Co. v. Bigham*, one of the decisions affirmed by Chief Justice Tarlton, was reversed by the Texas Supreme Court.[256]

Scott Stolley, an appellate attorney in Dallas, offered his perspective on this case:

> Although it was rare for Chief Justice Tarlton to affirm Judge Conner, that rarity occurred in *Texas & P. Ry. Co. v. Bigham*, 36 S.W. 1111 (Tex. Civ. App.), *rev'd*, 90 Tex. 223, 38 S.W. 162 (1896). This case involved a stock pen owned by the railroad. The plaintiff was attempting to secure a broken gate to the stock pen, when a passing freight train frightened cattle in the pen, causing a stampede through the gate and resulting in the plaintiff's injuries.
>
> The principal issue on appeal was whether the railroad's negligence (in allowing the gate to remain unrepaired) could be a proximate cause of the plaintiff's injuries. *Id.* at 1112. Chief Justice Tarlton held that although it can be difficult to distinguish between a proximate cause and a remote cause, the facts in this case fell within the category of proximate cause. *Id.*
>
> Proving that proximate cause can be in the eye of the beholder, the Texas Supreme Court reversed. 38 S.W. at 163-64. The court noted that under the proximate-cause test, the question was

whether a reasonably prudent person would have foreseen a similar injury. *Id.* at 164. Applying that test, the court held: "In our opinion, nothing short of prophetic ken could have anticipated the happening of the combination of events which resulted in the injury …" *Id.*

It might be argued that Judge Conner and Chief Justice Tarlton were in a similar quandary. What "prophetic ken" would they have needed in order to conclude that the Supreme Court would find as a matter of law that proximate cause was absent? To this day, lawyers and judges can differ about remote and proximate causes, as well as foreseeability. Ultimately, it might come down to the eye of the beholder, just as it apparently did in this case.

TWENTY-THREE

1897

THE YEAR 1897 WAS A sad and busy year for Chief Justice Tarlton. His daughter, Mary E. Tarlton, passed away on April 18, 1897, at the age of seventeen as the result of severe sickness contracted while away at school. The funeral was held April 18, 1897, at St. Patrick's Cathedral in Fort Worth.[257] She was buried at Oakwood Cemetery in Fort Worth in the Catholic section named Calvary Cemetery.

In that year, the Second Court of Civil Appeals handled five appeals from Judge Conner's court, affirming three[258] and reversing two[259] of the appeals. Chief Justice Tarlton reversed Judge Conner in the case of *Cope v. Lindsey*,[260] which involved a judgment against the defendant that was executed by the sheriff by the use of a range levy. A range levy allowed the sheriff to sell the stock without having to take possession of the stock. This could be quite a responsibility for the sheriff to seize cattle, take it into custody, and thereafter be responsible for the care of the stock. The sheriff wanted no part of that in this case. The disadvantage of a range levy is that a creditor could pick out prize cattle to satisfy a judgment that was not equivalent to the value of the stock being seized. The judgment debtor filed a motion to quash on the grounds that the stock was not running at large. Judge Conner denied the motion.

On appeal, Tarlton reversed the ruling, finding no justification for a range levy since[261] the stock was not running at large and could be confined to a pasture under fence. Tarlton found that the horses and cattle could be herded and penned without great inconvenience and expense. Tarlton wrote that: "No reason is perceived, under the facts alleged by the plaintiff, why, in this case, the sheriff could not follow the method prescribed as ordinarily necessary to the validity of a levy upon personal property, viz. why he could not take possession and control of the stock, situated, as they were, in enclosures of moderate size."

Tarlton found that the stock could be gathered because the area of the pastures was limited, and that the slight inconvenience and expense would be greatly overbalanced by the injurious consequences that would attach were the provisions of the state statute applied to the facts of the case. Tarlton found the levy illegal and that it should not have included the cost of $23.10 incurred in the appellate court.

Professor Stephen Alton, who teaches Property and Texas Land Titles at Texas A&M Law School, offered his analysis of the *Cope* decision:

Figure 51 Governor Charles Allen Culberson, 21st Governor of Texas, chose Fort Worth attorney Sam J. Hunter from Fort Worth for the vacant appellate seat of Justice Head, who retired from the court in 1895.

Other than a historian of the Texas ranching and cattle industry, who would have known that, in the late 19th century, there was a levy statute that required execution be had on all livestock in a debtor's enclosed pasture before execution could be had on that debtor's free-range livestock?

Tarlton's opinion for the Second Court of Civil Appeals is clear and concise as compared to many other opinions written in that era. His opinion appears to have correctly applied this statute, although his opinion never discusses the history or policy behind this law, perhaps because the result is so clear under the statute.

I suspect that the policy reason behind the statute requiring levy on livestock within an enclosure in preference to levying on free-range livestock is that the enclosed livestock will be easier to identify and catch, thus minimizing the possibility of mistakenly capturing someone else's livestock, which mistake would be much more likely to be made on the open range.

In *Cordill v. Moore*,[262] Cordill filed a trespass to try title suit against Moore over property that involved a survey of "public free school sections," title to which was held by the state. The defendant Moore claimed that he had purchased the property after applying and filing an affidavit that he settled on the property in good faith. The jury found in favor of Moore. Chief Justice Tarlton wrote the opinion reversing the jury verdict, finding that the plaintiff's application was not in compliance with the state statute. The state statute required the affidavit to be made when the land was subject to sale.

Dallas appellate attorney Dylan Drummond, 2022 Chair of the State Bar Appellate Section with the firm of Mayer LLP noted how Chief Justice Tarlton set out why the trial court erred:

The trial court sided with the defendant who asserted he complied with a statute governing the sale of certain state lands. In reversing the trial judge below, the appellate court found that the defendant failed to comply with the statute's terms because the defendant's statutorily-required affidavit was executed before the date upon which the public land was actually made available for private sale. But what makes the decision intriguing is that, after reaching its juristically straightforward conclusion early on in just the second paragraph of the opinion, Chief Justice Tarlton proceeded to spend the entire latter half of the opinion holding forth on the panoply of other reasons why the trial court erred—all the while acknowledging at the outset that the appellate court was not actually deciding whether any of these additional bases it examined would actually require reversal. In other words, Chief Justice Tarlton conceded that very nearly half of his opinion was mere dicta.

In May 1897, Tarlton was mildly criticized by the Texas Supreme Court in the case of *Groesbeeck v. Crow*,[263] where the court reversed his opinion after finding that he misapplied the statute of limitations. The court noted that the appellant's brief diverted attention from the issue.

On June 17, 1897, an event with 500 people gathered at the city park in Fort Worth for a concert to raise funds for the Robert E. Lee Camp, United Confederate Veterans, to pay off the amount due from the camp to the Jeff Davis memorial fund. A stand containing Confederate flags was arranged in a half circle in front of the band stand. The park was lighted by a great number of electric lights.

The orchestra opened with a selection followed by the Arion quartette and a response to an encore. Mrs. Maud Peters Ducker sang "The Red, White and Blue," which was enthusiastically received. Miss Lotta Carter recited "Two Gentlemen from Kentucky," which was vigorously applauded. Mrs. J.J. Wyly sang the negro dialect song, "Ma Angeline," in a "way that would have done credit to 'Bob' Taylor of Tennessee." The Young Men's Christian Association sang the battle piece, "The Artillery's Oath," to much applause. Mr. Wyly treated the audience to the song "She's the Only Pebble on the Beach" with a guitar accompaniment.

The exercise concluded with the song, "Dixie," in costume, by little Miss Genevieve Tarlton, daughter of Chief Justice B.D. Tarlton. While she sang, Miss Genevieve held above her head a small silk Confederate flag. Colonel R.M. Wynne, in introducing her, said that the flag had once belonged to the Fifth Regiment of the old Stonewall brigade, and had been carried by them through many battles, including that of the Wilderness.[264]

On December 30, 1897, Tarlton announced his candidacy for re-election. The *Brenham Weekly Banner* reported: "Chief Justice B.D. Tarlton of the court of civil appeals of the second supreme judicial district, states he will be a candidate for re-election next year. He evidently believes in the truth of the old adage: *The early bird gets the worm.*"[265]

TWENTY-FOUR

The Election of 1898

CHIEF JUSTICE TARLTON AND ASSOCIATE justices Hunter and Stephens faced election in 1898. To be renominated they would have to secure the majority votes of the Democratic delegates at the convention in San Antonio in July 1898.

In that year, Anson Rainey successfully transitioned from private practice to an associate justice of the Fifth Court of Civil Appeals in Dallas after appointment. Anson Rainey and Truman Conner knew each other from their days in Waxahachie.

On February 1, 1898, The *Houston Daily Post* reported that Judge Truman Conner of Eastland would run for chief justice of the court of civil appeals.[266]

The race began.

The story goes that Conner's challenge against Tarlton had nothing to do with Tarlton personally, but with Fort Worth dictating who would be appointed to the new Second Court of Civil Appeals.

On January 29, 1898, appellate attorney H.P. Brelsford of Eastland County and advocate for Judge Conner, traveled to Fort Worth to deliver the news. He told *The Dallas Morning News*, "You may say that Judge Conner of Eastland will be a candidate for the position of chief justice of the court of civil appeals, now filled by Judge B.D. Tarlton. Judge Conner has received the indorsement of all the territory west of Parker County, including Reeves County on the west. He is very popular in the upper Panhandle country."[267] Brelsford was delivering a message in Tarlton's new hometown of Fort Worth since joining the court.

Brelsford was politically influential; his name would be regularly mentioned in The *Fort Worth Daily Gazette* while visiting Fort Worth.[268] As a member of the state Democratic Executive Committee from the Twenty-eighth Senatorial District, he had access to the Democratic delegates. Brelsford was appointed as a Special Judge in an appeal in 1898 when all of the justices of the Second Court of Appeals were disqualified in a case,[269] and he served as a Special Associate Justice on the Texas Supreme Court.[270] Brelsford brought the Conner campaign to the heart of Tarlton country.

On February 1, 1898, The *Houston Post* reported that Judge Conner made his formal announcement of his candidacy for the position of Chief Justice of the Court of Civil Appeals.[271]

On February 28, 1898, the *Abilene Reporter* ran an endorsement of Judge Conner for the chief justice position by seven local bar associations. The resolution passed on February 5, 1898, at a meeting in Cisco, Texas, the same city as in the case of *State v City of Cisco* where the court had reversed Judge Conner because he was disqualified to hear the case. The endorsement cited the bars of Taylor, Jones, Shackelford, Comanche, Stephens, Eastland, and Callahan joining in the endorsement of Conner based on his eleven years on the bench, commenting that "because of his legal and literary education, is not only a thorough, painstaking, and able lawyer, but as well a broad minded and cultured gentleman." The endorsement was signed by H.P. Brelsford, Chairman, and W.P. Sebastian, Secretary for the Conner campaign. Other signatories to the endorsement were N.R. Lind from Comanche County bar; D.G. Hill and J.M. Wagstaff from Taylor County bar; Dan M. Jones and C.H. Steel from Jones County bar; J.A. Matthews from Shackelford County bar; P.W. Sebastian from Stephens County bar; and E.A. Hill and J.R. Stubblefield from Eastland County bar. Twelve attorneys had now signed on publicly as endorsing Judge Conner for the chief justice position.

On March 26, 1898, the *Jacksboro Gazette* issued an endorsement of B.D. Tarlton and noted that he had "occupied quite a prominent part in the political and judicial history of the state for about twenty years past."[272] The endorsement chronicled the judge's life from Louisiana to Texas and his time in the Legislature and serving in the judiciary. The endorsement discussed the issue of Tarlton living in Fort Worth:

> When so elected he was residing in Hillsboro, but as the discharge of his duties required his constant attention in Fort Worth, he, in compliance with the demands of duty, and at considerable personal expense, removed to this latter point soon after his election, and has been a citizen here since that time.
>
> When it was known that he would be a candidate for a second term, the members of the bar of Fort Worth assembled to indorse his candidacy, and to pay a just tribute to his learning, exalted character and judicial worth, and adopted the following resolutions:
>
> "Fairness and mental balance being two of the most important characteristics of a good judge, it is no more than the exact truth to say that the Hon. B.D. Tarlton, chief justice of this supreme judicial district, possesses in full measure these two cardinal attributions of a judge. These characteristics, supplemented by judicial learning and service upon the bench, have enabled him to enrich the jurisprudence and ornament the bench of this state; therefore, be it
>
> "Resolved, That the bar of Fort Worth sincerely and spontaneously pledges its earnest undivided support to the candidacy of the Hon. B.D. Tarlton for renomination to the chief justiceship of the court of civil appeals of this district, Having served one term on the bench of this district with entire satisfaction to the bar and the people, it is but a requital of his honorable service and arduous labor on the bench that his ambition to serve a second term be encouraged and supported by the people of this judicial district. His course on the bench has been marked not only by learning, equipoise and great carefulness in the preparation of his opinions, but by courtesy and dignity of demeanor that have endeared us both to the judge and to the man.

The endorsement by the Fort Worth Bar was signed by 135 attorneys, and that his candidacy had been endorsed by many bars in the district and that he had filled the fullest measure the highest requirements of a judge in appellate court, "being now at the very zenith of manhood's maturer years, and with an experience that enables him to render to the state and the people the largest possible amount of thorough and efficient work in the administration of justice."[273]

The endorsement pointed out that the "sole objection urged against him, that he resides at Fort Worth, it may be said that if this objection be at all tenable, it will apply with equal force against everyone who may seek to serve a second term on the court, since it would be wholly unreasonable to expect that a man of family, not originally from Fort Worth, but whose almost constant personal presence is required by a proper discharge of his duty to be at the place where the court is fixed by law, should not remove his family to such place, and thereby necessarily become a citizen there. His name is presented, not as a sectional judge, but as judge for the entire district."[274]

The *Albany News* Endorsement of Conner

A stinging editorial against Fort Worth by the editor of the *Albany News* appeared in the May 20, 1898, edition. The Democratic Convention was two months away. It showed that the counties west of Eastland to El Paso and in the northern parts up to the Panhandle were deeply resentful of "Fort Worth" deciding who would sit on the Court of Civil Appeals. The resentment had nothing to do with Tarlton.

Does Fort Worth Want the World?

If one will keep up with the daily reports from Fort Worth, published in the Dallas News, and other papers, he cannot be struck with the fact, that this glorious city, is not only entitled to have, but is heir to every State office in the gift of the people, and in addition, she has those among her citizenship, who are in every way qualified to file every office in the United States, from constable to President. It is only surprising to a great many people, that some one of her gifted citizens, does not lay claim to the Throne of England. Surely there is some residing in that city, who is more competent that Sampson, to take charge of the fleet he now commands.

But to read the many claims for office of the Fort Worth people, one would think that she has become so imbued with her own importance, that she thinks that all that is necessary for her to do, is, to simply come out and announce for office, and it is theirs—that the whole State should bow down and worship the said candidate for office, regardless of his qualifications. She presents a candidate for governor, and he is undoubtedly one of the ablest men in the State, and in every way qualified for the position. She presents a candidate for Commissioner of the General Land Office, one for Chief Justice of the Court of Civil Appeals, and the Lord only knows how many more. It is the latter office that I desire to refer to specially and to show how grasping the Fort Worth people are in their demands. Judge Tarlton, the present Chief Justice, is an able lawyer and judge, and the write has nothing to say against him, and this article is not aimed at him as a man or his ability as a judge, but he is the opponent of one whom the people of this section desire to succeed him, hence it becomes necessary to refer to him in connection with the discussion. Judge Tarlton moved his family to Fort Worth and is now a resident of that place. Judge Hunter has been a citizen of Fort Worth for many years and lived there when he was appointed by Gov. Culberson as Associate Justice. Next, we have Judge Stephens who hails from Weatherford, but has his home now in Ft. Worth, but Weatherford is within a stone's throw of Fort Worth, and you might say that he was almost a resident of the place before he was elected and moved there. Here we have the three judges residing in Fort Worth, and the Fort Worth people trying to keep them there–not wanting the outside part of the district, composing the second Judicial District, to have any say at all in the selection of judges–not wanting them to have a representative on the bench. Is it fair? Is it just?

But let's glance at a little past history! When Judge Head resigned, the Fort Worth and Denver section thought they were entitled to a representation on the Supreme Bench, and they put forward Judge Wallace for the place. That section west of Fort Worth thought that they were entitled to representation, and they put forward Judge T.H. Conner and Judge Kennedy, the former now being a candidate for the position held by Judge Tarlton. But Fort Worth was not willing for either the Fort W.& D.C. section or the Texas and Pacific section to get the office and she brought forward Judge Hunter (undoubtedly one of the ablest Judges in the state), and says to the Governor, that he must appoint one from Fort Worth–in her might she demands that she shall have all she claims, and actually thinks it presumption in the North and West, to bring forward able men to oppose those she advances for office. She thinks it a piece of arrogance for any section outside of Fort Worth, to aspire to see one of their gifted citizens on the Supreme Bench, and she makes war on every candidate that any section puts forward for any office. It is a fact, that Governor Culberson would have appointed Judge T.H. Conner to succeed Judge Head, had not Fort Worth entered the fight, and to reconcile the differences, Gov. Culberson appointed Judge Hunter. Governor Culberson expressed himself as believing at the time that this section and the Fort W. & D.C. section, should have recognition but they were divided, and even had all the candidates have remained in the race (Wallace, Conner, and Kennedy) we believe had not Fort Worth have sent in a candidate, that Judge Conner would have carried off the prize. Oh no! Fort Worth would not for one moment remain neutral–would not consent to any other section getting the office, but she rose in her grandeur and dictatorial way, and demanded that one of her gifted citizens should be appointed. Not long afterwards the election came off and although Judge Conner was urged to run from all sections of the district, he would not do so, as he recognized that Judge Hunter should be endorsed by an election by the people –that the Governor's appointment should be ratified, and he not only warmly supported Judge Hunter, but Judge Hunter will bear witness that the friends of Judge Conner supported him in this section. It was not because they were antagonistic to other sections and candidates but because they believed that Judge Hunter had made an able judge, and that the people should ratify his appointment. These people believed that a representative should be upon the bench from some other part of the district–none announced from Fort Worth & D.C. section, or from the Texas & Pacific section, and the friends of Judge Conner urged him to run. He decided to do so, and as soon as he announced, the bar of Fort Worth got together and said "Nay! You cannot have the office! Not only will we have the Governor, but we will have the Chief Justice of the Court of Civil Appeals! We have a candidate, and you must not presume to run for any office that a citizen of Fort Worth wants!" The bar resolved and began to flood the district with letters, circulars, etc., and actually sent the leading member of their bar, the Hon. Theodore Mack, out through Cooke and other Counties, to cry down Conner and hold up Tarlton. They throw up to us and others that we have Stephens, and we say we do not claim him– he is one of you, formerly lived very near you, and is now a resident of yours. They say again that Judge Tarlton is from Hill County, and we say, that he is a resident of your city, we learn has a home there, and that is his place of residence. We say that Judge Tarlton is one of you, and today his many friends are sending out through the country–his many friends in Fort Worth, urgent letters in his interest, and they do not come from Hill county, where he formerly resided. The Fort Worth people know that Judge Tarlton is a resident of their place and they are working for him–his old county has no interest in the race at all.

 A citizen of Fort Worth said no long since to a gentleman in this district, that we should pull down Conner and let Tarlton have it, and when the term of Judge Stephens ran out, then we could put Conner in, and he intimated that Fort Worth would oppose us. This of course would not be entertained for a moment, as

Judge Conner is in the race to win–he is going to win beyond the least particle of a doubt, and with all due respect to Judge Tarlton (whom I admire very much) I say that Judge T.H. Conner, now the District Judge of the 42nd Judicial District, (which position he has had for many years, and has given universal satisfaction) will be the next Chief Justice of the Court of Civil Appeals of the 2nd Supreme Judicial District.

The North, Northwest, West, Northeast, etc. now say to the good people of Fort Worth, we have been supporting nearly every candidate you have put out in the past, but the time has come when we demand recognition in some form, and if you fail to give us that which we are justly entitled to, please remember that you can expect little at the hands of this people in the future–the people that you trample upon and ignore in your deliberations. Take heed while there is time. We have good memories. Our demands are not great, and we feel that we have a candidate for office who is eminently fitted for the position–who has no superior in the state as a sound and able jurist—who is universally loved by all who know him, that the people of Fort Worth should not antagonize us in the manner they are doing–in her attempt to 'Claim the world'–including the sun, moon, and twinkling stars.

Governor Hogg said to the write when Judge Conner failed to get the appointment, at the time Judge Hunter was appointed, as follows: "Tell Conner not to be disappointed–his time will come soon, and he is destined to occupy some important position at no distant day, in this state–a man of his merit and ability cannot be kept down," and this is true–The time has now come. Every county west of Eastland to El Paso District are for him, those north of Texas & Pacific are for him, many counties on the Fort Worth & D.C. Ry. are for him. Cooke county spoke a few days since, and when the convention is held, T.H. Conner will be the nominee beyond a doubt.

This is not written in any manner to detract from the merits of the present Court of Civil Appeals–they are all able men, but it is written for the purpose of showing what a selfish position Fort Worth occupies in the matter of offices, and to ask her to give us and other sections surrounding her, a small slice of the cake. I believe she will do it, and that the Hon. T.H. Conner will be the Chif (sic) Justice of the Court of Civil Appeals of the Second Judicial District, beyond a doubt!

The article was signed with one word:

"JUSTICE"

No similar editorial appeared in the Fort Worth or Dallas newspapers on that date in 1898, and no doubt these more reputable newspapers would not have carried such a long meandering hit piece. The city of Albany is located in Shackelford County, near Abilene and in the western part of the state. The Shackelford Bar Association endorsed Conner for the chief justice position, and now the editorial page of the local newspaper was complaining that western counties had no representation on the new court of civil appeals. The article adopted the Conner campaign arguments.

The article was anything but about "JUSTICE" as it describes. It was a vicious attack on Fort Worth, and by default, Tarlton. It was no doubt encouraged by the Conner campaign and designed to undermine Tarlton's campaign. While the article said it had nothing to say against Chief Justice Tarlton and that it was not aimed at him "as a man or his ability," that claim was ridiculous. Chief Justice Tarlton was the incumbent and certainly more than just the "opponent" to which "this section desire to succeed him" and that it "hence becomes necessary to refer to him in connection with the discussion." The article read as if Tarlton was simply an impediment to Conner's election.

Most Texans would not realize that they lived within a purported "Fort Worth & D.C. section" in the Second Judicial District. The article blamed Fort Worth for Governor Culberson selecting Justice Sam Hunter to succeed Justice Head on the court. Governor Culberson selected a compromise candidate from Fort Worth to succeed Justice Hunter so as to not have to choose between a candidate between the sections in the district.

The *Albany News* article was illogical. It meant that anyone moving to Fort Worth to work therefore became part of the Fort Worth establishment and would be ineligible to serve a second term. The governor's choice of Hunter was obvious: all of the justices initially appointed to the new court of appeals were from outlying counties. They were not from Tarrant County or from Fort Worth. Chief Justice Tarlton was from Hillsboro in Hill County. Justice Head was from Sherman in Collin County, and Justice Stephens was from Weatherford in Parker County. They moved to Fort Worth because they had to perform their work on the court. It did not mean that the new court of civil appeals was owned by Fort Worth. The Governor picked a candidate from Fort Worth to give Tarrant County, the largest populated county in the district, representation on the court.

Conner Encouraged

In late May 1898, Conner campaigned in Granbury, Texas. The stop was reported by the *Abilene Reporter*:

> Judge T. H. Conner, of Eastland, candidate for chief justice of civil appeals at Fort Worth, spent a day in Granbury last week, and no man could have made more friends in the short time he was here. He is not only a learned and upright judge, but a most pleasant gentleman socially and an uncompromising democrat politically … So far he has carried nearly every county in the district in which primaries have been held and his chances for success are indeed bright. Judge Conner's claims for the position are superior to those of any other candidate. His long experience as a trial judge has especially fitted him for judging the character of litigation coming before this court; he is a permanent resident of this district, thoroughly identified with the interests of the west; and geographically he comes from a section that has never yet been represented on the bench of our ….

The corner of the newspaper was torn off and the remainder of the article is lost.

By June 1898, Conner was encouraged by the progress of his campaign. *The Dallas Morning News* quoted Democratic delegate and attorney, H.P. Brelsford, from Eastland County as saying:

> Judge Conner's friends feel exceedingly encouraged at the prospects of his candidacy. It will require ninety-nine votes to nominate and of this number he has seventy-three instructed votes or votes uninstructed but delegates favorable to him. To secure the remaining twenty-six votes necessary to nominate he has a majority of interior plains and panhandle counties to draw from, to say nothing of the large counties in the eastern end of the district which have not yet instructed. We feel that his nomination is virtually assured.

On July 15, 1898, the Conner headquarters announced that his nomination was assured because he had 106½ instructed votes and 12 votes assured from uninstructed counties for a total of 118 ½ votes. The number to nominate was 99.[275] Days later, Conner announced that he had 114 instructed votes and that Tarlton had 62 instructed votes. The remainder were uncommitted or not reported.[276]

Tarlton Withdraws from Race

On July 30, 1898, Tarlton withdrew from the race and retired from the court. The news media reported his withdrawal:

> A graceful thing which was done was the strong endorsement given the retiring chief justice, Judge Tarlton. The eulogies paid him as a man and as a judge were of the highest order and found a liberal response from the lawyers who had appeared before him and the delegates who were not lawyers, but who had become acquainted with the character of the man. No higher tribute could possibly be

paid any man the reference made to him by Judge G.H. Goodson of Comanche, who was a strong Conner supporter and who in a speech of some minutes declare that the convention should unequivocally indorse his course while on the bench, not as a matter of conventionally nor to taper off a defat, but because he was a pure man, upright and honest, noble and true and an able lawyer and a profound jurist. He thought that this was due the retiring chief justice because the fight was not made against him on the grounds that he was not satisfactory or had not made an excellent judge, but for other considerations.[277]

Conner Resigns District Court

In September 1898, Judge Conner tendered his resignation from his judicial bench to clear the way for a candidate to be elected in the November election.[278] Conner played high stakes politics: he would not let the Governor, who refused to appoint him to the court of civil appeals, appoint his replacement.

In November 1898, Judge Conner received the vote of the general election for chief justice. *The Houston Post* reported that "Chief Justice B.D. Tarlton of the court of civil appeals will retire from office at the session of the court on December 31, on which day his successor, Judge Conner will assume the duties of his office. Judge Tarlton however, will sit with the court on that day, handing down opinions in cases previously submitted."[279]

Ever the professional, during the election of 1898 Tarlton chose not to sit on cases that were presided on by Judge Conner, such as *Clack v. Wood*,[280] where Justice Stephens affirmed Judge Conner. After the election, Tarlton resumed handling appeals from Conner's court and affirmed Judge Conner in *Bull v. Jones*,[281] issued on October 22, 1898.

On December 31, 1898, Chief Justice B.D. Tarlton retired from the Second Court of Appeals. In that year the Second Court of Civil Appeals handled six appeals form Judge Conner's court, affirming four[282] and reversing two decisions.

Chief Justice Truman Conner began his term on January 1, 1899.

Figure 52 A much older Chief Justice Truman H. Conner.

TWENTY-FIVE

The Tarlton Opinions

FROM 1892 TO 1898, CHIEF Justice Tarlton wrote over 400 opinions during his first term on the Second Court of Civil Appeals, ranging from creditors rights, personal injury, public lands, title disputes, boundary disputes, adverse possession claims, and public lands. The following are some of the notable opinions that are now settled principles of law.

No requirement to plead evidence
In *Johnson v. James*,[283] Tarlton ruled that a person filing a lawsuit is not required to specifically allege in the suit the evidence he is relying on. In this case the defendant relied on deeds transferring title but did not specifically plead these allegations in his pleadings. The plaintiff (the party bringing the suit) objected to the introduction of instruments proving up the title on the grounds that they had not been pleaded. The trial court agreed and sustained the objection to the evidence. This meant that the defendant could not prove title to the property even though the plaintiff admitted that the documents were in due form and sufficient to pass title.

Tarlton found the trial court's ruling as "manifestly erroneous." Without citing to any authority, Tarlton wrote that "A pleader is not required to plead his evidence."

Name of title document does not control
In Texas, a deed conveys title to the property. A "quitclaim deed" does not convey title but transfers any interest that the transferor has in the

property; it stops the transferor from later claiming an interest in the property. However, calling a document a "quitclaim" deed does not mean that it is a quitclaim deed. It could be a deed that conveys title.

In *Dycus v. Hart*,[284] a party named a document a "quitclaim," but the court found that the deed actually conveyed title, and that having paid the purchase price and without notice of the claim, he would be protected as a bona fide purchaser of the property.

No requirement to make actual tender

In *Kalklosh v. Haney*,[285] the court held that a vendee (purchaser of real estate) is not required to make actual or tender payment of the entire balance due but is to plead and prove his willingness to pay the entire balance due; failing in this, his right should cease.

Insufficient property description

In *James v. Brooks*,[286] the court reversed a judgment foreclosing a vendor's lien that contained an insufficient description of the real property. The property description in the document must be sufficient so that the property can be located on the ground by the data contained within the document.

Court can impose a "constructive trust" on real property

In *Miller v. Carlton*,[287] Tarlton recognized the concept of "constructive trust" theory where real property obtained by agreement that is not complied with subsequently. When the failure to follow through with the agreement would amount to a fraud on the party, the court can impose a "constructive trust" on the property in order to prevent another from unjustly benefitting from breaching their agreement to convey. What was unique about this decision is that it is not necessary to prove all of the specific elements of fraud on the part of the defendant, but that the failure to enforce the agreement to convey title would amount to a fraud.

Adverse possession of property in possession

In Texas it is possible to acquire title by taking possession, cultivating, and enjoying the property for over ten years. There is no requirement of having a deed to the property. But this concept extends to only the property in actual possession. In *Hull v. Woods*,[288] the court found that in a trespass to try title suit based on the ten-year adverse possession statute, the party seeking possession cannot acquire property beyond what was in their actual possession.

Property sold in the wrong county by trustee's sale can be resold in the proper county

In *Texas Loan Agency v. Gray*,[289] the trustee sold property in Denton County when the property was located in Navarro County. The next month, the trustee sold the same property in Navarro County. The court held that the sale in Navarro County vested title in the plaintiff. The sale in Denton County was void, but it did not divest the trustee of the power to sell the property.

Manifest error: A party claiming title must establish the strength of their own title

The case of *Clements v. Clements*[290] shows that Chief Justice Tarlton believed in the concept of "manifest error." This is where a higher court finds error that justifies reversal even when it is not raised by the parties. In that case, the second Mrs. Clements, as a married spouse, upon the death of her husband had a homestead right to live on the property during her life, but she ended up owning the property over the heirs of her husband, who were entitled to the title to the property. The second Mrs. Clements was not entitled to any title to the property absent a will. But she prevailed. How was this possible?

The second Mrs. Clements lived in St. Louis and sold her homestead to move to Texas to live with her new husband. She sold her home in St. Louis and delivered $4,037 to Mr. Clements on the agreement that the premises would become her homestead, but that title would be vested in her as her separate property. However, her husband failed to execute a deed and fraudulently misrepresented the value of the property. The home was worth $1,000.

The surviving heirs of the first marriage between A. Clements and Catherine Clements filed suit to recover the property from Mrs. Clements by filing a trespass to try title claim. At trial, the heirs decided to abandon the claim. The second wife offered a witness who supported the wife's claim that the property would become her separate property. The court granted judgment for the second Mrs. Clements.

The heirs must have had second thoughts and retained an attorney to appeal. Having abandoned their claim at trial, what error could they assert on appeal? The argument was that the second Mrs. Clements still needed to establish her title to the property.

Chief Justice Tarlton agreed. There was no proof of title from the state of Texas (the sovereignty) or a common source with the adverse party or at least prior possession of the property. The court reversed the case because "it appears to have resulted from manifest error, and to be in its effects too grossly inequitable to receive the sanction and approval of a court of justice."[291] The lesson learned is that in a trespass to try title claim, even if the plaintiff cannot prove title, this does not mean that the defendant has established title and can prevail.

Definition of sale of personal property

In *Laing v. State*,[292] Tarlton revisited the definition of "sale" when it applied to a minor child who was sent to a saloon to buy beer by his employer. William Shirley, under the age of 21 years and with the consent of his father, was working for B.F. Chastain in a business near a saloon in Weatherford. B.F. Chastain sent Shirley with a bucket and 10 cents to the saloon to buy a bucket of beer. Shirley went to the saloon and told them that he was sent by his employer. The saloon keeper took the money and filled the bucket with beer, and Shirley delivered the beer to Chastain. The State of Texas filed suit on the liquor dealer's bond for $500 for violating the bond by selling alcohol to a minor.

The question was whether the liquor dealer violated the condition of their bond that forbade them to sell intoxicating liquor to a minor. The trial court held there was violation, but Tarlton reversed, finding no vendor / vendee relationship. There was no sale to the minor. "No title really or apparently passed by the transaction to the minor," Tarlton wrote.

Declarations beyond agency

Tarlton wrote two opinions enforcing the rule that an agency relationship is determined by the declarations of the acts of the authority, not the agent. In *Western Industrial Co. v. Chandler*,[293] the court held that authority on the part of an alleged agent cannot be established by showing that the alleged agent claims to have the powers which he assumes to exercise.

In *Moore v. Powell*,[294] Tarlton wrote:

> There can be no valid ratification or adoption by one person of the act of another unless the latter should have purported to act in the name of, or for the person ratifying. When one person has assumed to act for another, the latter may adopt or ratify the act of the former, however unauthorized, but such ratification, to apply, must be founded at least upon an assumption of authority.

Contract did not violate Statute of Frauds

Texas law prevents someone from filing suit on an agreement which cannot be performed within one year, unless the promise is in writing and signed or authorized by the parties. In *Weatherford M.W. & N.W.Ry. Co v. Wood*,[295] the county filed suit to condemn the Wood's real property, and Wood was entitled to receive $1,000 for compensation. Wood agreed to accept $800 paid in cash and an agreement that the railway company give him a free annual pass over its railway for ten years and to stop its trains at his home, which was near the railway. When the railway refused to issue the pass or to stop near his home, Wood filed suit to enforce the agreement.

The question was whether the contract violated the statute of frauds because it was not in writing and performable in one year. The court found that the contract did not fall within the meaning of the statute of frauds because the contract had been performed by Wood. Wood prevailed in enforcing his agreement.

Acts after the accident

The case of *Sills v. Ft Worth & D.C. Ry. Co.*[296] involved the derailment of a train due to the accumulation of sand on the tracks. At trial the plaintiff offered evidence that the sandy condition was permitted to occur after the accident, of which evidence was excluded. The court held:

> Therefore, the sole question in this connection is whether the testimony excluded, because it had reference to a period subsequent to the accident, throws or tends to throw light upon the issue whether the company was guilty of negligence in permitting the accumulation of the sand at that time. We answer this question in the negative. It is not perceived how the fact that sand blown by wind accumulated at the point in question once, twice, or thrice, after the accident, tends in any way to prove that the accumulation of sand at the time of the accident was due to the negligence of the company.

Gaines v. Newbrough

The case of *Gaines v. Newbrough*[297] shows how serious local politics can become in the county commissioner's courts. Under the Texas constitution and road laws, the county commissioner's courts were created to govern the counties. Among their duties were the responsibility to establish and to lay out the county roads and to appoint road overseers who were responsible for maintenance of county and public roads in their precincts. In those days the counties had the power to "draft" men to work on the county roads. Road overseers were responsible for the maintenance of the roads, the crews, and to pay compensation and submit reports to the commissioner's court.

Gaines was the road overseer in Precinct 1 in Palo Pinto County. In November 1893, Gaines was upset with the Palo Pinto County Commissioner's Court, which was composed of elected officials representing districts in the entire county. Gaines filed a sworn report with the county clerk that contained offensive and insulting language against the commissioners. The county commissioners reacted to the report and held Gaines in contempt for submitting his offensive report, fining him "$25 for contempt of this court in making and filing the report." The commissioners had him arrested and taken into jail.

Gaines was not present when the court ordered him arrested. The sheriff, B.M. Maddox, met up with Gaines and offered to read the capias for his arrest, but Gaines refused to let him. During the afternoon session of the commissioner's court, Gaines went to the door of the commissioner's court, accompanied by his fourteen-year-old son with a stick in hand, and went to the door of the commissioner's courtroom while the court was in session and said: "It is your day now, but my turn next."

The sheriff said: "You can't come here and cuss out the officers."

John Eaton, the clerk of the court, placed his hand on Gaines' arm, and Gaines raised the stick in a threatening position. Sheriff Maddox seized Gaines and said that he would take him to jail unless he paid the fine.

Gaines demanded that the writ be read, and the sheriff read the writ. Gaines tried to take the writ out of the sheriff's hand, and the sheriff took Gaines to jail. A man named Hindman paid the fine before Gaines was imprisoned, and Gaines was immediately released.

Gaines sued the Palo County Commissioner's Court members and county judge on the grounds that his confinement was false imprisonment and sought $5,000 in damages. The trial court, Judge J.S. Straughan, ruled against him. Gaines appealed, contending that the order was void because the contempt was not committed in the presence of the court.

Chief Justice Tarlton held that Gaines was acting as an official of the court and that no scire facias was necessary in dealing with the contemptuous report. Tarlton found that there was no false imprisonment because the county commissioner's court was considered a court of general jurisdiction and that it had jurisdiction over Gaines as road overseer. The court found that the actions of the court were judicial in nature and involved the exercise of judgment and discretion as to when, how, and to what extent punishment should be inflicted or a fine assessed for flagrantly contemptuous conduct.

TWENTY-SIX

Private Practice

"We are all Democrats gathered here, selected from the various wards and precincts. We are all Democrats and it is only natural that we should be Democrats. With us it is a matter of tradition as well as a matter of belief."
—B.D. Tarlton, Speech to the Democratic Convention, San Antonio 1904

Tarlton & Ayers

AFTER LEAVING THE COURT, TARLTON set up a legal practice with Ben Ayers to form the firm of Tarlton & Ayers. Ayers handled civil and criminal cases and numerous appeals to the Second Court of Civil Appeals. One of his cases was the appeal in *Gaines v. Newbrough* from Palo Pinto County, where Tarlton wrote the opinion affirming the judgment.

Tarlton began appearing in cases before the Second Court of Appeals with its new Chief Justice Conner. Conner wrote four opinions where Tarlton & Ayers were appellate counsel.[298] As a former chief justice, having his name on the pleadings involving significant litigation could be useful. In August 1899, Tarlton was named as co-counsel in a case of *Clark v. Finley*,[299] brought by Tarrant County Sheriff Sterling P. Clark to challenge the constitutionality of a new 1897 law that reduced the fees of sheriffs, constables, and district attorneys in certain counties, including Tarrant County. The other attorneys handling the suit were A.T. Watts and E.G. Senter of Dallas and Wallace B. Hendrick.

The newspaper reported "Judge B.D. Tarlton of Fort Worth" was listed on the petition for writ of mandamus that was presented to Judge R.R. Gaines of the Texas Supreme Court at his home in Paris, Texas. The suit argued that special legislation must be provided in the Texas constitution for the new law to be effective.[300] The paper reported that "No law passed in recent years has created more comment than the present fee bill did at the time and since its passage. It has been the cause of much contention and the pending legal fight re-opens the entire matter." The Texas Supreme Court ultimately affirmed the law.[301]

Tarlton appeared as counsel for a lessee, C.C. Slaughter, who was named in a petition for mandamus to compel the General Land Office to cancel the lease to Slaughter and to accept an application to purchase property. The Texas Supreme Court denied the petition in *Reed v. Rogan*.[302]

In 1903, Tarlton handled a will contest in Abilene involving Mrs. Louise Merrill, who left $50,000 to her niece. A will was found in the pocket of Mrs. Merrill and was alleged to have been a forgery.[303]

A newspaper ad in The *Dallas Morning News* showed that Tarlton had set up a law office in Beaumont.[304] Tarlton was probably drawn to Beaumont after the Spindletop oil field was discovered in January 1901, when 100,000 barrels of oil gushed from the ground every day for nine days.

Drawn to the coast, Tarlton no doubt wanted to leave Fort Worth.

Ex Parte Snodgrass

In 1901 Tarlton handled the case of *Ex Parte Snodgrass*[305] where he obtained the reversal of a contempt finding by an attorney who questioned whether a witness had been mistaken or had lied while on the witness stand. The attorney was Frank Snodgrass of Coleman, Texas. The case is a remarkable decision that sets out the proper boundaries between the judge, attorney and witnesses in the case.

During a criminal trial, two witnesses had testified: H.N. Beakley and J.M. Crawford. Snodgrass, in remarks to the jury said, in substance and effect, that either Beakley or Crawford were mistaken, or one of them had lied. Beakley heard Snodgrass's remark, arose, and told Snodgrass that he must not say that he had lied. Snodgrass turned toward Beakley in an excited voice and manner, pointing and waving his hand towards him, and said, "I stated that either you or Crawford was mistaken, or one of you had lied, and I have nothing to take back."

Snodgrass's remark provoked Beakley, who then sprung on Snodgrass and struck him in the presence of the court and jury. After the row, a gun was found on Beakley. Snodgrass resumed his arguments to the jury.

The judge in the case, Judge John Goodwin, submitted an affidavit stating that it was known in the town of Coleman that Snodgrass and Beakley were unfriendly and that it was commonly said that someday there would be a wholesale killing between those parties.

The judge fined Snodgrass fifty dollars and found him in contempt. He would be committed to jail in Coleman County until the fine was paid. Snodgrass was not required to serve his sentence in jail. He returned home and appealed his contempt to the Texas Court of Criminal Appeals, who ruled that the matter did not amount to contempt of court. The court found that the trial court had no subject-matter jurisdiction over Snodgrass based on his arguments to the jury. The court wrote:

> Now, the question arises, does the matter set up in the judgment make contempt of court? In order to be contempt of court, the trial court must have not only jurisdiction of the person of the relator, but he must also have jurisdiction of the subject matter, and to render the particular judgment rendered. He had jurisdiction of relator, but he did not have jurisdiction of the subject-matter, because he did not have the power or legal authority to enter the judgment against relator for the statements made as contained in the judgment. If he did, then it would destroy relator's right to argue the cause of his client in the courts of justice. It is a constitutional right guaranteed everyone tried in the courts of this state to be heard in person and

by counsel; and certainly where two witnesses testify, one for and the other against a certain proposition, showing an absolute and unqualified contradictio, there is but one of two conclusions to be drawn,- that one or the other testified falsely, or one or the other is mistaken.

Figure 53 Beakley slaps Snodgrass during his trial after Snodgrass said that either Beakley or Crawford was mistaken or one had lied. "I have nothing to take back," Snodgrass said.

The court held that attorneys are bound and will be held to obey legal orders of courts, and the court should invoke its judicial authority under the law, and in obedience thereto. The court explained that the relationships of court and attorneys, bench, and bar, are reciprocal, and each, in their proper sphere, is clothed with powers, rights, and privileges which are to be recognized and respected by the other. These relations should be recognized and respected alike by the bench and bar and being carefully kept in view and followed as rules of action and conduct, will avoid friction.

Justice Henderson, in his dissenting opinion, was not amused. He considered Snodgrass not being in jail as an escape. He found that the court did have subject matter jurisdiction over the matter. He recognized that an attorney has a right to criticise the testimony of witnesses but by calling a witness a liar or scoundrel would provoke a breach of the peace. The trial court witnessed the statement and the court could not try the case de novo and set aside the judgment on evidence contradicting the record.

Shoemaker v. Texas & P. Ry. Co.

In February 1902, the Second Court of Civil Appeals ruled in the case of *Shoemaker v. Texas & P. Ry. Co.*,[306] a case based on wrongful death over the death of her two boys who were run over by a train on June 4, 1900. The boys were eighteen and nineteen years of age and had left their home around 10 p.m. to go look for their brother-in-law, who was in Milsap but never returned home. Their remains were found scattered across the tracks for some distance; seven trains were known to have passed along that track on the night of June 4, 1900.

Susan Shoemaker filed suit based on the belief that the train conductor was unfit. The railway alleged that the youth were guilty of trespassing. The court instructed the jury to render a judgment for the defendant, which the jury did. On appeal, Justice Hunter wrote an opinion reversing the case based on the exclusion of evidence that indicated that the train was traveling at sixty miles per hour while passing through the appellant's premises, and that the train did not blow its whistle or ring a bell at the crossings. The track through the premises had been used day and night for years by the people of that community in going to and from Milsap and to and from Newbury Church, about one and a half miles east of the premises. This evidence tended to prove a condition of things which required those in charge of the engine to keep a lookout ahead as a matter of ordinary care, especially when the train was making such an unusual rate of speed. Hunter noted that the moon was shining brightly, and the headlight on Waldron's train was very good that night; so that, if it was the duty of the engineer and fireman to keep a lookout for people on the track at that place, the circumstances of the killing would tend to establish negligence on their part in not seeing the boys on the track, or, if they saw them, in not doing all within their power, consistent with safety to themselves and the train, to avoid the injury. The court excluded evidence that the train could have been stopped within 150 feet. This was an error.

Preparing for the reversal of the case near the end of the opinion, Justice Hunter added this sentence:

> We reversed the judgment and remanded the case *of Shiflet v. Railway Co., supra*, a case in some respect quite analogous to this, where Chief Justice Tarlton laid down the rule that: "If the course of legal evidence was such as tended to support the averments of the plaintiff's petition, it became the duty of the judge trying the case to submit the issues of fact to the jury, even though, had they returned a verdict against the defendant, he should have felt constrained to set aside the verdict on a motion for a new trial."

Justice Hunter had placed Chief Justice Conner in a box. A second vote was needed to form a majority opinion. But if he joined in the opinion, then he would be agreeing that former chief justice B.D. Tarlton had "laid down the rule," from three Texas Supreme Court cases.

Chief Justice Conner found a way to join the decision by agreeing with the disposition of the appeal but without having to agree with the wording of the opinion. Conner wrote in his concurring opinion:

> Without being able to assent to all that is said in the opinion of Judge HUNTER, I nevertheless agree to the disposition made of the appeal as announced by him. In the case of *Lee v. Railway Co.*,

89 Tex. 588, 36 S. W. 65, our supreme court, in an opinion by Associate Justice Brown, say: "Negligence, whether of the plaintiff or defendant, is generally a question of fact, and becomes a question of law to be decided by the court only when the act done is in violation of some law, or when the facts are undisputed, and admit of but one inference regarding the care of the party in doing the act in question; in other words, to authorize the court to take the question from the jury, the evidence must be of such character that there is no room for ordinary minds to differ as to the conclusion to be drawn from it."

Justice Stephens dissented on the ground that the evidence utterly failed to make a case for the jury but left all to conjecture and speculation as to how the accident occurred, or who was to blame for it.

The case was retried, and the jury returned a verdict for the plaintiff for $2,527 for the loss of her two sons. Justice Stephens affirmed the opinion on June 11, 1904. But on February 13, 1905, the Texas Supreme Court reversed and rendered, finding insufficient evidence to authorize a recovery without having to address whether the young sons were contributorily negligent. The court found there was no evidence of proximate cause. The only inference that could be made was that the boys were upon the track and away from the crossing.

Democratic State Convention

In March 1902, Tarlton was a delegate to the Democratic State Convention.[307] Other notable Fort Worth luminaries who attended the convention were: William Capps, William A. Hanger, W.P. McLean Sr., H.M. Chapman, W.H. Carter, C.E. Stewart, W.P. McLean Jr., M.A. Sprouts, B.H. Tucker, William Lahey, J.H. Thrasher, Thomas Spruance, R.M. Wynne, F.R. Wallace, Q.T. Moreland, B.L. Waggoman, W.E. Butler, J.H. Maddox, J.F. Lebane, F.E. Albright, L.L. Hudson and S.P. Clark.

Tarlton v. Kirkpatrick II

In 1902, the Dallas Court of Appeals issued the final decision in the *Tarlton v. Kirkpatrick* suit, ending fifteen years of litigation. As noted earlier, the Tarlton firm acquired rights in the 178 acres based on a patent from the State of Texas and a new survey and could prove title. Kirkpatrick, Huff, and Allen would have to establish title either through the five-year or ten-year adverse possession statutes. This time the retrial was before a jury and a different trial judge. Judge J.M. Hall was no longer the presiding judge. The jury found in favor of the Tarlton firm.

In 1902, the Dallas Court of Civil Appeals affirmed the judgment in a decision written by Chief Justice Rainey in *Kirkpatrick v. Tarlton*.[308] Rainey found that the evidence failed to show possession under the adverse possession statutes, entitling them to recover the real property. The court held that in an action of trespass to try title that a plaintiff is not required to plead his evidence and where he claims under a deed executed by an agent, he may show ratification by the principal of the agent's act without pleading such ratification.

In July 1902 B.D. Tarlton and G.D. Tarlton, after having acquired 139 of 178 acres through a final judgment on appeal, sold 27 ¾ acres to John D. Warren. Allen had conveyed the property to Huff, who conveyed the property to J.D. Warren. B.D. and G.D. Tarlton received $300 for the conveyance of the property to Warren. In March 1903, B.D. and G.D. sold the 132 3/5 acres to Paul M. Lewis for $1,400.

Free Fall Festival

In October 1902, Tarlton's daughter, Frances Tarlton, was selected Queen of the Free Fall Festival in Fort Worth and was driven from city hall to turn on the electric lights. The program included a trades display, a parade, and floral parades and brass bands.

Guaranty Abstract & Title Company

In April 1903, Tarlton & Ayers and others established *The Guaranty Abstract Title Company* in Tarrant County. The stockholders were Judge B.D. Tarlton of Tarlton & Ayres and LeRoy A. Smith of Pruitt & Smith, John J. Massie, and John Tarlton, as Abstractor.[309]

The advertisement read:

The Guarantee Abstract and Title Company ......
    Is a new company and has acquired a complete set of ABSTRACT BOOKS and is now prepared to make abstracts to any lands in Tarrant County.

The reference to John Tarlton was B.D.'s nephew, the son of John Belser Tarlton, B.D.'s half-brother, from his father's marriage to Caroline Belser Tarlton. John Tarlton's mother, Marie Lilly Delahoussaye Tarlton passed away in 1874. John Belser Tarlton and his wife Marie Lilly Delahoussaye Tarlton had eight children who were born in St. Mary's Parish. John Tarlton moved to Fort Worth around the turn of the century to make his home with B.D. Tarlton. One of his first jobs in Fort Worth was as a deputy clerk of the Second Court of Civil Appeals. John Tarlton obtained his law degree from Louisiana State University and returned to Fort Worth to practice in land titles. Elizabeth Wright Tarlton owned the Home Guaranty Abstract Company until he sold it in 1945. He married in 1909 and held memberships in the Fort Worth Club and Rivercrest Country Club. In 1945 he ran for City Council of Fort Worth as part of an eight-candidate ticket called the Citizens Ticket to replace the current city council.[310] He was a member of St. Patrick's Cathedral. His wife was a leader at First Methodist Church. He lived to be 100 years old and died in 1970 in White Settlement, Texas. He was buried at Ridge Park Cemetery in Hillsboro, Texas.[311]

Tarrant County Primary Convention

In June 1904, B.D. Tarlton attended the Sixth Ward Democratic primary convention in downtown Fort Worth at the fire station. The meeting was called to order by Senator William A. Hanger. On the motion of Judge Tarlton, ten delegates were elected to the county convention to cast the four votes of the ward for the following: Hon. William A. Hanger, Clarence Ousley, W.W. Wilkinson, Judge B.D. Tarlton, W.D. Bidaker, W.E. Mayfield, Hon. A.L. Matlock, Hon. William J. Bailey, Judge W.P. McLean and A.G. Dawson. The delegates were instructed to vote for Judge Alton B. Parker.[312]

Tarrant County Bar Association

In 1904, Tarlton became the first president of the Tarrant County Bar Association, which encompassed the entire county. The association was established to improve the character of practice in the various courts of the city and county. There were 150 attorneys practicing law in Fort Worth.

Delegate to Washington, D.C.

In April 1904, Tarlton traveled as a representative of Fort Worth to Washington, D.C. The sum of $50,000 was being presented to the Board of Management of the Catholic University of Washington as a donation from the order of the Knights of Columbus for the endowment of a chair of American history in that institution. The next day President Theodore Roosevelt attended a reception at the White House in honor of the delegates who were present. Traveling with Tarlton was T.P. Fenelon, city ticket and passenger agent of the Santa Fe Railway.[313]

Democratic Convention in San Antonio

In June 1904, Tarlton spoke in favor of New Yorker Alton B. Parker running against Theodore Roosevelt at the Democratic Convention in San Antonio. Tarlton told the Tarrant County delegates to vote for Parker and for Chief Justice Truman Conner.[314] Tarrant County Chairman William Capps of the Capps and Hanger Law Firm in downtown Fort Worth called the convention to order. Senator William A. Hanger, the State Senator from Tarrant County, offered a motion that a committee of three be appointed by the chair to select delegates to the state convention, and that no delegate be selected who did not support Judge Alton B. Parker of New York for President of the United States.[315]

Tarlton made a rousing speech at the convention:

I feel that my word to this convention should be more in the nature of word of congratulation on their adoption of Senator Hanger's resolution rather than words in discussion of that resolution.

We are all Democrats gathered here, selected from the various wards and precincts. We are all Democrats and it is only natural that we should be Democrats. With us it is a matter of tradition as well as a matter of belief. 7

The Fort Worth Star-Telegram reported Tarlton's speech:

Passing to the scenes of destruction and reconstruction as visited upon the south, he drew a picture of Texas, proud and strong in her infancy and glory, then Texas lying low, her fields lay waste, her houses desolate and destroyed. Quoting his votes from the time of Tilden down he was met with a burst of cheers upon announcing that his next vote would be for Judge Alton B. Parker. Why should we not support the most available man in the county? And Judge Parker is that man. He has been judge of the highest tribunal in the state of New York for fifteen years. He has carried that state by an overwhelming majority of 79,000 votes against a ticket led by Roosevelt. As judge, he has thoroughly reviewed the trust and corporation question and his decision on these questions have always been found on the side of truth and justice and consequently upon the side compatible with the best interests of the masses. We cannot elect a president unless we carry New York State and no one can better do this than one who has already carried the state by 79,000 majority.

On the silver question, I do not convict those who stood firm in their belief that that issue was paramount, but I would now invite them since that issue is past to join with us in the common support of the strongest man. I do not think we can stand upon a platform wholly silent on the silver issue. You have asked for my views. I am for the man who will dignify, typify and unify the party. Judge Parker will dignify it as a plain, simple Democratic gentleman; he will typify it, for he is typical Democrat, and he will unify the party because under his banner we can all unite and march to victory and triumph.[316]

TWENTY-SEVEN

Law School Professor

"I must now tend to my sheep."

—B.D. Tarlton in 1904

IN JUNE 1904, TARLTON ACCEPTED an appointment as Professor of Law at the University of Texas School of Law. *The Fort Worth Star-Telegram* reported the story:

> At a meeting of the board of regents of the State University held at Austin yesterday afternoon Hon. B.D. Tarlton of this city was elected professor of law, and he has signified his intention of accepting the position.
>
> The acceptance of this position takes Judge Tarlton into the faculty of the State University, and he will spend the summer preparing to enter upon his duties September 1, next. Just now it is not decided he will be called on to move his home to Austin. That is a question to come up later.
>
> Judge Tarlton is one of the most prominent attorneys of Texas. Tall, with all the dignity that goes with a jurist who has a conscientious knowledge of the honorable profession of which he is a member, with gray hair and smooth face. Judge Tarlton is one who will attract attention in a crowd, and will be singled out as a man of importance. He is slow of speech and selects his words carefully, every

sentence being correct as to language and pronunciation. That he is learned in the law is shown by his record as an attorney and as a judge on the bench, and in the selection of him for the position in the faculty the regents have taken from Fort Worth's bar one of its most distinguished members.[317]

Judge Cooper Event

In July 1904, the Fort Worth Bar Association chose to honor Judge James F. Cooper, one of the seven members of the supreme court of the Phillipine Islands. Cooper was appointed to the post in 1901 by President William McKinley.

Figure 54 Delaware Hotel around 1895.

Tarlton was chosen to serve as toastmaster for the event for Judge Cooper to be held at the Delaware Cafe located in the Delaware Hotel.

The Delaware Hotel was one of the best established and largest hotels (140 rooms) in the city and in the entire state. Located at Main, Fourth, and Houston streets, the Delaware Cafe was known for its exquisite cuisines such as scallops, Spanish mackerel, geese, fresh shad, New York counts, blue points, crab meat, and other delicacies.

Tarlton sat on one side of Judge Cooper, who wore a Philippine tuxedo of pure white. Judge W.P. McLean sat on the other side of Cooper. McLean served as a member of the convention that drew up the Constitution of Texas in 1875, and later served in the ninth and twelfth sessions of the Legislature and the Railroad Commission of Texas.[318]

Judge Tarlton Event

The event for Tarlton was held in September 1904, also at the Delaware Cafe, and included an orchestra, toasts, and speeches. Justice Sam Hunter, serving as toastmaster, began the event:

"Gentlemen of the Fort Worth Bar Association—We are assembled around this festival board this evening to testify the high appreciation and esteem in which we hold our distinguished fellow citizen and brother lawyer, Judge B.D. Tarlton, who, as you know, has been, without solicitation, appointed to that high office of Dean Professor of Law in the University of Texas, and who will in a few days go out from among us to make his abode in the capital city of our state, where, perhaps for life, he will labor in the highest occupation known to civilized man—the legal education of the youth of Texas. Were I a pessimist, I might truly say: 'This is a time for memory and for tears,' but I am not, but believe with Pope that: 'Whatever is, is right.' I know no man within the broad confines of Texas so peculiarly and eminently qualified for the high and honorable position in which the state has called him. None who would fill it with greater credit and honor to the state, to his friends and to himself. Dignified, noble, self-poised, brave and honorable, as a man; profound, clear and erudite, as judge; wise, zealous, brilliant, untiring and true as an advocate; as a citizen in social life his conversation, conduct and character are as gentle, sympathetic, pure and sweet, as a woman's. A man who the proud youth of Texas will love to honor and to emulate. So, it was right to appoint him; right that we should lend him to the state; right that his high ideals of justice, equity and professional life should be inculcated now among the young men who are soon to take our places at the bar and on the bench as members of the noblest and grandest profession known to mankind.[319]

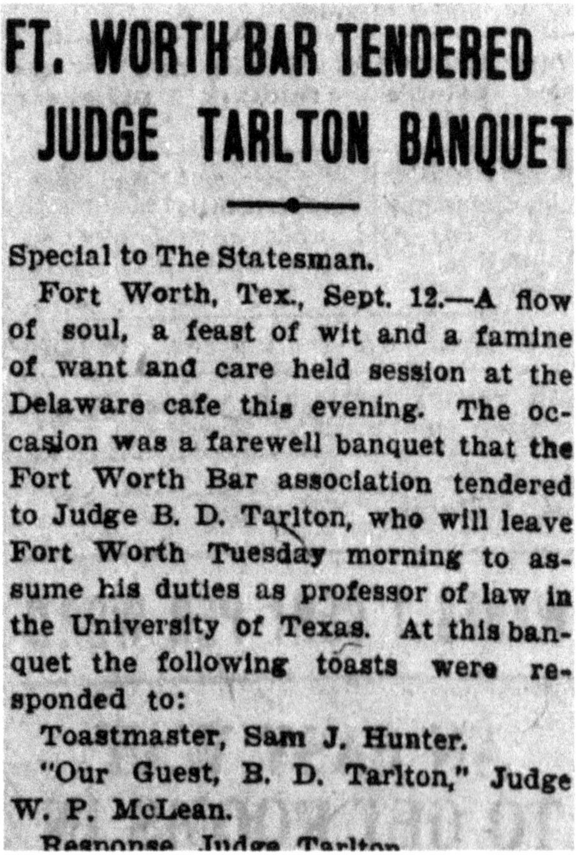

> **FT. WORTH BAR TENDERED JUDGE TARLTON BANQUET**
>
> Special to The Statesman.
>
> Fort Worth, Tex., Sept. 12.—A flow of soul, a feast of wit and a famine of want and care held session at the Delaware cafe this evening. The occasion was a farewell banquet that the Fort Worth Bar association tendered to Judge B. D. Tarlton, who will leave Fort Worth Tuesday morning to assume his duties as professor of law in the University of Texas. At this banquet the following toasts were responded to:
>
> Toastmaster, Sam J. Hunter.
>
> "Our Guest, B. D. Tarlton," Judge W. P. McLean.
>
> Response, Judge Tarlton.

Figure 55 The Austin American Statesman, Sept. 13, 1904, reporting the event for B.D. Tarlton.

"Then let us be merry tonight. We do not give to the state, we only lend him to her. He will continue to remain, I hope a member of the Fort Worth Bar Association, which honored him with its first presidency, and which position he now so honorably fills. There are many things here which will call him back and hold him as one of us. Many friends whose smile and a hearty handshake will always welcome him. Here, too, as chief justice of the Court of Civil Appeals, he built for himself a name and a monument more enduring than marble, for as long as government by law exists among men, his clear, just and equitable opinions will be cited and read in the courts of the land, and his fame as a jurist will continue to echo,

> Through the corridors of Time.
> Then wreath the bowl
> With flowers of soul.
> The brightest wit can find us;
> We'll take a flight
> Toward heaven tonight,
> And leave dull earth behind us."[320]

Judge W.P. McLean responded to the toast, "Our Guest," and paid a high tribute to the personal character, dignity, and professional purity of Judge Tarlton. He stated that his influence and instruction of the youth of the state, aspiring to enter the legal profession, would so profoundly impress the lawyers of the future that it would show to the benefit of the state and the credit of the university.[321]

Tarlton discussed the law in the days of Solon and Lycurgus, and up to the present time. He reviewed the influence of the lawyer in society, as a legislator and as a judge. He said that while there are three co-ordinate branches of government, the legislative, judicial and executive, that upon the lawyer depends on the perpetuation of the work of the legislator, or its call, and that by and with the advice of the lawyer and judge, the executive is directed in proper channels.

Figure 56 Justice Hunter serves as Toastmaster for the B.D. Tarlton event.

He spoke of the constitutional provision which made possible the education of the youth of this state and emphasized the fact that the Constitution of 1876 provided that there should be maintained by the state a "University of the first class," which should teach arts and sciences. He spoke of the university in length and brought out forcibly the benefit it is to be in the state of Texas in the future as it has been in the past. When he came to his farewell to the bar, his address was one of tender pathos and appreciation for the compliments shown him and was in beautiful language.[322]

Judge Spier spoke of the history of the Court of Civil Appeals and gave humorous references to practice, and then referred to the service of Tarlton as chief justice on the court, mentioning a number of opinions written by Tarlton that would long stand as the law such as his decisions that operated to the betterment of the property rights of women.[323]

Judge Hunter called for a response to the toast, "The University of Texas." He said that the response would come from a young attorney not mentioned in the program but known as a silver-tonged orator. He was referring to Sidney Samuels, known as the "silver-tongued lawyer," and Fort Worth city attorney from 1907 to 1909. Samuels was recognized as one of the great lawyers in Texas. His specialty was libel law representing The *Fort Worth Star-Telegram* and The *Dallas Morning News*. He was the personal attorney for Amon Carter Sr., and Burk Burnett.[324]

The crowd looked to the left of Hunter, Samuels blushed and hesitated, and the attorneys applauded. Judge Hunter relieved the embarrassment by saying he did not think it necessary to call the "silver-tongued" by name, and he affectionately laid his hand on Samuels' shoulder.[325] Samuel chose his words carefully with a classic response, showing a wide range of thought and wealth of knowledge.[326]

W.H. Slay responded to the "The Tribulations of the Young Lawyer." Charles Cassel made a delightful address to respond to "The Ladies;" he showed that the everyday work of man, the ambitions of those in professions and the accumulations of those who invest, are in the interest of women, and it is women who make the homes beautiful, who bring the good in man to the front. "His talk was not exactly poetical, but it was that character which would inspire poetry in any man." The event ended after a closing and with the singing of "Auld Lang Syne."[327]

Austin, Texas

In 1904, Tarlton moved to Austin to begin his tenure as law professor at a salary of $3,200.[328] He and Susan took up a temporary residence at 110 W. 18th Street until they could purchase a permanent home. Today that site is the Bullock State History Museum.

In 1906, the Tarltons purchased a home at 22 ½ Rio Grande, S.W. 817, Austin, Texas, near the university, from Louis and Fru Wortham.[329]

Tarlton was one of three faculty members in charge of the first session of a new summer law school from June 10 to August 4 that embraced contracts, real estate, equity, evidence, elementary law, Texas pleadings, torts, criminal procedure, and Federal practice.[330] Tarlton was known for quotes that provided insight about his law students, mentoring, and legal intellect.

When he was conversing freely in class about one of his vast subjects of knowledge and connecting it to his teachings, he brought the class back to task. Such was his refrain, "I must now tend to my sheep."[331]

Figure 57 University of Texas annual.

Figure 58 Construction began on the Old Law Building in 1906 and was dedicated in 1908. The building had a spacious law library.

Among the anecdotes attributed to Tarlton was that he gave two grades on each paper.[332] One was the grade they deserved, and the other was the grade that he wanted to give, encouraging one-on-one instruction and mentoring.

His students had high regard for him, and he was said to be one of the most tolerant persons they ever knew and that his relationship with his law students was legendary.[333] Tarlton's activities throughout the years, either personal or professional in nature, would frequently make headlines across the state.

Figure 59 Construction began on the Old Law Building in 1906 and was dedicated in 1908. The building had a spacious law library.

In July 1905, he spoke to the Twenty-Fourth Annual Meeting of the Texas Bar Association in Sherman, Texas. His speech was on "The Texas Homestead Exemption."

Figure 60 University of Texas annual.

On March 30, 1907, B.D.' half-brother, John Belser Tarlton passed away at the age of sixty-nine. He was buried in the Franklin Cemetery in St. Mary's Parish, Louisiana.

In May 1907, the University of Texas installed a chapter of Delta Chi and initiated twenty novices. Tarlton attended the event and gave a toast for "The Lawyer from a Fraternal Standpoint." The honorary members of the new chapter were Judge W.S. Simkins, Judge C.H. Miller, Judge B.D. Tarlton, Judge J.C. Townes and Dr. Samuel Peterson.[334]

In 1907, Tarlton's name was included as an appellate attorney in the case of *Ft. Worth & D.C. Ry. Co. v. Gribble*,[335] where he teamed again with his former partner Ben Ayers. The court of appeals reversed a ruling by District Judge Irby Dunklin. Dunklin would eventually become chief justice of the Second Court of Appeals.

In October 1907, the Tarlton children made headlines when Frances Tarlton married. The marriage was reported in the newspaper:

> Leigh Ellis and Miss Frances Tarlton were married here last evening by Father O'Keefe in the presence of a few friends. Both young people live here and will make their home at Seventh and Rio Grande.
>
> Mr. Ellis is the son of the late L.A. Ellis, formerly a prominent sugar planter. Miss Tarlton is the daughter of Judge B.D. Tarlton, professor of the law department of the State University. Judge Tarlton was formerly of Fort Worth of the court of civil appeals.

Miss Tarlton was one of the most popular of Fort Worth girls during the family's residence here and a large circle of Fort Worth friends will join in well-wishes to her as a bride.[336]

Injury in Horse Accident

In August 1908, Tarlton was seriously injured while hitching a horse at his residence in Austin after the horse broke away and threw him to the ground, dislocating his shoulder and bruising him in the head and legs.[337]

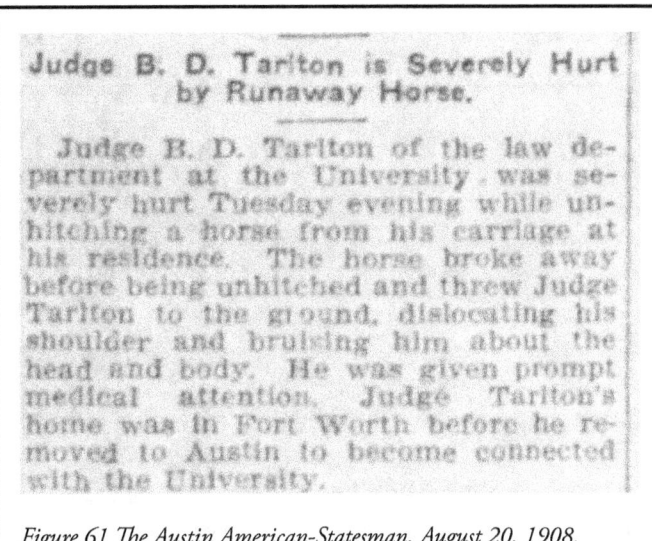

Figure 61 The Austin American-Statesman, August 20, 1908.

In 1909, Benjamin Dudley Tarlton Jr. enrolled in the University of Texas Law School.

In December 1909, *The Fort Worth Star-Telegram* reported the Tarlton family meeting in Fort Worth for the wedding of John Tarlton to Elizabeth Wright. As noted earlier, John Tarlton was Judge Tarlton's nephew, the son of John Belser Tarlton, his half-brother. John Tarlton worked as the head of the Abstract and Title Company in Fort Worth that Tarlton and others established. The newspaper reported the wedding and wrote that: "Until recently, Miss Wright, who is the daughter of Robert M. Wright, resided at Hillsboro. During the short time she has lived in Fort Worth she has won many admirers. Mr. Tarlton is prominently connected, being a member of a family well known throughout the state."[338]

Columbus Day Speaker

On October 1, 1911, *The Austin American-Statesman* reported that B.D. Tarlton would be the orator of the day at the Columbus Day Celebration at the state capitol on October 12, 1911. The newspaper account wrote that: "Judge Tarlton is one of the most finished orators in the South. His oration will be delivered in the hall of the House of Representatives during the afternoon and after the procession."

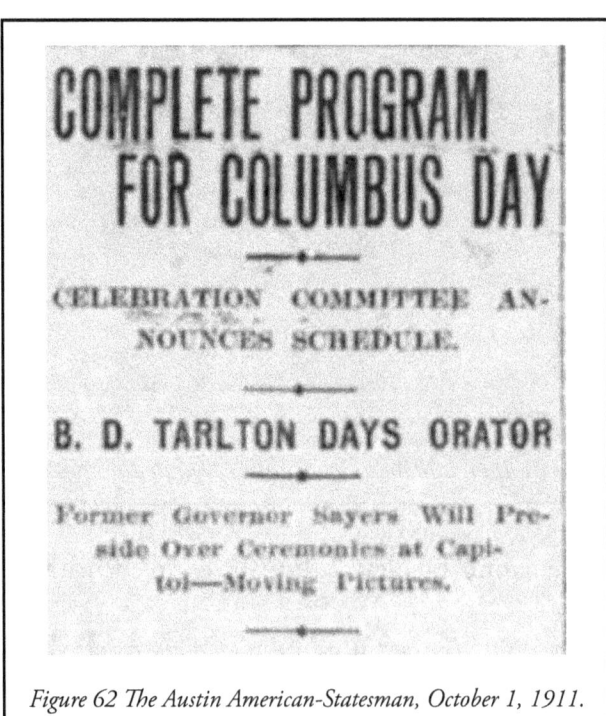

Figure 62 The Austin American-Statesman, October 1, 1911.

In 1911, B.D. Tarlton Jr. graduated from the University of Texas School of Law. He moved to Hill County, where he was appointed District Attorney for the 36th Judicial District Court in Hill County, Texas.

In September 1911, B.D. and his wife traveled to Fort Worth to see his nephew John Tarlton, who lived at 1012 South Adams Street.[339] This address is located behind Trimble Tech High School near the football stadium and is now a parking lot.

Matter of Debate

In 1912, Tarlton proposed that appellate courts have the power to reverse a case, even if no error had been committed during the first trial. Tarlton said that an error that does not substantially affect the rights of the appellant should not be considered reason for setting aside a verdict, but on the other hand he expressed the belief that if no error was committed during the trial in the lower court, but the consciences of the appellate judges convinced them justice had not been done, the judgment should be set aside.[340]

Tarlton's statements started a general discussion that led to an extemporaneous debate. Many attorneys began to question the wisdom of the suggestion of Tarlton. Tarlton stood alone, answering the questions.[341]

C.K. Lee objected that Tarlton's plan would have the effect of absolutely abolishing trial by jury. C.M. Templeton asked if Tarlton would not favor giving the state the right to appeal in a criminal case? Tarlton did not answer.[342]

In February 1913, Tarlton was a speaker at the Alumni Banquet at Texas Christian University. His speech was "Yesterday and Tomorrow."[343]

Dixie Day

On May 30, 1914, the student government of the University of Texas held "Dixie Day" or "Confederate Day." A law review article in 2010 by Thomas D. Russell wrote about a wildly popular lecture given by one of the University of Texas law school professors, Professor William Stewart Simkins, who taught at university from 1899 until his death in 1929. Simkins admitted that he had participated in and organized the Ku Klux Klan during Reconstruction, but the organization went into remission in the 1870s. The article points out Professor Simkins' address about the Ku Klux Klan and that Professor B.D. Tarlton was selected by the faculty to talk about the Confederacy.

> The first record of Professor Simkins's wildly popular public lecture about the Ku Klux Klan comes from 1914. That year, the leader of student government organized a "Dixie Day" celebration for campus. The day was also called "Confederate Day." At that time, Memorial Day was still an exclusively Northern holiday, and Dixie Day was to be a Southern alternative, or response to Memorial Day. The first such observance of Confederate or Dixie Day at the university took place on May 30, 1914. Benjamin Dudley Tarlton, who was a law professor from 1904 to 1920 and for whom the law school's library is now named, spoke first on behalf of the faculty. Professor Tarlton gave a speech on the confederacy. Professor Simkins, who was a platform guest, was so moved by the occasion that he gave an extemporaneous account of Reconstruction and his involvement in organizing the Florida Klan. The thrilled students willingly stayed well past the scheduled end of the event to listen to Simkins.[344]

Although he had not served in the Confederacy, Tarlton had significant knowledge of the Confederacy after living through the Civil War and having two brothers who served in the Confederacy.

Death of Judge J.M. Hall

On February 6, 1915, District Judge J.M. Hall died. The funeral was held at the home of his daughter. The funeral service was conducted by Reverend A.D. Porter, the pastor of the Main Street Methodist church. The pastor read the scripture lesson and a short sketch of the life of Judge Hall. At the close the Masons took charge of the internment. Judge Hall's obituary said that his casket was "wrapped with a Confederate flag, the emblem he loved so well." Judge Hall was laid to rest in a Cleburne cemetery. Like all of the obstacles that B.D. faced in his life, his experience in front of District Judge Hall could have been the impetus that propelled him into becoming an appellate attorney and appellate justice.

Fort Worth Banquet Speaker

In March 1916, Tarlton was the principal speaker at a banquet for alumni and friends held in Fort Worth at the Westbrook Hotel. The Westbrook Hotel was a seven-story hotel located at Main, Fourth, and Houston Streets in 1910, and cost one million dollars to build. It stood on the same site as the Pickwick Hotel and later the Delaware Hotel. The hotel was exquisitely furnished with 302 rooms, of which 200 had baths; all had toilets, hot and cold running water, and a telephone. On the top floor was a banquet and convention hall, with the capacity of holding 500 persons.[345]

Tarlton spoke on the welfare of the university.[346] One hundred and fifteen persons, nearly half of them women, attended the banquet, which was enlivened by college songs, numerous surprising "stunts," and half a dozen humorous short talks by alumni. That evening a cold front came through the city, dropping the temperature to twenty-five degrees.

The silver-tongued lawyer, Sidney Samuels, was scheduled to speak but was unable to attend on account of the illness of his sister. Three short speeches were substituted instead. Leroy Smith's subject was "What I Would Do if I Were President of the University." His answer was "Resign." W.H. Slay, speaking on what he would do if he were governor, declared that he would "burn up the shacks that mar the campus and make it like a white man's habitation." L.W. Newton spoke on what he would do if he were the board of trustees.

M.L. Massingill started to make his scheduled talk on traditions when three-fourths of the men at the table rose, yawned elaborately, and noiselessly departed from the banquet hall. They returned shortly thereafter with a basket of flowers to smooth his feelings.

At the beginning of the banquet, W.D. Smith, toastmaster, read a telegram signed with the name of W.J. Battle, acting president of the university, who was planning to attend the alumni association banquets in Fort Worth and Dallas. When he entered, he was wildly applauded and had to wait for the applause to die down. During his talk, someone slipped up behind him and snatched from his head a wig that had concealed most of his hair. He immediately lost his identity as president of the university.

Tarlton's talk was the only serious speech of the evening. He gave a brief history of the University of Texas from the time of the passage of an act of the Texas Congress in 1839 providing for its organization, down to the present. He referred to the state constitution that no money from the general revenue of the state should go toward the construction of buildings for the university.

"Send to the legislature," he urged, "men who are grounded and perfected in English education and the law.

"I have heard it said," he continued, "that women are capable of taking dictation and briefs and arguments. I wouldn't be surprised if many of them would make doughty adversaries in the courthouse.

"If all women were mothers and had households, there would be some pith in the objection that '-a woman's place is in the home,' but that is not the case.

"I have seen women working in store-houses, standing on their feet ten and eleven hours a day and receiving a mere pittance for their labor. They can and are permitted to perform other characters of labor that are hard and arduous, but let them aspire to a profession, and, to society holds up its hands in holy horror. Hypocritical society!"

On Sunday, May 28, 1916, *The Austin Weekly Statesman* reported that there would be a public reception for Rev. T.R. Murphy, pastor of St. Mary's Church, under the auspices of the Knights of Columbus. The event would be on Monday evening from 8:30 to 10:30 p.m. B.D. Tarlton was named on the committee in charge of the arrangements. The newspaper reported that "a general and cordial invitation is extended through the press to the citizens and residents of Austin to be present. It is the desire of the committee to have Rev. Father Murphy meet and become acquainted with as many residents of Austin as possible. The function will be informal that all may attend in such attire as comfort may dictate."[347]

On November 11, 1918, *The Austin American-Statesman* reported that Judge Tarlton was scheduled to give a four-minute talk at the "Four Minute Talkers" scheduled for four days during the week. Judge Tarlton appeared at the Crescent Theater on Tuesday, November 15, 1918.

Four-Minute Talkers Scheduled for This Week at Theaters

The following named gentlemen have been selected for four-minute talks for four days this week:

Casino Theatre.
Wednesday, Nov. 13: B. S. Dickinson.
Thursday, Nov. 14: Grover Hart.
Friday, Nov. 15: Miss Virginia Williams.
Saturday, Nov. 16: J. D. Moore.

Crescent Theatre.
Tuesday, Nov. 15: Judge B. D. Tarlton.
Wednesday, Nov. 13: C. S. Potts.
Thursday, Nov. 14: T. U. Taylor.

Figure 63 The Austin American-Statesman, November 11, 1918.

TWENTY-EIGHT

The Hurricane

On Sunday morning, September 14, 1919, to their amazement and horror, Judge Tarlton and his family found themselves in the middle of the hurricane in Corpus Christi, Texas. At 1 p.m., the water reached eighteen inches deep at Chaparral Street. By 2 p.m., it rose to five feet deep.

Figure 64 Photo courtesy of Blucher Collection depicts the view east from the Bluff at Blucher and Broadway street in downtown Corpus Christi.

By 3 p.m., the full sixteen-foot storm surge rolled through downtown Corpus Christi as the eye of the storm made landfall twenty-five miles south. The North Beach became submerged, and the Nueces and Corpus Christi were absorbed into one body of water.[348]

Terrified, Genevieve Daugherty, Tarlton's daughter, kept her four children calm in the hotel. In some parts of the city people heard nothing.[349] "My mother said that she heard nothing..." said Claude D'Unger, who grew up in Corpus Christi and remembers the hurricane. D'Unger is the mother of Geraldine McGloin who told Theresa Tarlton about the miracle of Grand Coteau. He still recalls the storm but did not know of the destruction of the downtown area until later. "It was before the break wall was built," he said.

But for the people in downtown Corpus Christi, many were washed into the bay water that reached the second story of some downtown buildings and receded back into the coast, leaving victims in the water with no help.[350] The North Beach was nearly wiped clean, wooden debris scattered everywhere and one standing building–the three-story Spohn Sanitarium.[351] The streets of Mesquite and Laguna (now known as John Sartain street) were filled with wood from collapsed buildings. The street known as "Peoples Street" flooded to the mid-way point of a Model T registered as 117972, trying to make its way through the water before it stopped.

Figure 65 A rowboat is shown in this photo. Photo courtesy of L.M. Gross Collection, Special Collections and Archives, Mary and Jeff Bell Library, Texas A&M University-Corpus Christi.

Governor William Hobby sent five hundred militia men to protect the city after declaring martial law.[352] Nuns assisted with the Catholic relief effort. Tarlton left the hotel and began to help rescue victims swept into the bay by taking a rowboat to assist with the recovery effort. Genevieve recalled that he "exhausted himself swimming a distance in the bay and repeatedly rescuing and returning women and children to safer shores."[353]

The trains were down for the next two days. On September 16, 1919, the trains, referred to as "refugee trains" began to leave. The Tarltons left Corpus Christi by train for Beeville, where they took safety at the home of his daughter and son-in-law, Genevieve and James Daugherty.[354]

But Corpus Christi was still not safe. Governor Hobby issued a general call on the people of Texas to respond to the appeal for relief from Corpus Christi and named committees in cities across Texas to coordinate for the relief effort. Forty-three bodies had passed through the morgue at the courthouse.

STORM STRIKES CORPUS CHRISTI

Thousands Homeless and Without Food

NO WATER OR LIGHTS

More Than Two Score Killed in Hurricane

CORPUS CHRISTI, TEX., Sept. 15 —From 15 to 25 persons are dead and approximately 4,000 are homeless and property damage which will reach $4,000,000 is the result of the tropical hurricane that raged here for 24 hours. The city is in distress and Mayor Gordon Boone has sent the following appeal to Governor Hobby at Austin:

"Please send at once two companies of the national guard iwth supplies, and join in appeal for assistance. Conditions here are serious."

A score or more persons were adrift in Nueces Bay today, where they were washed out by waves. What few boats were undamaged were used in rescuing them.

Figure 66 Clipping from The Times and Democrat, Orangeburg, South Carolina, Sept. 16, 1919.

Deaths were reported in other cities: Sinton and Odem, Portland, White Point, Port Aransas, Aransas Pass; the total death toll reached 800.

The bodies were so badly decomposed that identification was impossible, and the corpses were being taken directly to the burial park for interment.[355]

By Saturday, September 20, Tarlton appeared fine and went into the town of Beeville to chat around the town and with numerous friends.[356] Later that day he was busy dictating examination questions for his work at the University of Texas School of Law for the 1919-20 term.

Reports Reveal Increasing Magnitude of Disaster

$15,000,000 PROPERTY LOSS

Corpus Christi and Havana Stood Brunt of Hurricane

CORPUS CHRISTI, Texas — The list of known dead in Corpus Christi and environs is now nearing the two hundred mark, exceeding all earlier estimates and is being swelled hourly.

Figure 67 The hurricane made national news as shown by this cliping from The Capital Times – Madison, Wisconsin, Sept. 17, 1919.

TWENTY-NINE

The Death of Tarlton

Whatever did not fit in with my plan did lie within the plan of God. I have an ever deeper and firmer belief that nothing is merely an accident when seen in the light of God, that my whole life down to the smallest details has been marked out for me in the plan of Divine Providence and has a completely coherent meaning in God's all-seeing eyes. And so I am beginning to rejoice in the light of glory wherein this meaning will be unveiled to me.

—*St. Theresa Benedicta of the Cross*

BUT THINGS CHANGED ON SUNDAY morning, September 21, when B.D. could not get out of bed. A severe chill seized his entire body. At first his condition was thought to be temporary, but he had contracted double-pneumonia or flu-pneumonia. During the prior winter, four of his nieces and nephews succumbed to the same ailment. He had to recall his mother, who died of pneumonia.

Tarlton looked at his son-in-law, James Daugherty, and in a lucid moment said: "*They all seemed to like me.*" Then his voice trailed off indistinctly into a Latin apostrophe to the delights of friendship. It was reported that to the very end his thoughts were of his students, next to his family, the closest to his heart.

Figure 68 B.D. Tarlton.

The *Fort Worth Record* reported Tarlton's passing on front page news when he had not been a resident of Fort Worth for fifteen years:

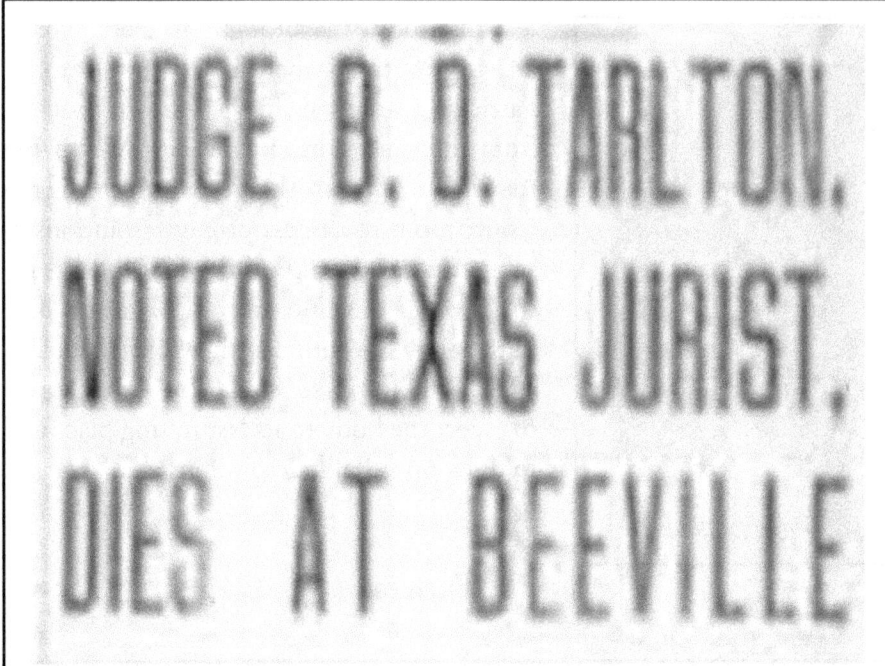

Figure 69 News of Tarlton's passing reached newspapers across the state including the Fort Worth Record.

Judge B.D. Tarlton, 69 years old, former chief justice of the court of criminal appeals here, and noted Texas jurist, died Monday at Beeville, according to information received here by his nephew, John Tarlton. Judge Tarlton escaped with his life during the recent storm at Corpus Christi, only after suffering severe hardships.

He went to Beeville to recuperate and contracted pneumonia, brought on by exposure during the storm. The aged jurist made a valiant fight, but in his weakened condition he could no longer hold on. For the last twelve years he had been professor of law at Texas University. Widely known, Judge Tarlton also was one of the most beloved members of the faculty at the Texas school and through his mentorship many brilliant attorneys of the state today owe their start to him.

Figure 70 B.D. Tarlton.

His body was brought to Fort Worth, arriving by train where it was moved to St. Patrick's Cathedral in downtown not far from the train station. The Fort Worth Bar Association met in the Seventeenth District Court room to discuss proper resolutions of sympathy. A meeting of the Ex-Students association of the University of Texas was held in the Sixty-Seventh District Court, called by W.W. Wilkinson to discuss an honor guard to escort the body to its last resting place and to draw up suitable resolutions.[357]

The Funeral

Figure 71 This photo of St. Patrick's Cathedral was taken in 1913. The church was dedicated in 1892, the year that B.D. Tarlton began his term as Chief Justice.

Officiating at the funeral was Dean Robert M. Nolan, who extolled Tarlton's life achievements. Among those who attended his funeral were Dr. R.E. Vincent, president of the University of Texas; Dr. A.L. Campbell and Dr. R.E. Cofer of the faculty of the Department of Law of the University; Messrs. James B. Daugherty and Benjamin Dudley Tarlton Jr. of Beeville; W.C. Morrow of Austin; and Tarlton's brother, Judge G.D. Tarlton of Hillsboro.

The active pallbearers were LeRoy A. Smith, Sidney L Samuels, F.M. Bransford, Paul McDermott, W.D. Smith, and District Judge George E. Hosey, all former students under Judge Tarlton at the University. The honorary pallbearers were: Chief Justice Truman Conner and Associate Justices Raymond H. Buck, Irby Dunklin, J.W. Stephens and Ocie Speer; former justice Henry O. Head of Sherman; and Judges W.P. McLean Sr., Ben M. Terrell, R.E.L. Roy, Bruce Young and George Hosey.[358]

Burial in Oakwood Cemetery

Figure 72 Oakwood Cemetery in Fort Worth is the burial site of B.D. Tarlton, his wife, Susan Tarlton, and Mary Eleanor Tarlton.

B.D. Tarlton was buried in the Catholic section of Oakwood Cemetery in west Fort Worth next to his daughter Mary Eleanor, who died in 1897. Tarlton was a charter member of the Texas Bar Association and the American Bar Association and was the vice-president for Texas delegation at one time, a fourth-degree member of the Knights of Columbus, and member of the Town and Gown Club of Austin, a group composed of citizens of Austin and faculty of the University of Texas.[359]

Figure 73 *The Tarlton family plot contains the graves of Mary E. Tarlton, who died in 1897, B.D. Tarlton, who died in 1919, and Susan Tarlton, who died in 1928.*

Shock to the Law School

The death of Professor Tarlton shocked the law school students, faculty, and the legal community across the state. A memorial for Professor Tarlton was held on November 3, 1919. In the same month, *The Alcalde*, the newsletter for the law school included tributes to him. One tribute was that "the world is better, much better, for his having lived. He will ever be an example to the youth of Texas, and the child that is unborn shall bless the beauty of his life." Another student wrote that "his influence could not be defined. In class-room and in council his wisdom and fine personality was missed." Another wrote that "we shall not look upon his like again."

Paul McDermott gave a write up of Tarlton, having taught Evidence, Wills, Real Property, and Criminal Law and Procedure:

> He was a profound student of these subjects and an inspiring teacher, he had left his mark upon many of the real property decisions of his time, either as practitioner or as Judge. His name calls up visions of an alert and friendly countenance surmounted by a shock of unruly white hair, of profound learning, pronounced courtesy, and a kindly and gracious spirit. He sometimes exhibited a fine sense of humor and made the class feel that he was one of them; but at the proper moment he would announce, "I must get back to my sheep," and the amusement would end for a time. At times he illustrated points with copious quotations from the classics, while at others he might impress a lesson by means of a sincerity that attained the realms of true eloquence. There can be no wonder, then, that he early acquired, and in our memories yet retains the full admiration and respect of the class.[360]

Tarlton's lectures were said to be witty and eloquent, and students relished them. One student wrote of his professor:

> ...whoever said that the study of law is boring and uninteresting had evidently never attended any of Judge Tarlton's lectures, or he could not truthfully have made such a statement. The writer has attended some two hundred and fifty or more lectures given by the venerable judge, and regrets that he has no more of them ahead of him, and never once has he found himself sleepy or bored. How can a subject be uninteresting when every point brought out is

punctuated with a pun, or illustrated by a story, and every principle expanded is embellished with a quotation or a poem?

Tarlton Lectures

Tarlton's lectures to the Middle Law Class were transcribed in a 105-page supplement to *Real Estate* by Judge Yancey Lewis and entitled *Lectures to the Middle Law Class on the Transfer of Title from Individuals (Supplement) and Estate as Affected by Marriage,* by B.D. Tarlton, LL.B. Professor of Law, University of Texas. One fragile copy exists that has been digitized online. It has handwritten notes at the top that it was presented to the owner by Tarlton in 1917. The name appears to be Ira P. Hildebrand.

The preface to the book states:

The following lectures have been used, and are designed for use, especially by students of the University of Texas. They were originally delivered orally and later transcribed by a stenographer. It is hoped that they will be found useful for the purpose indicated. In them, the law is sought to be condensed from considerations of the necessary economy of time in the treatment of the subject.

—B.D. Tarlton
University of Texas April 5, 1913

The supplement is divided into two parts: the first part covers the transfer of property by voluntary transfers by individuals, involuntary transfers of property, and transfers by operation of law. The second part deals with the marital estates, including the homestead exemption. An addendum includes changes in the marital law by legislation.

In 1920, the 39th Session of the Texas Bar Association honored him in El Paso, noting that the judge's nature was reflected most admirably in his physique. He was a living example of the old maxim, "Laugh and grow fat… his twinkling blue eyes and rosy cheeks seem to belie the hoary mark which time has laid so gently upon his heavy thatch of hair. He may grow old, but his nature will ever remain young. He belongs to that particular race of men known as optimists."[361]

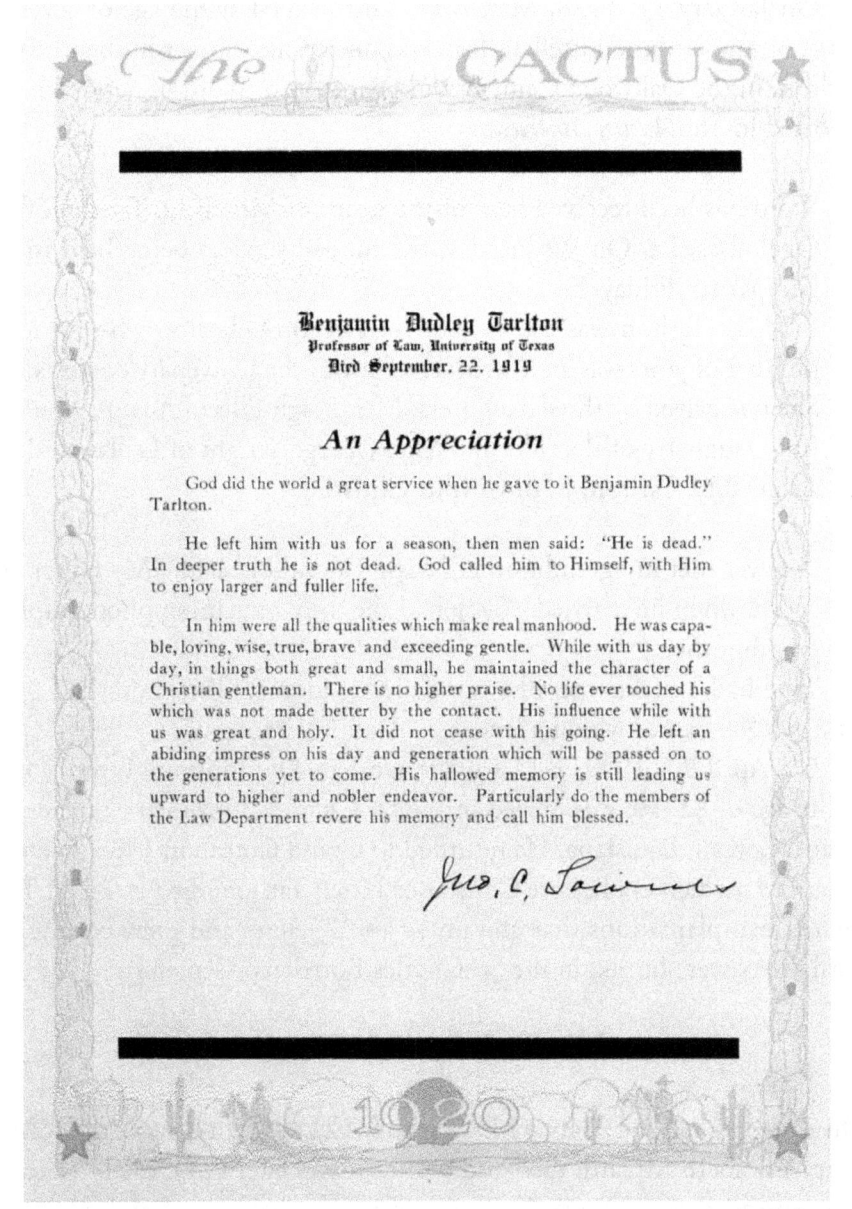

Figure 74 An appreciation written 1920 in The Cactus, an annual yearbook of the University of Texas.

On January 11, 1928, Mrs. B.D. Tarlton died at the age of seventy-three. Suzanne Marie Littell Tarlton was buried next to her husband, B.D. Tarlton, in the Oakwood Cemetery in Fort Worth. Word of her death was reported in The *Austin American*:

> Word has been received here of the death of Mrs. B.D. Tarlton of Opelousas, La. On Wednesday, the funeral services being held in Fort Worth Friday.
>
> Mrs. Tarlton was the wife of the late B.D. Tarlton who for a number of years was an instructor of law in the University of Texas. She is survived by three daughters: Mrs. Leigh Ellis of Austin; Mrs. Jim Daugherty of Beeville, and Mrs. George Wright of Dallas; and a son, B.D. Tarlton, Jr. of Corpus Christi.[362]

"I never met my grandmother," Sissy Farenthold said. "My father was thirty-five when he married." Sissy had the only remaining photograph of her grandmother.

"She had a nickname. She was called 'Mooma.' They both had nicknames." The name "Mooma" means, "Beautiful Mother."

On April 23, 1929, B.D.'s older brother, Dr. Toulmin Tarlton, died at the age of 82. He was buried in the St. Charles Borromeo Cemetery in Grand Coteau, Louisiana. He returned to Grand Coteau in 1883 where he practiced medicine. His wife Constance Littell Tarlton, died in 1931. They owned two plantations that amounted to 375 acres and grew cotton and corn. They were buried in the St. Charles Borromeo Cemetery.

G.D. Tarlton and Wife Die

On August 27, 1931, Mrs. G.D. Tarlton, G.D.'s second wife, the former Mary Elizabeth Millard, died and within hours later G.D. died.[363] Stories were spread that G.D. was in a state of indescribable grief and could not resume his life. His first wife, Sallie, died in 1907, and in 1909 he married Mary Elizabeth Millard, of Washington, D.C. who was related to Dr. Edward Millard, the medical doctor who attended to Mary Wilson in 1866 at the Sacred Heart Academy. The funeral for Mrs. Tarlton was held at St. Helen's Catholic Church. Immediately afterward was the funeral for G.D. Tarlton held at St. Mary's Episcopal Church.

G.D. practiced law in Hillsboro for fifty years and became a large landowner, but his family lost everything from the Depression. He supposedly went to the third floor of the home and hung himself.

His home was used as a bed and breakfast for many years. One resident who was suffering from depression stayed in the home and said that she felt cold spots on the third floor and saw a figure that she thought was straight out of the grave. "I hear your thoughts, little girl," she reported the figure saying to her. She ran down to her room and believed that the figure she encountered was G.D. Tarlton, who was trying to warn her not to take her own life. The resident said that she believed that it was Mr. Tarlton and that it was his way of warning her not to do what he had once done.

"He saved my life," she said.[364]

Figure 75 G.D. Tarlton home, built in 1895, still stands today.

Figure 76 B.D. Tarlton.

THIRTY

Legacy

IN 1951, THE UNIVERSITY OF Texas School of Law named the Tarlton Library after B.D. Tarlton. Leading members of the state's legal and educational professions and high government officials gathered in Austin to dedicate the law library at the University of Texas in his name and to honor the Texas jurist whose efforts to aid storm-stricken Corpus Christi led to his death.

John W. Brady, LL.B of the U.T. law class of 1891 wrote in *The Alcade* in November 1919 that Professor Tarlton:

> ...filled every position of trust with signal ability and rare fidelity. As a lawyer he was unfailingly courteous, highly ethical, and unusually successful. It should be remembered, too, that he often measured lances with the greatest advocates and most brilliant legal minds in Texas. As a judge, he was fearless, learned and just. As a lawmaker, active and far-seeing. As a teacher, the last and perhaps most useful work of his life, he was sympathetic, strong and magnetic; he charmed by his eloquence, and amazed at his learning and power of chaste illustration. As a Christian, he was devout without ostentation; always unshaken in his faith, and he lived as he believed. As a husband, he was chivalrous, tender and true. As a father, affectionate, devoted, and the constant companion of his children. His home life was beautiful, as was inevitable with one of such knightly character and uncommon graces.[365]

The library, where his picture is prominently displayed, has become one of the leading academic law libraries in the country. "Like Judge Tarlton's indefatigable dedication to his students and his family, the library seeks to provide exceptional research facilities and services to the students and faculty of The University of Texas School of Law multidisciplinary collections, its innovative uses of technology, and its rare books and special collections."[366]

In April 1965, a memorial scholarship was established by the James R. Daugherty Foundation to honor Tarlton.

Sissy Farenthold was proud that her grandfather, B.D. Tarlton, pushed for the rights of women. "He pushed for women's equality before there was women's suffrage," she said. "He was revered and had a following and this makes me so sad because everyone has died off. I remember hearing about him as a child. There was this reverence for him in the family."

B.D. Tarlton's son, B.D. Tarlton Jr. left Hillsboro and moved his practice of law to Corpus Christi, where he led a distinguished career as a defense attorney in Corpus Christi, handling defense of death penalty cases and fought against the Ku Klux Klan.

B.D. Jr. practiced law with his son, Vincent Tarlton until he died on April 22, 1956. He greatly influenced Sissy, especially in how he fought for inequality and took on the Ku Klux Klan in the 1920s and thereafter.

"He had wonderful grades," Sissy said. "He would visit the class of 1911 and they kept in touch with each other. He would go see his friends in Houston. I remember listening to the radio with him when Roosevelt was president. I grew up with politics with him."

Figure 77 B.D. Tarlton, Jr.

Figure 78 B.D. Tarlton, Jr.

"He ran for the Legislature and was 'tarred and feathered' over the KKK. He was very vocal over his opposition to them. My father taught me a lesson. Once we were at a football game with my brother Vincent and we saw a small lady struggling with a suitcase. He said, 'Go help that person.'"

"Daddy, she's colored," Sissy said.

"It doesn't matter. She reminds me of 'Mooma.'"

"He was very race conscious," she said.

Sissy recalled a female attorney who worked with her father at the same law firm. "He was the only lawyer that accepted her as a colleague. He was a life-long Democrat but when Roosevelt ran for a fourth time, he said 'that was too much power for too long.' That was a difficult decision for him."

In 1998 at a ceremony at the Second Court of Appeals where B.D. Tarlton's photograph and the other chief justices of the court were being presented, Benjamin Dudley Tarlton III, grandson of B.D. Tarlton, attended the event and said:

Figure 79 Left to right: B.D. Tarlton IV, B.D. Tarlton III, B.D. Tarlton V, Theophilus de Boer Tarlton, Dolores Audrey de Boer Tarlton, and Theresa Ann Tarlton.

My grandfather was gone before I ever had a chance to know him personally, in a narrow sense; however, in knowing my father I really feel that I knew my grandfather in a broad sense.

My mother recalled 'Bon Pa,' a derivative of 'Le Bon Papa' meaning 'The Good Dad,' the name used by older grandchildren who were fortunate enough to know him personally. As the youngest grandchild, 'Bon Pa' sounded like 'Bum Paw' to me. I couldn't understand how a man who was so revered by so many, was referred to as 'Bum Paw,' and I was too scared to ask why. So, I went with it and nobody corrected me. He had been 'Bum Paw' to me since my childhood until the puzzle pieces came together. One of my father's sisters, Genevieve, for whom I was named, spoke often and proudly of our grandfather. He was the youngest of ten; three stepsiblings and six sisters and brothers. His Louisiana parents were Dr. John Tarlton and Frances Caller Tarlton, both devout Protestants, who continued their family medical and teaching traditions in Waxahachie and then in Hillsboro, Texas. Mrs. Tarlton founded a finishing school for women in Waxahachie, which continues as a school today. The 'Benjamin' of her youngest son's name came from an educator and friend of Dr. Tarlton. The specific ties to 'Dudley' are for the moment forgotten."[367]

Figure 80 Family portrait. From top left, Theresa Ann Tarlton, Benjamin Dudley Tarlton Farenthold, Kate Dougherty Bluntzer, George Edward Farenthold, Catherine Bluntzer Tarlton, Emilie Chevalier Farenthold. Seated on the floor: B.D. Tarlton V, Vincent Bluntzer Farenthold, Robert Farenthold, and Theophilus de Boer Tarlton.

Figure 81 B.D. Tarlton IV (left), B.D. Tarlton III (center) and B.D. Tarlton V.(right).

In 2004, the University of Texas School of Law celebrated the *Centennial Celebration* honoring B.D. Tarlton becoming a faculty member in 1904. Genevieve Tarlton Hearson, his fifth child who witnessed the 1919 Hurricane, spoke at the event.

She said, "At a time before signature buildings were dependent upon major monetary contributions as a consideration for designation, the law professors and administrators chose to name Townes Hall and the Tarlton Law Library after two of the 'Five Horsemen.' The Horsemen forged a foundation of social conscience, legal intellect, and moral courage. Their dedication, work ethic and production foreshowed a national standing for The University of Texas School of Law."[368]

Theresa Tarlton, the daughter of B.D. Tarlton III and granddaughter of B.D. Tarlton, said that "the Tarlton men were known to be gentlemen. How true this was of Le Bon Papa, B.D. Tarlton. At home, he was known to stand, out of respect, whenever one of his daughters entered the room." She said that Tarlton's interest in languages is still discussed today. "Latin and Greek were favored areas of study for our father. The linguistic affinity must have issued in part from his grandfather, B.D. Tarlton, teacher of both classical languages as a young man at the Jesuit College of New Orleans during his own law school studies."

Figure 82 B.D. Tarlton IV and his son B.D. Tarlton V.

B.D. Tarlton IV graduated from South Texas College of Law in 1988. He is a Texas licensed attorney and the Vice-President of Environmental and Safety for TransMontaigne Partners in Denver, Colorado. His three daughters, Genevieve Tarlton, Katie Tarlton Hamilton, and Vanessa Hauser are all Texas attorneys residing in Houston.

"I have always aspired to hold myself to, and endeavored to live my life by, the moral standards, work ethic and great achievements of my great grandfather, BDT, which have been passed down to me through his son, BDT, Jr. and my father, BDT, III. I am proud to say that I can see those principles and achievements reflected in the way all my children conduct themselves and that the legacy begun by BDT will live on through them in future generations, even though I couldn't pass his name on to all of them, he said.

B.D. Tarlton V is a senior policy analyst for global health issues with the United Nations in Geneva, Switzerland, and Istanbul, Turkey. He holds a master's degree in International Diplomacy from Seton Hall in 2005. He represents the last of the B.D. Tarlton name as he and his wife have two daughters.

Figure 83 B.D. Tarlton IV and B.D. Tarlton V taken in 1998 during at the unveiling of the official photograph of B.D. Tarlton at the Second Court of Appeals in Fort Worth.

Genevieve Tarlton, the daughter of B.D. Tarlton IV, graduated from the University of Texas School of Law in 2018 and observed her great-grandfather's photograph on a regular basis in the law school. She works for the firm of Jackson Walker LLP in Houston in the area of wills, trusts, and probate.

"Growing up, I always knew about my family name and some of the history. But when I went to law school, and saw my great, great grandfather's portrait hanging at the entrance of the Tarlton Law Library, for the first time, I had a daily, tangible reminder of his contribution and legacy, as well as a continual inspiration for the type of character that I intend to cultivate and maintain for myself. That's the power of these great legacies, one person achieves so much, but it's ultimately not just for themselves, it positively affects all future generations. And I am so grateful to have these tremendously inspirational figures in my family," she said.

Figure 84 Genevieve Tarlton, the daughter of B.D. Tarlton IV, in front of her great-grandfather, Professor B.D. Tarlton.

Figure 85 Sissy Farenthold and her (labor/environmental/human rights activist) second son George Farenthold at the 2016 Democratic Convention. Sissy Farenthold served on the DNC Rules Committee at age 90.

George Farenthold has been a loyal union member and active Democrat since his mid-20s, serving in elected positions with the United Steelworkers of America (USW) and later with the Office and Professional Employees based in Fort Worth (OPEIU Local 277). He has also been active in the Environmental Movement, being named by Houston Magazine as an Environmental Hero for his work on Earth Day 1990 (the 20th Anniversary). He also helped found the Environmental Fund For Texas (now EarthShare of Texas) serving as Vice-Chair of EFT/EarthShare in the mid-'90s.

In other environmental and labor activities George also served on the Foresight Committee at the Houston Advanced Research Center in The Woodlands and as President of the Citizen's Environmental Coalition from 1993-1997.

As an active OPEIU member, he serves today on the Metropolitan Washington AFL-CIO Council's Executive Board and regularly serves as a delegate to the Metropolitan Baltimore AFL-CIO Council and the DC Democratic Committee, working among other issues on D.C. statehood, minimum wage, hero pay and other current labor issues.

George's child Rhiley Farenthold served on the Montgomery (MD) College Student Senate and today remains very active in disability rights, LGBTQ issues and the Black Lives Matter human rights and voting rights issues.

Figure 86 Rhiley Farenthold (left) and his father, George Farenthold. George calls his son "my student human rights activist" for his work in supporting civil rights and raising funds for charitable causes including advocacy services for the deaf.

The Farenthold family spawned activism on both sides of the political aisle when Randolph Blake Farenthold served in the U.S. House of Representatives for the Texas 27th Congressional District from 2011 to 2018.

Figure 87 Sissy Farenthold.

Sissy continued the same fight her entire career. She grew up in Corpus Christi and graduated from Hockaday School in Dallas, Vassar College in New York, in 1946 and from the University of Texas School of Law in 1949, being only three women out of a class of 800.

In 1950 she married Georges Edward Farenthold, a Belgian-born immigrant, linquist and Army Air Corps veteran of World War II. The couple had five children: Benjamin Dudley Tarlton Farenthold, Geroge Farenthold II, Emilie Farenthold, James Robert Daughtery Farenthold, and Vinceent Bluntzer Tarlton Farenthold.

Sissy served in the Texas House of Representatives where she pursued anti-corruption and doggedly pursued the Sharpstown Scandal where careers of politicians were ended due to her insistence on transparency. She ran two campaigns for governor of Texas in 1972 and 1974. In 1972 her name was placed in nomination for Vice President of the United States, finishing second to Thomas Eagleton at the 1972 Democratic National Convention.

In her later years she engaged in international acctivism by joining the board of directors of the Helsinki Watch Committee, precursor of Human Rights Watch. She led protests against apartheid in South Africa and against nuclear proliferation. She helped organize the Peace Tent at the 1985 NGO Forum in Niarobi and embarked upon peace and human rights missions throughout Central America, Asia, and the Middle east.

Sissy taught law at the Thurgood Marshall Law School at Texas Southern University and at the University of Houston. She served as the chair of the board of the Institute for Policy Studies in Washington, D.C and in the interfaith Rothko Chapel in Houston, the advisory board of the Bernard and Audre Rapoport Center for Human Rights and Justice at the University of Texas School of Law. Her countless friends and collaborators established the Frances Tarlton "Sissy" Farenthold Endowed Lecture Series in Peace, Social Justice, and Human Rights, co-presented each year by the Rapoport Center and the Rothko Chapel.

Mary Frances "Sissy" Farenthold passed away on September 26, 2021, in Houston, Texas at the age of 94. Before passing she said that she struggles with the fact that in 2021 there is still a lot to do in terms of racial equality. She is proud that her family passed down for generations a legacy that fought for equality and against racial injustice and injustice for over 100 years. Even still, the work is not done. She died during the height of the COVID 19 pandemic and there could be no public funeral. A private service was held at Rose Hill Cemetery in Houston, Texas attended by immediate family.

"I thought that we could have the law and it would be enough, but it is not. We have a lot to do," she said.

Figure 88 Monsignor John Howell gave the eulogy at the grave site ceremony at Sissy Farenthold's funeral on September 30, 2021, at Rose Hill Cemetery in Houston, Texas.

Figure 89 Sissy's three survivors, George Farenthold II, Emilie Farenthold and Benjamin Dudley Tarlton Farenthold.

Figure 90 L to R – Robert Dougherty, Benjamin Dudley Tarlton Farenthold, Chispa Bluntzer and Diana Bluntzer Sherman

THIRTY-ONE

Why Did Conner Run Against Tarlton?

What prompted District Judge Truman Conner to want to oust Chief Justice Tarlton from the court? One news opinion report said that Conner's race against Tarlton was not personal. It must be obvious that the race had to be personal. Conner wanted to replace the first chief justice to serve on the new court, and he took him on in a public way within his own party that made headlines across Texas. To win, Conner had to make it appear that the race was not personal. There have been several reasons offered.

The Railroads
One possible reason offered was that Tarlton was targeted by the railroad companies. According to Corpus Christi attorney and historian William Chriss: "in those days, if he wasn't in the railroads' pocket, that would be enough to justify trying to get rid of him."

Conner and Tarlton lived in in two different worlds. Conner resided in Eastland County where the railroad brought modern transportation to the new county, making the county accessible from all over the state. Tarlton resided in Fort Worth where the great tarantula hub brought the many carriers, used mostly for transportation of goods, into the new metropolitan city that was becoming a powerhouse of commercial and political activity. The railroads were being sued across the state for personal, property and contractual damages. Tarlton served on the court that presided over one third of the appeals in the state.

The railroads tried to limit their damages any way they could, from trying to shorten the statute of limitations on contractual claims to vigorously defending the most serious of damage claims. The abuses of the railroads led to the election of Governor Jim Hogg, who wanted to reign in these new dominant powers in the state by establishing a Railroad Commission. Tarlton was a product of Jim Hogg.

Tarlton wrote over sixty opinions involving claims against the railroads. Ten of his opinions affirmed the property damage and contract disputes against the railroads. He affirmed over twenty personal injury judgments against the railroads that involved damages claims that ranged from $75 to as high as $10,000 in one case, including one suit that had $5,000 in punitive damages involving the wrongful expulsion from the train. The court ordered a remittitur of $250 in that case. Only when the trial court improperly instructed the jury on the measure of damages were the personal injury cases reversed, and Tarlton did so. Tarlton reversed and remanded almost thirty judgments against the railroads due to errors in the case. He reversed and remanded more cases against the railroads than were affirmed based on errors in the cases. He was clearly calling balls and strikes in the railroad cases.

But there are three interesting cases that involved the railroads that originated in Judge Conner's court. In *Watson v. Texas & P. Ry. Co.*,[369] Judge Conner denied recovery to the plaintiff for not bringing his personal injury claim in the same suit as the claim for damages to his property, being the horses damaged in shipment. Chief Justice Tarlton reversed the judgment, finding that damages to goods is a distinct cause of action to damages to the person. This meant that a personal injury suit did not have to be combined with a suit for property damages.

In *Reeves v. Texas & P. Ry. Co.*[370] Tarlton reversed Judge Conner that involved a negligence claim against the railroad resulting from damages to cattle during shipment while the cattle were in transit in Louisiana.[371] The Texas and Pacific Railroad Company included a limitation of liability in their contract that required claims to be made within forty days after the damage occurred. The Texas Legislature made such clauses void and prevented the statute of limitations from being less than two years. Judge Conner found the limitation valid and instructed the jury to find in favor of the defendant if the claim was not filed within forty days.[372] Tarlton found that the statute was not an attempt to regulate interstate commerce.

In 1896, Justice Hunter reversed and remanded the case of *Hall v. Tex. & P. Ry. Co.*,[373] where Judge Conner gave an instruction to find for the defendant (the railroad) if the damages were caused by anyone invited to use a private crossing and suffered damages due to the failure of the structure.[374] In that case the railroad was not required to erect a private crossing, but the court found that if it did so, and voluntarily assumed to keep it in repair, then it became its duty to use proper and ordinary care and prudence in keeping it in a safe condition for use for which it was designed, and failing to do which it would be liable to an action for damages for injuries received by any one invited to use such structure occasioned by such failure.[375] The court found that Conner erred in giving the peremptory charge to find in favor of the railroad.

The railroad theory makes for interesting discussion, but even if true, there is no footprint that Conner's race was prompted or promoted by the railroad industry or any of the decisions involving railroad companies.

Catholicism

In March 2020, I interviewed Sissy Farenthold and asked if she knew why District Judge Conner ran against her grandfather and how Conner was able to unseat the sitting incumbent chief justice so easily.

"Conner won because Tarlton was Catholic and the Democrat delegates were prejudiced against Catholics," she said. The newspaper accounts of the election make no mention of religion being raised in the race. No doubt prejudice existed against Catholicism, but whether this was the reason for Conner's race and Tarlton's loss in 1898 is not easy to determine one hundred and twenty-three years later. Yet this is the *only* explanation offered by Sissy Farenthold, an attorney, and this belief has been passed down for years of Tarlton family discussions. She took this belief to her grave.

Truman Conner and his father were Free Masons. They were members of a secret fraternal (men-only) order that form Masonic Lodges that meet and conduct business and have many ceremonial requirements and events. The groups perform numerous charitable programs and raise money for worthy causes. George Washington and Benjamin Franklin were freemasons. No one doubts the charitable nature of these organizations.

One aspect about Freemasonry that is not well known is that the Catholic Church condemned Freemasonry in 1738 because of concern over Masonic temples and the secret rituals performed within them. Is it possible that the opposite was the case? That Conner, personally, his backers, or the Democrat delegates to the 1892 Democratic Convention may have been prejudiced against Tarlton once they discovered his Catholic faith?

Prejudice against Catholics certainly existed in the 19th century. Until almost the end of the Mexican War in Texas, Catholicism was the established religion in Texas and Anglo—Americans seeking permission to settle in Texas had to accept the Catholic faith.[376] By the time of the Texas Declaration of Independence, freed of all legal restraints, Protestants rapidly sprawled across the Republic of Texas. By the 1840s the state had become a grid of Methodist, Baptist, Presbyterian, Lutheran, and Episcopal circuits and conferences, associations, and conventions.[377] Newspapers added a new dimension to the outreach to many immigrants to Americanize and Christianize the newcomers.[378] By 1861, the Methodists remained ahead of all other religious bodies in the state, with 30,661 members and 410 church buildings. With 500 congregations and 280 buildings, the Baptists were a distant second. The Cumberland Presbyterians, with 6,200 members and 1550 places of worship, comprised the third largest group. The Disciples grew dramatically in 1850 and had 39 churches, followed by the Catholics with 33, and Episcopalians with 19 churches.[379] Of the 604,215 Texas residents in 1860, no more than 12 percent were not affiliated with organized religion.[380]

In 1889, Mark Twain released his book *A Connecticut Yankee in King Arthur's Court*, which featured the character Hank Morgan thrusted back in time with opinions that were "strongly denunciatory towards the Catholic Church."[381] Twain reportedly wrote, "Please don't let on that there are any slurs at the Church," to Sylvester Baxter, who was reviewing the novel for the *Boston Herald*.

"I want to catch the reader unawares and modify his views if I can," he said.³⁸² Twain admitted that he had "...been educated to enmity toward everything that is Catholic."³⁸³

In a 2015 article *"When America Hated Catholics*," Josh Zeitz, a professor of American history and politics at Cambridge University and Princeton University, describes how political cartoonist Thomas Nast regularly lambasted Irish Catholic immigrants as drunkards and barbarians unfit for citizenship.³⁸⁴ Between 1840 and 1924, over 30 million European immigrants relocated to the United States, and many who were Catholic were met with hostility and derision. "From the burning of Boston's Charlestown Convent in 1834 and the rise of the single-issue, anti-immigrant Know Nothing party in the 1850s (an organization that, for a brief moment, controlled dozens of congressional seats and enjoyed extensive influence within the political anti-slavery coalition)—to the No Irish Need Apply signs of the 1890s—immigrant Catholics faced the brunt of Protestant America's rage."³⁸⁵

J. Frank Norris

Ironically, B.D. Tarlton and J. Frank Norris lived in Hill County at the same time, but their paths probably never crossed. Norris was born in 1877 in Dadeville, Alabama. His family moved to Hubbard City in Hill County, where Warner Norris wanted to start over. The Norris family arrived in 1888 by train, where they moved into a house two miles from Hubbard City. His father became a sharecropper. When the family ran out of money, Warner Norris began to drink at a local drinking establishment, where all of his money dissipated. A young, barefooted Frank Norris was sent by his mother to the establishment to warn the proprietor to not serve Warner Norris. The proprietor laughed at the young boy, who went home crying.³⁸⁶

Later, Warner became embroiled in a feud after furnishing information about a gang of horse and cattle thieves. One of the accused, John Shaw, confronted the elder Norris and shot him. J. Frank Norris charged Shaw with a knife and was shot three times, nearly killing the boy, who languished for three days near death. These formative years in Hill County transformed the young Norris, who went to Baylor College in Waco in 1898. Norris pastored in Dallas, and in 1909 accepted the position as Pastor of the First Baptist Church in Fort Worth from a call by Judge R.H. Buck, who served as the judge of the Forty-eighth District Court in Tarrant County. Norris was thought to be the arsonist who burned down his own church in 1914. He was tried for shooting Dexter Elliott Chipps and was acquitted.

Norris was a teenager when he lived in Hubbard City while B.D. Tarlton was in his thirties, reaching his prime in his legal career in Hillsboro as a practicing attorney. Tarlton left Hillsboro and moved his family to Fort Worth in 1892. When the *Tarlton v. Conner* race occurred in 1898, Norris was living in Waco. He would not have been a factor in that race.

Norris's anti-Catholicism did not appear until the 1920s when he preached from the pulpit, a radio station, and wrote in a weekly newspaper in Fort Worth.[387] In 1926, Norris campaigned against the election of Democrat Al Smith and voiced his support for Herbert Hoover, the Republican nominee who won and carried Texas. When Al Smith ran for president in the 1920s, anti-Catholicism was widespread. A political cartoon showed Smith with a room full of bishops serving a jug of "XXX" liquor. One prominent Baptist minister from Oklahoma told his parishioners, "If you vote for Al Smith you're voting against Christ and you'll all be damned."[388] Norris attacked Mayor H.C. Meacham of Fort Worth, whom he accused of misappropriating funds for Roman Catholic causes.

Sixty-two years after Tarlton was defeated for re-election, remnants of prejudice remained in the race for president ran between John F. Kennedy and Richard M. Nixon. Anti-Catholic rhetoric persisted in that campaign. In September 1960, Citizens for Religious Freedom organized a conference in Washington, D.C., to feature 150 prominent Protestant clergy, including Norman Vincent Peale, author of *The Power of Positive Thinking*.[389] "Our American culture is at stake," Peale said. "I don't say it won't survive, but it won't be what it was."[390]

On September 12, 1960, Kennedy traveled to Texas to give a speech to the Southern Baptist clergy. The campaign stop was not a normal stop.

Kennedy was the second Catholic to run for president after Al Smith's unsuccessful run in 1928. "And for a Catholic candidate from New England, a conference of Southern Baptist ministers was considered the 'lion's den,' ground zero for anti-Catholic political rhetoric and even outright bigotry."[391]

During that election, former Chief Justice Atwood McDonald, who served eleven years on the Second Court of Civil Appeals from 1941 to 1951, headed a committee of "Good Government" to make recommendations of political candidates. The "Good Government" committee endorsed all Democrats except for Kennedy-Johnson for president. The committee supported Nixon-Lodge, the Republican ticket, snubbing their party's vice-presidential nominee, Lyndon B. Johnson. Why would the Democrats support Herbert Hoover and Richard M. Nixon? Isn't the answer obvious? If anti-Catholic prejudice existed from the 1920s through the 1960s, it certainly existed 1898 when Tarlton was running for re-election.

Was B.D. Tarlton a victim of anti-Catholicism during his race against Conner?

For the first time, Tarlton was not involved in a direct election but in a primary election to be decided at the Democrat Convention. The Democratic delegates could be swayed prior to the primary votes being cast. Tarlton's ability to reach out directly to those delegates was limited while serving on the court. Conner had the assistance of H.P. Brelsford, who was a member of the Democratic Executive Committee, and others on the Conner campaign were concentrating on securing endorsements from local bar associations in the western counties across the second district. Conner could reach out to a swath of delegates in surrounding western counties and in the panhandle and simply paint himself as a victim of a system of government that provided no representation from the outlying counties in the Second Judicial District. This was an easy sell because it sounded like the concept of taxation without representation.

That Sissy Farenthold maintained that religious prejudice was the cause of Tarlton's loss must be considered as one reason. Logic dictates it: there were more likely more Protestant voters than Catholic voters, but there is no paper trail that shows that the Conner forces used Tarlton's Catholic religion against him.

The motivation to run against Tarlton

What motivated Conner to run against Tarlton? Was there another reason besides lack of representation on the court? The selection of Sam Hunter to replace Justice Henry Head in 1895 may have unwittingly set the stage for the race between Conner and Tarlton in 1898. The court's reversal of Conner in the *State v City of Cisco*, a case handled by H.P. Brelsford shortly after the appointment of Justice Hunter could have been enough to cause Conner to begin his campaign against Tarlton.

The race between Conner and Tarlton was penned as a race between the western and northern counties of Texas versus Fort Worth. The race became ironic because Tarlton and Conner were not from Fort Worth.

Fort Worth did not exercise a dictatorial prerogative if it pushed the governor to select Justice Hunter for the court in 1895. The largest city in district had no representation on one of the most significant courts in the state. Representatives from Parker, Collin, and Hill counties represented the court and the entire Second District.

The newspaper journalists in that era had no time to examine what was really occurring in the court between Tarlton and Conner. One newspaper simply advocated Conner's winning strategy. After several years of examining the Conner appeals to the Second Court of Civil Appeals from 1892 to 1898, these facts emerge:

> The *first two reversals* by the new appeals court during its first week in operation in October 1892 were appeals from *Judge Conner's court.*
>
> During the first six-year term of the court, there were fifty-two reported appeals from Judge Conner's decisions. The court reversed Judge Conner *twenty-five times.* However, two cases where the court affirmed Judge Conner were reversed by the Texas Supreme

Court. One of those reversals was an opinion written by Chief Justice Tarlton.

Thus, Judge Conner *should have been reversed twenty-seven times* out of the fifty-two reported appeals.

Nine of the twenty-five decisions reversing Judge Conner were written by Chief Justice Tarlton.

It is my opinion that Judge Truman Conner ran against Chief Justice Tarlton because he did not approve of the reversal of his judgments and the opinions written by Tarlton. Judge Conner was at odds with the Second Court of Civil Appeals from the first week the court was in operation. He was discouraged that he was not selected to replace Justice Head in 1895. He and H.P. Brelsford, an attorney friend in Eastland, Texas might have been particularly upset over the *State v City of Cisco* decision where the court found Judge Conner disqualified to hear the case days after the Governor appointed Sam Hunter to replace Justice Head on the court.

Conner had been vying for a seat on the court when the court was established in 1892. He loathed the political influence that Fort Worth exerted in 1895 that deprived him of the appointment after the resignation of Justice Head. When the Governor passed over him in 1895, Judge Conner had had enough and took matters into his own hands, directly challenging Chief Justice Tarlton. He saw no reason to challenge Justice Hunter, who had reversed him five times. He could have easily run against Justice Stephens who reversed him nine times—the same number as Chief Justice Tarlton. If Conner were to run at all, he would run for the top position and replace Chief Justice Tarlton. Conner looked to his appellate attorney friends in Eastland to begin that campaign that spread across the Second Judicial District as far as El Paso, far beyond Tarlton's reach. He saw himself rising to the chief justice position in Fort Worth as Anson Rainey had risen to the court of appeals in Dallas. Conner and Rainey, colleagues in Waxahachie, would be colleagues again. Both would eventually become chief justice of the courts of civil appeals in Fort Worth and Dallas.

Who was the real author of the Editorial in the Albany News of May 20, 1898?

Edgar Rye was a well-known writer, journalist, and political cartoonist. He was born in 1848 in Kentucky, and by 1876 he had moved to Texas, where he served as a justice of the peace and county attorney for Shackelford County. His notoriety came from his work as a journalist and political cartoonist. He founded a number of newspapers across the state such as the *Tomahawk* in 1879 and successors *Western Sun* and *Albany Sun,* working as a cartoonist and town booster for the *Albany Star* in 1883. He was a correspondent for The *Fort Worth Daily Gazette*. In 1889–90 he operated The *Albany Weekly News*.

Figure 91 Edgar Rye.

In 1891 Edgar Rye and S.F. Cook were the editors and publishers of the *Albany News*. On April 11, 1891, The *Fort Worth Daily Gazette* reported that he was in Fort Worth, where he had been a resident for some time. In 1892 he began the *New Era* in Rockport and contributed to the *Texas Land News*. In 1894 he started the *Graham Radiator*. In 1896 he started the *Texas Coast News* in Texas City, and by 1898 he was living and writing for the *Wichita Falls Herald*.[392] He was not with the *Albany News* at the time of the May 1898 editorial about the Tarlton—Conner race.

Molly Sauder, a historian of Texas history for many years, investigated the May 1898 *Albany News* editorial and commented: "I'll admit that my first impression of this letter, given its length and well written endorsement, was that it was probably a form letter sent to the newspapers of many surrounding communities from Conner's headquarters in Eastland." She suggested possible local attorneys such as Thomas Blanton, Sam Webb, or Edgar Rye.

"He [Rye] was quite the renaissance man and moved around a lot, and according to this entry in the Texas Handbook, he was in Wichita Falls writing for the *Herald* at the time of the election. I'm not sure that he would have taken the time to write back to the *Albany News* about such an election, but he certainly had the writing chops for it if he wished," said Sauder.

Only the *Albany News* printed it. Why? Possibly because it was never sent to other newspapers. The writer of the article knew Judge Tarlton and wrote that he is an "able lawyer and judge, and the writer has nothing to say against him…" Rye lived in Fort Worth for a period during his career, and he might have met Chief Justice Tarlton while he was serving on the court of civil appeals.

The article goes into the details of how Judge Conner was not appointed to the Second Court after Judge Head resigned from the court and that Governor Culberson could have appointed Judge Conner and that Governor Hogg said that Conner's day was coming. The article discusses the appointments of Tarlton, Head, and Stephens, where they lived, and about an appointment to the Texas Supreme Court and the division of the sections in the Second Judicial District into the Fort Worth & Denver and the Texas & Pacific districts. The endorsement followed the exact argument of the Conner campaign: that the western districts had no representation on the court. It did not consider the logical argument that simply moving to Fort Worth and working on the court would be an objection to anyone seeking a second term on the court.

The article refers to Fort Worth as the "glorious city" being an "heir to every State office" and it is "only surprising to a great many people that some one of her gifted citizens, does not lay claim to the Throne of England." It is possible that Rye, the attorney turned newspaperman, journalist, cartoonist, and satirist, from Shackelford County was Conner's pipeline into the press working behind the scenes to promote Conner's career. Rye may have been instrumental in Judge Conner being touted as a potential candidate for governor in 1892, shortly before the Democratic Convention in Dallas when Tarlton was nominated.

There are some interesting phrases in the *Albany News* article that point to Conner as the possible author. Look at this paragraph in the article:

> But to read the many claims for office of the Fort Worth people, one would think that she has become so imbued with her own importance, that she thinks that *all that is necessary* for her to do, is, to simply come out and announce for office, and it is theirs—that the whole State should bow down and worship the said candidate for office, regardless of his qualifications.

Chief Justice Conner used the phrase "all that is necessary" in *Gamer Co. v. Gamage*, 147 S.W. 721, 724 (Tex. Civ. App.—Fort Worth 1912, no writ) and in *Richmond v. Hog Creek Oil Co.*, 229 S.W. 563, 570 (Tex. Civ. App.—Fort Worth 1920).

Then look at this phrase:

> Oh no! Fort Worth would not for one moment remain neutral—*would not consent* to any other section getting the office, but she rose in her grandeur and dictatorial way, and demanded that one of her gifted citizens should be appointed.

Chief Justice Conner used the term *"would not consent"* in *Burnett v. Gibbs*, 196 S.W. 725 (Tex. Civ. App.—Fort Worth 1917, no writ) and *U.S. Fid. & Guar. Co. v. Rochester*, 281 S.W. 306, 307 (Tex. Civ. App.—Fort Worth 1926, no writ).

Was Conner the author? If you are unconvinced, then read this sentence:

> Judge Tarlton, the present Chief Justice, is an able lawyer and judge, and the writer has nothing to say against him, and this article is not

aimed at him as a man or his ability as a judge, but he is the opponent of one whom the people of this section desire to succeed him, *hence it becomes necessary* to refer to *him in connection with the discussion ...*

Chief Justice Conner used the phrase *"hence it becomes necessary"* in *Logan v. Ludwick*, 283 S.W. 548 (Tex. Civ. App.—Fort Worth 1926, no writ) when he wrote:

Their principal insistence is that the personal property in controversy was not situated in Denton county at the time of the institution of plaintiff's suit within the meaning of exception 12 to article 1830, which exception we have quoted above, and *hence it becomes necessary*, or at least proper, that we consider the question so presented.

Conner used the phrase *"in connection with the discussion ..."* in the case of *Richmond v Hog Creek Oil Co*, 229 S.W. 563, 564 (Tex. Civ. App. – Fort Worth 1920, no writ) where he wrote "... *in connection with our discussion of the propositions presented*" and in *Hog Creek Oil Co*, 229 S.W. 563, 564 (Tex. Civ. App. – Fort Worth 1920, no writ) where he wrote: "[S]uch other facts, if any, that may be deemed pertinent, will be stated *in connection with our discussion* of the case."

While all the above phrases are commonly used terms by attorneys and appellate justices, it is very possible that the mysterious writer or a contributor to the *Albany News* endorsement in May 1898 was indeed District Judge Truman Conner.

Epilogue

B.D. Tarlton was a unique character who brought his intellect and Catholic heritage to Texas. Educated at one of the finest schools in the South at St. Charles College in Grand Coteau, Louisiana, Tarlton witnessed the Civil War being fought in Grand Coteau, only to be followed by the miracle of Grand Coteau when Mary Wilson was cured by John Berchmans, who became a saint afterwards. Tarlton began his practice of law in Louisiana when the state experienced a real *coup d'etat* when its governor was removed from office only to be forcibly restored to power by the U.S. military during Reconstruction. Tarlton saw his parents endure years of litigation to save their family plantations in Louisiana and in Texas while his father made law in two states. Who else in American History could be the witness to such extraordinary events?

Tarlton's rise in Texas politics and the law was based on his intellectual brilliance and his likeable personality. He lost his first two races for political office because he ran against established incumbents. In Louisiana he lost against an older and more experienced politician, E.D. Estilette, who went on to become the Louisiana Speaker of the House. He lost against District Judge J.M. Hall in Texas, a Civil War veteran, who had already paved his way to win after losing against Tarlton's mentor, Jo Abbott. Hall was most likely one tough, hard driving, and difficult trial judge who constantly challenged Tarlton in court. Tarlton's entanglement with Judge Hall turned him into an appellate attorney and appellate justice.

Tarlton learned the importance of seeking out influential colleagues and associating with them at the right time. His success in Texas politics was from following the influence of Jo Abbott and being promoted two times by Governor Jim Hogg.

Tarlton's life came in conflict with Eastland County District Judge Truman H. Conner who desired to be appointed to the new court of civil appeals when it was established in 1892. After the first month the new court was in operation, Conner may have viewed himself as under attack by the new court that began to supervise the 118 counties in the state because of the number of reversals of his decisions during Tarlton's first term in office. When Conner was not appointed to the new court of civil appeals in 1895, he could wait no longer. He would act, and Tarlton was in his way.

Conner defeated Tarlton, working behind the scenes in a campaign like no other. He quietly won the election before there was an election. Conner would not make it easy on the governor who declined to appoint him to the new appellate court. He resigned his district court seat to allow the public to decide his successor and to snub the governor. While there are many theories about what prompted the Tarlton-Conner, how Conner accomplished his victory over Tarlton may always be a mystery.

Dr. John Tarlton spawned a legacy quite different than his own. Like B.D. Tarlton who believed in women's rights before there was women's suffrage, the Tarlton children and grandchildren fought for individual civil rights and against the Ku Klux Klan, and continued to push for equality for over one hundred years to this day. Had Tarlton not been defeated in 1898, perhaps his son B.D. Tarlton Jr. would have moved to Fort Worth instead of Corpus Christi and fought against the rise of anti-Catholicism and the Ku Klux Klan. The rise of J. Frank Norris in Fort Worth may have been diminished. The history of Fort Worth would have been different. But the history of the University of Texas School of Law would have been different as well. There would have been no Professor Tarlton and no Tarlton Law Library. Tarlton would not have died in the Hurricane in 1919.

In January 2021, I asked Sissy Farenthold whether she still believed that Tarlton lost his race to Conner because of his Catholic faith. She confirmed again that "he lost over the Catholic issue. It wasn't said that way. It was understood." Possibly all the above reasons suggested earlier came together in one perfect storm that ended Tarlton's judicial career and foretold what would lie ahead for him. Legends are passed down; legends become verified; and eventually legends become truth.

THE END

Acknowledgements

Many thanks to all for the numerous contributions to this book. To my wife Camille and my children, Stephen, Andrew, Michael, and Margaux for the time and hours away working on this book over the past four years. To Laurie Cockerell, my sister-in-law, for the many edits, rewrites, and drafts.

To Sissy Farenthold, who sat through numerous interviews weathering the COVID 19 pandemic with her mask at ninety-four years of age, showing me her family photographs and phone conversations. Her passing was such a loss. I wanted so much to be able to bring her the final book in print before she died.

To Benjanmin Dudley Tarlton IV, George Farenthold II, Theresa Tartlon and Emily Farenthold for long conversations and emails. To Genevieve Tarlton, Katie Hamilton, George Farenthold, Claude D'Unger and all the Tarlton family members, and Tom Cohen, for providing valuable feedback and encouraging historical accuracy.

To the many Texas attorneys, professional colleagues, and friends, for their contributions in examining the Tarlton decisions: Dylan Drummond, 2022 President of the State Bar Appellate Section, Jerry Bullard, 2021 Chair of the State Bar Appellate Section; Steve Hayes, former chair of the State Bar Appellate Section; JoAnn Story and Andrew Johnson, co-chairs of the Judicial History Committee of the State Bar Appellate Section, Judicial History Section; Allan Howeth, former Managing Partner of Cantey & Hanger, LLP in Fort Worth; Chad Ruback; Roland Love; former Associate Justice Jason Boatright, Fifth Court of Appeals, Dallas; William Chriss, Scott Stolley and Stephen Alton, for their contributions and reviews the Tarlton decisions.

To retired District Judge Frank B. "Bob" McGregor, Chair of the Hill County Historical Commission, for his assistance with research on Judge J.M. Hall, finding his photograph, researching the B.D. Tarlton home, and finding the application to practice law by George I. Jordan. Judge McGregor found the tombstones of the Tarltons buried in Hillsboro, Texas. McGregor says that "the Tarlton family is one of Hillsboro's oldest and most respected families, having long-time connections here."

To Bogumil Nosek and Alliance Francaise of Dallas for translations of two of the french affidavits for the *Miracle of Grand Coteau.*

To Will Lowrance for his research of B.D. Tarlton and finding Hill County Census information and biographical information of the Tarlton, Jordan & Tarlton firm, and the status of the former B.D. Tarlton home in Hillsboro, Texas.

To Tyra Madison and April Cook with the district clerk's office in Hill County for locating real estate records:

To Jennifer Vasser and Louann Potter, clerks in Johnson County, for their research of District Judge J.M. Hall.

To the Travis County clerks, Jason Williams and Servando Hernandez.

To Tessa K. Culverhouse, clerk in Eastland County,

To Curtis M. Chaney, a professional surveyor, for locating the Tarlton property near Amelie, Louisiana.

To Lynn Cowles for assistance in research in Austin and coordinating with the University of Texas School of Law.

To Peggy Crowder with the Hill County Surveyors for helping to locate documents related to the *Tarlton v. Kirkpatrick* case.

To Dan Duplantis of Morgan City, Louisiana, with background of the former area known as Tiger Island.

To Judith Gossee for the illustrations in the book. What a marvelous addition to the book!

To Valerie Ellis with the Mobile Public Library for her research of Dr. John Tarlton and Caroline Belser Tarlton.

To Crystal Harris with Peede & Associates Land Surveyors in Hillsboro, Texas, for locating the property in dispute in the *Tarlton v. Kirkpatrick* litigation and creating the graphic.

To the Hillsboro City Library, Russell Keelin, Assistant Library Director.

To Kent McMillan, a professional surveyor, for locating B.D. Tarlton's former residences in Austin, Texas, and conducting research of Professor Tarlton in Austin, Texas.

To Caroline Richard with the Society of the Sacred Heart for research in St. Louis of the archives of St. Charles College and for documents relating to the Miracle of Grand Coteau.

To Molly Sauder for her research of the May 1898 endorsement from the *Albany News*.

To the Texas State Preservation Board for permission for use of the photos of B.D. Tarlton, Ben Ayres and Wright Morrow, and to Michelle Lambing, Graphics Coordinator, Texas State Preservation Board.

To the Texas Archives for many requests by email for records and the numerous appellate briefs by B.D. Tarlton and for finding the *Tarlton v. Daily* files and permission to examine them during the COVID pandemic.

To Gagandeep Singh and Amrit Kaur from India for numerous hours typing up handwritten legal documents that are over 150 years old to make them understandable.

To Erin Shirley with the Morgan City Archives in Morgan City, Louisiana, for her research on the Tarlton family and finding that they initially located to Bell Isle, Louisiana.

The cases of *Sanger Bros v. Henderson*, *Texas Central Railway Company v. Stewart*, *Robinson v. Moore*, and *Gulf, C. & S.F. Ry. Co. v. Johnson* in Chapter Seventeen are reprinted with permission of Thomson Reuters. Special thanks to Rebecca Matzek, Copyright Specialist with Thomson Reuters.

To Molly Tepera with the Dallas History and Archives Division for finding the *Albany News* editorial regarding the 1898 race between B.D. Tarlton and Truman Conner.

To Kia Winfrey with the City of Opelousas Tourism office for finding the U.S. Army Corps of Engineers report in 1988 and solving some of the early questions over the John Tarlton properties.

To Paige Witt, Texas A&M Law graduate 2022, for her research assistance with the book.

Notes

1. Allison Ehrlich, "Corpus Christi's 1919 Hurricane Brought Destruction but Reshaped the City for the Future," *Caller Times*, https://www.caller.com/story/news/local/2019/09/13/corpus-christi-1919-hurricane/2232867001/.
2. Ibid.
3. *The Tarleton Family*, Compiled by C.W. Tarleton, Concord, N.H.: Ira C. Evans, Printer, 12 School Street (1900).
4. Ibid.
5. "Jeremiah Tarleton," *Find a Grave*. https://www.findagrave.com/memorial/184376519/jeremiah-tarleton.
6. *The Tarleton Family*, Compiled by C.W. Tarleton, Concord, N.H.: Ira C. Evans, Printer, 12 School Street (1900).
7. "Transylvania University," Wikipedia.https://en.wikipedia.org/wiki/Transylvania_University.
8. A Memorial and Biographical History of Johnson and Hill Counties, Texas (Chicago: The Lewis Publishing Company, 1892).
9. *The Tarleton Family*, Compiled by C.W. Tarleton, Concord, N.H.: Ira C. Evans, Printer, 12 School Street (1900).
10. *Fay's Mobile Directory or Stranger's Guile* IMobile, Ala. 1838,1839).
11. Emma Jane died on Sept. 27, 1853, at age 12.
12. *The Tarleton Family*, Compiled by C.W. Tarleton, Concord, N.H.: Ira C. Evans, Printer, 12 School Street, p. 210, (1900).
13. Ibid, 211.

14 Archeological and Historical Research on Avoca Plantation U.S. Army Corps of Engineers District, New Orleans, Final Report, September 1988.
15 *Tarlton v. Wofford,* 15 La. Ann. 592 (1860).
16 "St. Charles College (Louisiana)," *Wikipedia.* https://en.wikipedia.org/wiki/St._Charles_College_(Louisiana).
17 "Rose Philippine Duchesne," *Wikipedia,* https://en.wikipedia.org/wiki/Rose_Philippine_Duchesne.
18 https://64parishes.org/entry/civil-war-louisiana
19 Ibid.
20 *Grand Coteau, The Holy Land of South Louisiana,* Trent Angers, Acadian House Publishing, LaFayette, Louisiana (2005).
21 Ibid, 39.
22 Ibid, 42.
23 https://lasc.libguides.com/c.php?g=967774&p=6992539
24 No. 467 – Vol. XVIII, Frank Leslie's Illustrated Newspaper (September 10, 1864).
25 *No. 6706, Elizabeth McWalters, wife et al v. Dr. John Tarlton, District Court, St. Landry's Parish;* McWater's name appears as both "McWaters" and "McWilliams" in documents. Her name was McWaters in title of the mortgage by Dr. Tarlton to in the 1857 transaction and McWilliams in the body of the document. At that time, McWilliams was the widow of Aaron M. McWaters. By 1865 she was the wife of James M. Grunsby.
26 *Allen v. Tarlton,* 22 La. Ann. 427 (1870).
27 *Smith v. McWaters,* 22 La. Ann. 431 (1870).
28 *Cause No. 10146, John W. Hardyman, Administrator of the Succession of William Hardy, Deceased v. Jane Caller & ALS, St. Landry Parish, Louisiana.*
29 *The Opelousas Courier,* Dec 28, 1867; Jan. 4, 1868.
30 Trent Angers, "Grand Coteau, The Holy Land of South Louisiana," Acadian House Publishing, 2005.
31 Frances Goldie, *The Life of the Blessed John Berchmans,* London: Burns and Oates, Portman Street, and Paternoster Row (1877) at 14.
32 Ibid.

33 https://www.shreveporttimes.com/story/news/2016/11/17/heart-st-john-berchmans/93894670/; Temoingage du 2 medecin, le docteur Edward Millard.
34 Judge Benjamin Dudley Tarlton Centennial Celebration (2004).
35 Memorial Address on Professor Benjamin Dudley Tarlton, Prof. W.S. Simkins, November 3, 1919; Judge Benjamin Dudley Tarlton Centennial Celebration (2004).
36 *Allen v. Tarlton*, 22 La. Ann. 427 (1870).
37 *Smith v. McWaters*, 22 La. Ann. 431 (1870).
38 Cause No. 6706, *Elizabeth McWilliams v. Dr. John Tarlton*, St. Mary's Parish, State of Louisiana.
39 Case No. 12004, *Frances Ann Caller v. John Tarlton*, District Court, St. Landry's Parish. In 2020, only two sheets remain of this lawsuit: the cover page and a second page.
40 *St. Landry Democrat*, 16 Jul. 1870.
41 Cause No. 6767, *Mrs Francis Caller, Wife v. Mrs. Elizabeth McWalters, Wife et al*, St. Mary's Parish, Louisiana.
42 22 La. Ann. 427 (1870)
43 Cause No. 6706 *Elizabeth McWilliams v. Dr. John Tarlton*, St. Mary's Parish, Louisiana.
44 April 13, 1872 edition of the St. Landry Democrat.
45 "A brief history of the requirements to join the Louisiana Bar: 1855," *The Law Library of Louisiana*; https://lasc.libguides.com/c.php?g=457651&p=3130577.
46 https://en.wikipedia.org/wiki/William_Pitt_Kellogg.
47 https://en.wikipedia.org/wiki/John_McEnery_(politician).
48 *A Memorial and Biographical History of Johnson and Hill Counties, Texas* (Chicago: The Lewis Publishing Company, 1892).
49 "Susan M. Littell," *Geneanet*. https://gw.geneanet.org/tdowling?lang=en&p=susan+m.&n=littell
50 The Opelousas Courier, 3 May 1873.
51 *St. Landry Democrat*, Apr 19, 1873.
52 Ibid.

53. https://en.wikipedia.org/wiki/Colfax_massacre.
54. Ibid.
55. Ibid.
56. *The Opelousas Courier,* May 3, 1873.
57. The letter was signed by: E.T. Lewis, Henry L. Garland, A. Bailey, E.D. Estillette, Laurent Dupre, John F. Smith and B.D. Tarlton.
58. Dr. Tarlton to Elizabeth Grundy dated Oct. 23, 1873, recorded at MOB 25, Pg 271, #15779. That transaction refers to a 2-page Ratification of Title transaction recorded in MOB 25, Pg 276, #15785.
59. *The Times-Picayune* in New Orleans July 10, 1870.
60. *St. Landry Democrat,* Feb. 13, 1874.
61. https://www.findagrave.com/memorial/132675965/edmond-ducre-estilette.
62. *Cause No. 10146, John W. Hardyman, Administrator of the Succession of William Hardy, Deceased v. Jane Caller & ALS, St. Landry Parish, Louisiana.*
63. The Opelousas Courier, Aug. 22, 1874.
64. *https://en.wikipedia.org/wiki/Colfax_massacre#Aftermath*
65. *The Opelousas Courier,* Aug. 22, 1874.
66. https://en.wikipedia.org/wiki/Colfax_massacre#Aftermath
67. *The Opelousas Courier,* Oct. 3, 1873.
68. *St. Landry Courier,* Friday Nov 6, 1874.
69. http://www.waxahachiecvb.com/p/about/history-of-waxahachie
70. 26 Tex. 562 (Tex. 1863).
71. *The Austin American-Statesman* (06 Sep 1873).
72. *The Dallas Daily Herald* (17 Dec 1875).
73. *The Galveston Daily News* (07 Mar 1877).
74. *The Dallas Daily Herald* (15 Feb 1888).
75. *The Dallas Daily Herald* (Oct. 7, 1886).
76. Instrument Number 1873000L0250*1, Page Number 250. The deed was recorded but has been lost.
77. *The Austin Weekly Statesman* (May 22, 1884).
78. David Minor, "Ferris, Justus Wesley," *TSHA Online.* https://tshaonline.org/handbook/online/articles/ffe09.

79 "Jane Henrietta Toulmin Caller," *Find a Grave.* https://www.findagrave.com/memorial/70754849/jane-henrietta-caller.

80 "A Memorial and Biographical History of Johnson and Hill Counties, Texas, *Portal to Texas History,* p. 225. https://texashistory.unt.edu/ark:/67531/meapth46829/m1/236/?q=%22jo%20abbott%22.

81 "Judge Tarlton is to be of Faculty of University. Prominent Fort Worth Attorney to be Professor of Law at State School," The *Fort Worth Star-Telegram,* June 10, 1904; L.E. Daniel, "Personnel of the Texas State Government," (San Antonio: Maverick Printing House, 1892). *Legislative Reference Library of Texas.* https://lrl.texas.gov/scanned/members/bios/Personnel_of_the_Texas_state_government_1892.pdf.

82 John. W. Brady, "An Appreciation," *The Alcalde,* November 1919, No. 48, Vol. VII, No. 4 (p. 285-287).

83 https://gw.geeanet.org/tdowling?lang=en&p=frances+ann&n=tarlton website doesn't come up

84 "Mary Elenaor Tarlton," *Geneanet.* https://gw.geneanet.org/tdowling?lang=en&p=mary+elenaor&n=tarlton.

85 "Elizabeth Millard Tarlton," *Geneanet.* https://gw.geneanet.org/tdowling?lang=en&p=elizabeth+millard&n=tarlton.

86 https://www.findagrave.com/memorial/138557029/elizabeth-millard-wright.

87 *A Memorial and Biographical History of Johnson and Hill Counties, Texas,* (Chicago, The Lewis Publishing Company, 1892).

88 *Legislative Reference Library.* https://lrl.texas.gov/scanned/members/photos/large/T/Tarlton_B_17.jpg.

89 *Tarlton v. Daily,* 55 Tex. 92, 94 (1881).

90 32 Tex. 290, 294 (1869).

91 "Dr. John Tarlton," *Find a Grave.* https://www.findagrave.com/memorial/70755012/john-tarlton.

92. Archeological and Historical Research on Avoca Plantation U.S. Army Corps of Engineers District, New Orleans, Final Report, September 1988.
93. "Col John H. Bullock," *Find a Grave*. https://www.findagrave.com/memorial/15666416/john-h.-bullock.
94. E.H. Loghery, *Personnel of the Texas State Government For 1885*, (Austin: JM Snyder, 1885).https://lrl.texas.gov/scanned/members/bios/Personnel_19th_1885.pdf.
95. Ibid.
96. *A Memorial and Biographical History of Johnson and Hill Counties, Texas* (Chicago: The Lewis Publishing Company, 1892.)
97. Hendrickson, Kenneth E., Jr, *The Chief of Executives of Texas: From Stephen F. Austin to John B. Connally, Jr.* (College Station: Texas A&M University Press, 1995).
98. "Prayers Answered in Death of Venerable Couple at Hillsboro," *Fort Worth Star-Telegram,* August 27, 1931.
99. "Tarlton Family of Hillsboro," *Ancestry.Com/UK*. https://www.ancestry.co.uk/boards/localities.northam.usa.states.texas.counties.hill/3365/mb.ashx.
100. 61 Tex. 698, 699 (1884).
101. *Jones v. Fancher,* 61 Tex. 698, 701 (1884).
102. 63 Tex. 333, 335 (1885).
103. "A Memorial and Biographical History of Johnson and Hill Counties, Texas," p. 377, *The Portal to Texas History.* https://texashistory.unt.edu/ark:/67531/meapth46829/m1/396/?q=%22J.M.%20Hall%22.
104. Vol 2, *Southern Historical Papers,* page 161, or the United States War Records.
105. *A Memorial and Biographical History of Johnson and Hill Counties, Texas* (Chicago: The Lewis Publishing Company, 1892).
106. *The Times-Picayune* in New Orleans, April 19, 1885.
107. *The Dallas Morning News,* December 3, 1887.
108. *Munawar v. Cadle Company,* 2 S.W.2d 12, 18 (Tex. App – Corpus Christi 1999, m pet deied); Title Examination Standards, Standard 1.20 Review by Examiner.

109 "Wright Chalfant Morrow (1859-1942)" *Tarlton Law Library*.https://tarltonapps.law.utexas.edu/justices/profile/view/147).

110 *A Memorial and Biographical History of Johnson and Hill Counties, Texas* (Chicago: The Lewis Publishing Company, 1892).

111 https://prabook.com/web/wright.morrow/936352.

112 *The Opelousas Courier,* Jul 27, 1889.

113 9 S.W. 157, 157–59 (Tex. 1888).

114 29 Tex. App. 250, 15 S.W. 719 (Tex. App. 1890, no pet.).

115 *Farrar v. State,* 15 S.W. 719 (Tex. App. 1890, no pet.).

116 29 Tex. App. 250, 15 S.W. 719 (Tex. App. 1890, no pet.).

117 *The Fort Worth Daily Gazette* (08 Jun 1890).

118 Ibid.

119 Ibid.

120 *The Portal to Texas History.* https://texashistory.unt.edu/ark:/67531/metapth46829/m1/316/zoom/?q=wear&resolution=2&lat=2674&lon=626

121 Ibid.

122 Ibid.

123 Ibid.

124 Ibid.

125 *The Austin Weekly Statesman* (14 Aug 1890)

126 *Texas Democracy, The Dallas Morning News,* August 14, 1890.

127 Ibid.

128 *The Austin American-Statesman* (26 Nov 1890).

129 *The Fort Worth Daily Gazette* (18 Dec 1890).

130 *Austin Weekly Statesman* (12 Jul 1883).

131 http://genealogytrails.com/tex/panhandle2/eastland/earlyhistoryperiod2chap1.html.

132 Ibid.

133 Ibid.

134 Ibid.

135 1 Tex. Civ. App. 642, 20 S.W. 962 (1892, writ ref'd).

136 3 Willson 321 (Tex. 1887).

137 12 Tex. App. 235 (1882).

138. "History of Texas: Fort Worth and the Texas Northwest Edition," Vol. 3, *Google Books*.
139. 85 Tex. 193, 196, 19 S.W. 994, 995 (1892).
140. *The St. Louis Globe-Democrat* (May 13, 1891).
141. *The Fort Worth Daily Gazette* (May 5, 1891).
142. 81 Tex. 505, 17 S.W. 52 (1891).
143. *Fustok v. Bank of Am., N.A.*, CV H-16-2867, 2017 WL 6459644 (S.D. Tex. Sept. 27, 2017); *In re Estate of Miller*, 446 S.W.3d 445, 455 (Tex. App. – Tyler 2014, no pet.).
144. 82 Tex. 405 (1891).
145. 19 S.W. 357 (1892).
146. 84 Tex. 424 (1892).
147. Frank A. Stamper, *A Handbook for Texas Abstractors and Title Men* (Texas Land Title Association 1973).
148. 83 Tex. 370 (1892).
149. 84 Tex. 365, 368, 19 S.W. 520, 521 (1892).
150. 82 Tex. 677 (Tex. 1892).
151. 392 S.W.2d 118, 120 (Tex. 1965).
152. 82 Tex. 195 (1891).
153. 84 Tex. 149 (1892).
154. 81 Tex. 503 (1891).
155. 83 Tex. 302 (1892).
156. 85 Tex. 145, 147, 19 S.W. 1085, 1086 (1892).
157. State Bar Meeting, The *Dallas Morning News*, Jul. 27, 1891.
158. Ibid.
159. "Feast at Woollam's Lake," The *Dallas Morning News*, Jan.31, 1892.
160. "The Political Grab Bag," The *Dallas Morning News*, Feb.22, 1892.
161. "Down in Hill County," The *Dallas Morning News*, Mar. 8, 1892.
162. "Judge Tarlton's Candidacy," The *Dallas Morning News*, May 13, 1892.
163. L.D. Daniell, *Personnel of the Texas State Government* (San Antonio: Maverick, 1892). https://lrl.texas.gov/scanned/members/bios/Personnel_of_the_Texas_state_government_1892.pdf (accessed 12/14/20)

164 Mike Nichols, *Lost Fort Worth,* The History Press (2014).
165 Centennial of the Second Court of Civil Appeals, 1992. Fort Worth City Directory.
166 Ibid.
167 Ibid.
168 History of Texas Together with a Biographical History of Tarrant and Parker Counties, Chicago: The Lewis Publishing Company (1895).
169 *The Fort Worth Daily Gazette,* Sept. 13, 1887.
170 *The Fort Worth Daily Gazette,* March 24, 1892.
171 The Judicial Convention, Aug. 1, 1892, The *Dallas Morning News.*
172 Ibid.
173 *The Dallas Morning News,* Sept. 2, 1892.
174 *The Fort Worth Star-Telegram,* Nov. 16, 1936.
175 *The Dallas Daily Herald,* Dec. 12, 1882.
176 *The Austin American-Statesman,* Jun. 16, 1897.
177 *The Fort Worth Star-Telegram,* Nov. 16, 1936.
178 *The Fort Worth Star-Telegram,* Apr. 18, 1908.
179 Ibid.
180 https://www.txcourts.gov/2ndcoa/about-the-court/history/
181 Ibid.
182 "The News in Fort Worth," The *Dallas Morning News,* Sept. 5, 1892; "Governor's Appointments," The *Dallas Morning News,* Sept. 2, 1892.
183 "A Governor's Patronage," The *Dallas Morning News,* Sept. 27, 1892.
184 100 Year Centennial of the Second Court of Appeals.
185 Ibid.
186 Turner Publishing Company (2007).
187 Turner Publishing Company (2010).
188 *The Dallas Morning News,* Sept. 29, 1892; *The Galveston Daily News,* Oct. 1, 1892.
189 Minute Book 1, Court of Civil Appeals.
190 1 Tex. Civ. App. 412, 21 S.W. 114 (Tex. Civ. App. – Fort Worth 1892, writ denied).
191 1 Tex. Civ. App. 642, 644, 20 S.W. 962, 963 (1892, writ ref'd).
192 1 Tex. Civ. App. 93, 20 S.W. 994 (1892, no writ).

193 1 Tex. Civ. App. 103, 20 S.W. 1123 (1892, no writ).
194 *The Dallas Morning News,* Oct 4, 1892.
195 *The Dallas Morning News* Oct 5, 1892.
196 *The Dallas Morning News,* Oct 4, 1892.
197 *The Dallas Morning News,* Vol. VIII, Oct 4, 1892.
198 1 Tex. Civ. App. 412, 21 S.W. 114 (Tex. Civ. App. – Fort Worth 1892, writ denied).
199 *The Gazette: Fort Worth, Texas* Jun 11, 1884.
200 *The Galveston Daily News,* 21 Feb 1892.
201 http://genealogytrailscom/tex/panhandle2/eastland/earlyhistoryperiod2chap1.html
202 *The Galveston Daily News,* 4 Mar 1895
203 *The Galveston Daily News,* 4 Mar 1895
204 *The Dallas Daily Herald,* 1 Feb 1887.
205 17 Tex. Jur. 3d Creditors' Rights and Remedies § 248.
206 9 Tex. Civ. App. 130, 28 S.W. 695 (Tex. Civ. App. – Fort Worth 1894, writ ref'd).
207 *The Austin American-Statesman,* 24 Oct 1896.
208 *Brownsville Herald,* 16 Sept. 1896.
209 *Evening Messenger,* 26 Sep 1896.
210 1 Tex. Civ. App. 642, 20 S.W. 962 (Tex. Civ. App. – Fort Worth 1892, writ ref'd).
211 16 S.W. 642 (1891).
212 81 Tex. 281 (1891).
213 84 Tex. 674 (1892).
214 1 Tex. Civ. App. 93, 20 S.W. 994 (Tex. Civ. App. – Fort Worth 1892, no writ).
215 81 Tex. 659 (1891).
216 1 Tex. Civ. App. 103, 20 S.W. 1123 (Tex. Civ. App. – Fort Worth 1892, no writ).
217 16 S.W. 775, 779 (Tex. App. 1890, no writ).
218 *The Dallas Morning News,* Oct 11, 1892.
219 1 Tex. Civ. App. 100, 102, 20 S.W. 1004 (Tex. Civ. App. – Fort Worth 1892, no writ).

220 6 Tex. 502 (1851)
221 30 Tex. 257 (1867)
222 *The Austin Weekly Statesman*, Aug. 18, 1892.
223 *The Galveston Daily News*, Mar 13, 1892.
224 *The Fort Worth Daily Gazette*, 15 Feb 1892.
225 1 Tex. Civ. App. 100, 102, 20 S.W. 1004 (Tex. Civ. App. – Fort Worth 1892, no writ).
226 20 S.W. 932, 933 (Tex. Civ. App. – Fort Worth 1892, no writ).
227 1 Tex. Civ. App. 379, 382, 21 S.W. 143, 144 (Tex. Civ. App. – Fort worth 1892, no writ).
228 *The Dallas Morning News*, Dec. 4, 1892.
229 Ibid.
230 *Martin v. Anderson*, 4 Tex. Civ. App. 111, 23 S.W. 290 (Tex. Civ. App. – Fort Worth 1893, no writ); *Strickland v. Hardwicke*, 3 Tex. Civ. App. 326, 327, 22 S.W. 541 (Tex. Civ. App. – Fort Worth 1893, no writ); *Savoy v. Brewton*, 3 Tex. Civ. App. 336, 339, 22 S.W. 585, 586 (Tex. Civ. App. – Fort Worth 1893, no writ).
231 *Wilson v. Casey*, 3 Tex. Civ. App. 141, 142, 22 S.W. 118 (Tex. Civ. App. – Fort Worth 1893, no writ); *Williams v. Hardie*, (Tex. Civ. App. 1892, rev'd, 85 Tex. 499, 22 S.W. 399 (1893).
232 3 Tex. Civ. App. 326, 327, 22 S.W. 541 (Tex. Civ. App. – Fort Worth 1893, no writ).
233 Ibid.
234 22 S.W. 585 (Tex. App.—Fort Worth 1893, no writ).
235 *Tomlinson v. League*, 25 S.W. 313 (Tex. Civ. App. – Fort Worth 1894, no writ); *Rushing v. Willis*, 28 S.W. 921 (Tex. Civ. App. – Fort Worth 1894, no writ); *French v. Koenig*, 8 Tex. Civ. App. 341, 27 S.W. 1079 (Tex. Civ. App. – Fort Worth 1894, writ ref'd); *Swink v. League*, 6 Tex. Civ. App. 309, 311, 25 S.W. 807 (Tex. Civ. App. – Fort Worth 1894, no writ); *Watson v. Texas & P. Ry. Co.*, 8 Tex. Civ. App. 144, 27 S.W. 924 (Tex. Civ. App. – Fort Worth 1894, no writ).
236 *Yager v. Heimer*, 28 S.W. 1026 (Tex. Civ. App. – Fort Worth 1894, no writ); *Martin-Brown Co v. Henderson*, 9 Tex. Civ. App. 130, 28 S.W. 695 (Tex. Civ. App. – Fort Worth 1894, writ ref'd); *Corrigan v. Nichols*,

6 Tex. Civ. App. 26, 24 S.W. 952 (Tex. Civ. App. – Fort Worth 1894, no writ); *Wortham v. Anderson*, 6 Tex. Civ. App. 18, 24 S.W. 847 (Tex. Civ. App. – Fort Worth 1894, no writ); *Yost v. Watertown Steam-Engine Co.*, 24 S.W. 657 (Tex. Civ. App. – Fort Worth 1894, no writ).

[237] 8 Tex. Civ. App. 144, 27 S.W. 924 (Tex. Civ. App. – Fort Worth 1894, no writ).

[238] *Swink v. League*, 6 Tex. Civ. App. 309, 310, 25 S.W. 807 (Tex. Civ. App. – Fort Worth 1894, no writ).

[239] 8 Tex. Civ. App. 144, 27 S.W. 924 (Tex. Civ. App. – Fort Worth 1894, no writ).

[240] 8 Tex. Civ. App. 144, 145, 27 S.W. 924, 924 (Tex. Civ. App. -- Fort Worth 1894, no writ).

[241] Ibid.

[242] Ibid. at 144.

[243] *Swink v. League*, 6 Tex. Civ. App. 309, 310, 25 S.W. 807 (Tex. Civ. App. – Fort Worth 1894, no writ).

[244] *Stanley v. Hamilton*, 33 S.W. 601, 602 (Tex. Civ. App. – Fort Worth 1895, writ ref'd); *Connellee v. Eastland County*, 31 S.W. 552, 553 (Tex. Civ. App. – Fort Worth 1895, no writ); *Standard Life & Acc. Ins. Co. v. Koen*, 11 Tex. Civ. App. 273, 279, 33 S.W. 133, 137 (Tex. Civ. App. – Fort Worth 1895, no writ); *Tex. & P. Ry. Co. v. Cornelius*, 10 Tex. Civ. App. 125, 130, 30 S.W. 720, 723 (Tex. Civ. App. – Fort Worth 1895, writ ref'd); *Tex. & P. Ry. Co. v. Neill*, 30 S.W. 369 (Tex. Civ. App. 1895, writ ref'd); *Cunningham v. Holt*, 12 Tex. Civ. App. 150, 152, 33 S.W. 981 (Tex. Civ. App. – Fort Worth 1895, writ ref'd).

[245] *State v. City of Cisco*, 33 S.W. 244 (Tex. Civ. App. 1895, no writ); *Am. Fire Ins. Co. v. Ctr.*, 33 S.W. 554, 556 (Tex. Civ. App. 1895, no writ); *Jackson v. Steffens*, 32 S.W. 862, (Tex. Civ. App. 1895, no writ); *Brown v. Henderson*, 31 S.W. 315 (Tex. Civ. App. – Fort Worth 1895, no writ); *Reeves v. Tex. & P. Ry. Co.*, 11 Tex. Civ. App. 514, 32 S.W. 920 (Tex. Civ. App. – Fort worth 1895, no writ).

[246] 31 S.W. 315 (Tex. Civ. App. – Fort Worth 1895, no writ).

[247] 11 Tex. Civ. App. 514, 32 S.W. 920 (Tex. Civ. App. – Fort Worth 1895, no writ).

248 31 S.W. 315 (Tex. Civ. App. – Fort Worth 1895, no writ).
249 11 Tex. Civ. App. 514, 32 S.W. 920 (Tex. Civ. App. – Fort Worth 1895, no writ).
250 *Albany News,* May 20, 1898.
251 33 S.W. 244 (Tex. Civ. App. – Fort Worth 1895, no writ).
252 85 Tex 520 (1893).
253 5 Tex. Civ. App. 17 (Tex. App. – Fort Worth 1893, no writ)
254 *Page v. Conaway,* 34 S.W. 143 (Tex. Civ. App. – Fort Worth 1896, no writ); *Dewitt v. Chilton,* 35 S.W. 23 (Tex. Civ. App. – Fort Worth 1896, no writ).
255 *Hall v. Texas & P. Ry. Co.,* 35 S.W. 321 (Tex. Civ. App. – Fort Worth 1896, no writ); *Cage v. Tucker's Heir,* 14 Tex. Civ. App. 316, 317, 37 S.W. 180 (Tex. Civ. App. – Fort Worth 1896, no writ); *Gentry v. Gatlin,* 14 Tex. Civ. App. 419, 38 S.W. 223 (Tex. Civ. App. – Fort Worth 1896, no writ); *Moore v. Stone,* 36 S.W. 909 (Tex. Civ. App. – Fort Worth 1896, no writ); *Hall v. Tex. & P. Ry. Co.,* 35 S.W. 321 (Tex. Civ. App. – Fort Worth 1896, no writ); *Clack v. Wood,* 14 Tex. Civ. App. 400, 37 S.W. 188 (Tex. Civ. App. – Fort Worth 1896, no writ); *Texas & P. Ry. Co. v. Bigham,* 36 S.W. 1111 (Tex. Civ. App. – Fort Worth 1896, rev'd *Texas & P. Ry. Co. v. Bigham,* 90 Tex. 223, 38 S.W. 162 (1896).
256 *Texas & P. Ry. Co. v. Bigham,* 90 Tex. 223, 38 S.W. 162 (1896).
257 *The Fort Worth Register,* April 18, 1897.
258 *Texas & P. Ry. Co. v. Moore,* 43 S.W. 67, 68 (Tex. Civ. App. – Fort Worth 1897, writ ref'd); *W. Union Tel. Co. v. Thompson,* 41 S.W. 1103 (Tex. Civ. App. – Fort Worth 1897, no writ).
259 *Cope v. Lindsey,* 17 Tex. Civ. App. 203, 204, 43 S.W. 29, 30 (Tex. Civ. App. – Fort Worth 1897, no writ); *Cordill v. Moore,* 17 Tex. Civ. App. 217, 219, 43 S.W. 298, 300 (Tex. Civ. App. – Fort Worth 1897, no writ).
260 17 Tex. Civ. App. 203, 204, 43 S.W. 29, 30 (Tex. Civ. App. – Fort Worth 1897, no writ).
261 Article 2350, Rev. St. 1895.
262 17 Tex. Civ. App. 217, 43 S.W. 298 (Tex. Civ. App. – Fort Worth 1897, no writ).

263 91 Tex. 74, 76, 40 S.W. 1028, 1029 (1897).
264 *The Fort Worth Record and Register,* Jun 18, 1897.
265 *Brenham Weekly Banner,* Dec. 30, 1897.
266 *The Houston Daily Post,* Feb. 1, 1898.
267 *The Dallas Morning News,* Jan. 30, 1898.
268 The *Fort Worth Daily Gazette,* Mar. 31, 1895.
269 *Winston v. City of Ft. Worth,* 47 S.W. 740, 741 (Tex. Civ. App. 1898, writ ref'd).
270 *Snyder v. Baird Indep. Sch. Dist.,* 102 Tex. 4, 6, 111 S.W. 723 (1908).
271 *The Houston Post,* Feb 1, 1898.
272 *Jacksboro Gazette,* Mar 28, 1898.
273 Ibid.
274 Ibid.
275 *The Dallas Morning News,* Jul 15, 1898.
276 Ibid.
277 *The Dallas Morning News,* Jul 31, 1898.
278 *The Dallas Morning News,* 13 Sept 1898.
279 *The Houston Post,* Dec 16, 1898.
280 46 S.W. 1132 (Tex. Civ. App. – Fort Worth 1898, no writ).
281 47 S.W. 474 (Tex. Civ. App. – Fort Worth 1898, no writ).
282 *Mansur & Tebbetts Implement Co. v. Beeman-St. Clair Co.,* 45 S.W. 729, 731 (Tex. Civ. App. – Fort Worth1898, no writ); *Davis v. Cuthbertson,* 45 S.W. 426 (Tex. Civ. App. – Fort Worth 1898, no writ); *Ross v. Strahorn-Hutton-Evans Comm'n Co.,* 18 Tex. Civ. App. 698, 46 S.W. 398 (Tex. Civ. App. – Fort Worth 1898, writ ref'd); *Ferguson v. Cochran,* 45 S.W. 30 (Tex. Civ. App. – Fort Worth 1898, no writ).
283 21 S.W. 372 (Tex. Civ. App. – Fort Worth 1893, no writ).
284 2 Tex. Civ. App. 354, 21 S.W. 299 (Tex. Civ. App. – Fort Worth 1893, no writ).
285 4 Tex. Civ. App. 118, 120–21, 23 S.W. 420, 421 (Tex. Civ. App. – Fort Worth 1893, no writ).
286 5 Tex. Civ. App. 59, (Tex. Civ. App. – Fort Worth 1893, no writ).
287 2 Tex. Civ. App. 382 (Tex. Civ. App. – Fort Worth 1893, no writ).
288 25 S.W. 458 (Tex. Civ. App. – Fort Worth 1894, no writ).

289 12 Tex. Civ. App. 430 (Tex. App. – Fort Worth 1896, writ ref'd).
290 18 Tex. Civ. App. 617 (Tex. Civ. App. – Fort Worth 1898, no writ).
291 *Lumpkin v. Murrell*, 46 Tex. 51, 57 (1876).
292 9 Tex. Civ. App. 136 (Tex. Civ. App. – Fort Worth 1894, writ ref'd).
293 31 S.W. 314 (Tex. Civ. App. – Fort Worth 1895, no writ)
294 6 Tex. Civ. App. 43 (Tex. Civ. App. – Fort Worth 1894, writ ref'd). Tarlton visited this concept again in *Land Como Land & Improvement Co. v. Caughlin*, 9 Tex. Civ. App. 340, 29 S.W. 185 (1895, no writ) where Winthrop made a declaration beyond his agency relating to homes being built in the Arlington Heights area in Fort Worth.
295 29 S.W. 411 (1895, no writ).
296 28 S.W. 908 (Tex. Civ. App. – Fort Worth, 1894, no writ).
297 12 Tex. Civ. App. 466, 467, 34 S.W. 1048 (1896, writ ref'd).
298 His firm handled the cases of *Bond v. Rintleman*, 24 Tex. Civ. App. 298, 59 S.W. 48 (1900, no writ)(C.J. Conner); *Shaw v. W. Land & Live-Stock Co.*, 62 S.W. 941, 942 (Tex. Civ. App. 1901, writ ref'd)(C.J. Conner); *Toyaho Creek Irr. Co. v. Hutchins*, 21 Tex. Civ. App. 274, 279, 52 S.W. 101, 103–04 (1899, writ ref'd)(C.J. Conner); *Stewart v. Robbins*, 27 Tex. Civ. App. 188, 189, 65 S.W. 899, 900 (1901, writ ref'd)(C.J. Conner).
299 93 Tex. 171, 176, 54 S.W. 343, 344 (1899).
300 *Fort Worth Morning Register*, August 11, 1899.
301 93 Tex. 171, 176, 54 S.W. 343, 344 (1899).
302 94 Tex. 177, 59 S.W. 255 (1900).
303 "A Legal Battle On At Abilene, Judge B.D. Tarlton Of This City Engaged in Big Will Case – Points At Issue," The *Fort Worth Star-Telegram*, Sept. 20, 1903.
304 Advertisement, The *Dallas Morning News*, June 7, 1901.
305 43 Tex. Crim. 359, 362–67, 65 S.W. 1061, 1062–65 (1901).
306 29 Tex. Civ. App. 578, 69 S.W. 990 (Tex. Civ. App. – Fort worth 1902, no writ).
307 "County Convention Instructs After Much Oratory," *Fort Worth Register*, Mar. 6, 1902.
308 29 Tex. Civ. App. 276, 279, 69 S.W. 179, 180–81 (1902, writ ref'd).

309 Advertisement, *The Fort Worth Star-Telegram*, Apr. 26, 1903.
310 *The Fort Worth Star-Telegram*, Mar. 30, 1945.
311 "John Tarlton," *Find a Grave*. https://www.findagrave.com/memorial/125503641/john-tarlton.
312 *The Fort Worth Star-Telegram*, June 5, 1904.
313 "Leave to Attend $50,000 Donation Fort Worth Will be Represented at Washington by Delegates," The *Fort Worth Star-Telegram*, Apr. 11, 1904.
314 "Put None but Parker Men on Guard as Delegates. Tarrant County Endorses the New Yorker-Strong Endorsement for Gillespie," The *Fort Worth Star-Telegram*, June 12, 1904.
315 Ibid.
316 Ibid.
317 "Judge Tarlton is to be of Faculty of University. Prominent Fort Worth Attorney to be Professor of Law at State School," The *Fort Worth Star-Telegram*, June 10, 1904.
318 "Constitution Makers of '75 Reduced to 2 by Death at Paris," *Fort Worth Star-Telegram*, Apr. 6, 1919.
319 "B.D. Tarlton, Members of Fort Worth Bar Tender Banquet to Retiring President of the Organization Who Goes to University," The *Fort Worth Star-Telegram*, Sept. 13, 1904.
320 Ibid.
321 Ibid.
322 Ibid.
323 Ibid.
324 Ann Arnold, History of the Fort Worth Legal Community (Eakin Press, Austin, Texas 2000).
325 *The Dallas Morning News*, Oct. 13, 1892 – Sidney Samuels is referred to as the "reporter" in the synopsis of the opinion in *Bateman & Bro. v. West Star Milling Company*.
326 Ibid.
327 "B.D. Tarlton, Members of Fort Worth Bar Tender Banquet to Retiring President of the Organization Who Goes to University," The *Fort Worth Star-Telegram*, Sept. 13, 1904.
328 Judge Benjamin Dudley Tarlton Centennial Celebration (2004).

329 1906 Austin City Directory.
330 "Summer Law School Judge B.D. Tarlton, One of Three Men in Charge," The *Fort Worth Star-Telegram*, Fort Worth, February 7, 1906.
331 Judge Benjamin Dudley Tarlton Centennial Celebration (2004).
332 Ibid.
333 Ibid.
334 *The Austin Daily Statesman*, April 15, 1907.
335 46 Tex. Civ. App. 78, 102 S.W. 157 (1907, no writ).
336 *The Fort Worth Star-Telegram*, Oct. 11, 1907.
337 *The Fort Worth Star-Telegram*, Aug. 19, 1908.
338 *The Fort Worth Star-Telegram*, Dec. 12, 1909.
339 *The Fort Worth Star-Telegram*, Sept. 17, 1911.
340 *The Fort Worth Star-Telegram*, Dec. 15, 1912.
341 Ibid.
342 Ibid.
343 *The Dallas Morning News*, Mar. 1, 1913.
344 Thomas D. Russell, "Keep Negroes Out of Most Classes Where There Are A Large Number of Girls": The Unseen Power of the Ku Klux Klan and Standardized Testing at the University of Texas, 1899-1999, 52 S. Tex. L. Rev. 1, 15–16 (2010)
345 *The Fort Worth Star-Telegram*, Dec. 11, 1910.
346 *The Fort Worth Star-Telegram*, Feb. 25, 1916.
347 *The Austin Statesman*, May 28, 1916.
348 Ibid.
349 Judge Benjamin Dudley Tarlton Centennial Celebration (2004).
350 *The El Paso Herald*, Sept. 19, 1919.
351 https://www.caller.com/story/news/local/2019/09/13/corpus-christi-1919-hurricane/2232867001/.
352 *The El Paso Herald*, Sept. 19, 1919.
353 Statement of Genevieve Tarlton Hearon.
354 *The Beeville Bee*, Thursday, Sept. 25, 1919.
355 *The Corpus Christi Caller*, Sept. 20, 1919.
356 Ibid.
357 *The Fort Worth Record*, No. 342, Sept. 23, 1919.

358 "Prominent Texans Attend Funeral of Judge B.D. Tarlton," *The Fort Worth Star-Telegram,* Sept. 24, 1919.
359 John. W. Brady, "An Appreciation," *The Alcalde,* November 1919, No. 48, Vol. VII, No. 4, p. 285-287.
360 *The 1911 Law Class of The University of Texas,* Austin, Tex.: University of Texas School of Law, p. 86.
361 Texas Bar Association Proceedings of the Thirty-ninth Annual Session, held at EI Paso Texas, July 1st, 2nd, and 3rd, 1920, 188-189.
362 *The Austin American,* January 15, 1928, p. 10.
363 *The Fort Worth Star-Telegram,* Aug. 27, 1931.
364 https://backpackerverse.com/haunted-hillsboro-ghost-warnings-tarlton-house.
365 John. W. Brady, "An Appreciation," *The Alcalde,* November 1919, WHOLE NO. 48, VOL VII, No. 4 (p. 285-287).
366 Roy M. Mersky, Harry M. Reasoner Regents Chair in Law and Director of Research, Tarlton Law Library, Judge Benjamin Dudley Tarlton Centennial Celebration (2004).
367 Judge Benjamin Dudley Tarlton Centennial Celebration (2004).
368 Introduction, Genevieve Tarlton Hearon, Judge Benjamin Dudley Tarlton Centennial Celebration (2004).
369 8 Tex. Civ. App. 144, 27 S.W. 924 (1894, no writ).
370 11 Tex. Civ. App. 514, 32 S.W. 920 (1895, no writ).
371 7 Tex. Civ. App. 116, 120, 26 S.W. 161, 162 (1894, no writ).
372 67 Tex. 166, 2 S.W. 574 (1886).
373 35 S.W. 321, 321–22 (Tex. Civ. App. 1896, no writ).
374 1887 WL 1435 (Tex. App. 1887, no writ).
375 *Gulf, C. & S.F. Ry. Co. v. St. John,* 13 Tex. Civ. App. 257 – Fort Worth, 1896, writ denied).
376 https://www.tshaonline.org/handbook/entries/religion.
377 Ibid.
378 Ibid.
379 Ibid.
380 Ibid.

381 https://en.wikipedia.org/wiki/A_Connecticut_Yankee_in_King_Arthur%27s_Court.
382 https://twain.lib.virginia.edu/yankee/beard4.html
383 https://en.wikipedia.org/wiki/Anti-Catholicism_in_the_United_States
384 https://www.politico.com/magazine/story/2015/09/when-america-hated-catholics-213177
385 Ibid.
386 David R. Stoke, *The Shooting Salvationist*, Steerforth Press, Hanover, New Hampshire, 2011.
387 https://en.wikipedia.org/wiki/J._Frank_Norris.
388 https://www.history.com/news/jfk-catholic-president/
389 Ibid.
390 Ibid.
391 Ibid.
392 https://www.tshaonline.org/handbook/entries/rye-edgar.

Index

A

Abilene, Texas 115, 151, 156, 157, 182, 199, 214
Abilene Reporter 192, 200
Abbott Jo viii, 77, 78, 81, 82, 91, 93, 94, 96, 98, 103, 124, 141, 289, 290
Abbott's Grove 114
Abbott & Tarlton 77, 78
Adrian College 137
Albany News 194, 200, 285, 286, 287, 295
Albany Weekly News 284
Albany Star 284
Albany Sun 284
Albright, F.E. 219
The Alcalde 252, 259
Alleghany County, Maryland 3
Alexander, L.W. 159
Allen, Dr. Ethan 16, 25, 26, 50, 52
Allen, J.P. 99, 100–102
Allison, George F. 77
Allen v Tarlton 26, 50, 52
Alton, Stephen 188, 293
Angers, Trent 22
Aransas Pass, Texas 246
Army Hospital No. 15, 2
Atchison, David Rice 4
Asheville, North Carolina 116
Attakapas Tribe 10
Attakapas District 17, 22
Austin, Stephen F. 4, 123, 136, 137, 138
Austin, Texas 90, 150, 157, 158, 171, 181, 182, 225, 259
The Austin American 256
The Austin American Statesman 142, 228, 235, 236, 240, 241
The Austin Weekly 115
Austin, Texas ix, 115, 231, 235, 251, 252
Ayers, Ben ix, 136, 137, 138, 213, 221, 234
Ayers, Jefferson D. 137

B

Bailey, Honorable William J. 222
Baltimore, Maryland 35
Banks, General Nathaniel P. 21, 23, 24
Barksdale, Honorable H. 69, 70, 118
Battle of Antietam 95
Battle of Bayou Bourbeaux 23
Battle of Corinth 157
Battle of Fort Bisland 21
Battle of Fort Jackson and St. Philip 21
Battle of Grand Coteau vi, 21, 22, 23
Battles of Fredericksburg and Chancellorsville 95
Baylor College 280
Baylor County, Texas 82, 146
Bayou Boeuf 10, 11, 13, 14, 23, 25, 55
Bayou Teche 35
Baxter, Sylvester 279
Belles Lettres 49
Belser, Caroline Mary 5, 6, 221, 294
Berchmans, Blessed John vi, 30, 31, 32, 34, 36, 39, 40, 42, 43, 44, 46, 289
Bidwell, B.G. 115
Bill and wife Francis and son Edmund, (no last name) 15
Billy the Kid 118

Black, R.M. 167
Black Leagues 61
Blair, George W. 143
Blanton, J.S. 81
Blanton, Thomas 285
Bledsoe County, Tennessee 141
Bledsoe, Joseph 143
Bloomfield College 91
Boston Herald 279
Bluntzer, Mary Justine 29
Bosque County, Texas 81, 106
Boatright, Associate Justice Jason 182
Bon Pa, (Le Bon Pa, Le Bon Papa 29, 261, 263
Benausse, Father Felise 33, 36, 38, 42, 43
Beeville, Texas 245, 246, 249, 251, 256
Brady, John W. 259
Breakers Hotel 1
Brelsford, H.P. 184, 191, 192, 201, 281, 283
Brenham Weekly Banner 190
Breaux, Brigette (Novice) 42
Bright, Jesse D. 4
Briscoe, Mary Herbert 3
Brown, James W. 96
Bullard Jerry 179
Bullock, John H. 81, 82, 89, 90, 91, 146
Bullock, (daughter of John H. Bullock) 82, 146, (see also J.W. Perrill)

Bullock State Museum 231
Bullock & Tarlton 81, 91
Burbridge, (Union) Brigadier
    Stephen G. 23
Burnett, Burk 231
Butler, W. E. 219

C

Calhoun, John Henry 119
Calhoun, Jennie LaRue 117
Caller, Frances Ann (Tarlton) 6,
    10, 12, 73, 80
Caller, Green Duke 6, 7, 14, 75,
    89
Caller, Jane H. Toulmin 6, 7, 18,
    27, 51, 52, 61, 73, 74, 75, 89
Caller v Tarlton 51
Calvary Cemetery, Oakwood
    Cemetery 187
Cambridge University 279
Campbell, Dr. A. L. 251
Campbell, Dr. James 33, 34, 35,
    42, 43, 45
Cannon, John W. (steamboat) 98
Cantey & Hanger LLP 87, 125,
    293
Capps, William 219, 223
Capture of New Orleans 21
Carlin, Adland 16, 17
Carroll Manor 4
Carter Sr, Amon 231
Carter, J.W. 153
Carter, Lotta 190

Carter, W. H. 219
Cassel, Charles 231
Casey, Martin 171
Cemetery of the Religious of the
    Sacred Heart 34, 43
Centennial Celebration 263
Cetti, Zane 171
Chapman, H. M. 141, 219
Citizens for Religious Freedom 280
Citizens National Bank 68
Chicago, Illinois 177
Chisum, John 118
Civil War vi, 9, 21, 25, 30, 31, 49,
    54, 56, 60, 68, 74, 77, 95, 107,
    116, 157, 238, 289
Claiborne, General 158
Clark Clubs 150
Clark, George 133, 150, 157, 163,
    167, 169, 213
Clark, Sheriff Sterling P. 213
Clark, S.P. 219
Cleburne, Texas 96, 160
Cleburne Cemetery 239
Cleveland, President Grover 163
Cofer, Dr. R.E. 251
Coke, Governor Richard 68
Colfax, Louisiana 58
Colfax Riot 58
Collier, Professor John 91
Collins, B.F. 119
Collin County, Texas 143, 149,
    159, 160, 200, 282
The Colonel 163
Cook, S.F. 284

A Connecticut Yankee in King Arthur's Court 278
Confederate Day 237
Conner, Samuel S. and Margaretta Lucinda and family, Truman Holman Conner, Mary Maude Coleman, Ella Nora Parsons, Claude Leon Conner, William Earl Conner, Jennie LaRue Calhoun 117 Conner, Truman Holman x, 117–122, 131, 139, 140, 149, 151, 153, 155, 159, 164, 165, 167, 173, 174–179, 181–187 191, 192, 194, 196–203, 213, 218, 223, 251, 275–278, 281–287, 290
Connelly, Cornelia 31
Constructive trust 206
Continental Army 3
Corpus Christi 1, 29, 243, 244, 245, 249, 256, 259, 260, 270, 275, 290
Corpus Christi Area Heritage Society 29
Cotton, B.F. 167
Coushatta, Louisiana 63
COVID 19 pandemic 271
Covington, Texas 91
Criss, William, Ph.D 24, 181
Culberson, Governor Charles Allen 183, 188, 195, 196, 199, 285
Cumberland School of Law 95, 143

Cunningham, Sheriff 153

D

Daily v Tarlton 69, 79, 118 (see also *Tarlton v Daily*)
Daily, Lacey v Tarlton II 79
Daily, Lacey v Tarlton III 81
Dallas Morning News 132, 133, 141, 150, 163, 169, 191, 201, 214, 231
Dan (no last name) 15
Daniel Daily 55, 65
Davenport, J.H. 167
David, William 87
David Teel Realtors 78
Davis, Jim 163
Daugherty Genevieve 1, 244
Daugherty James B. 1, 245, 247, 251
Daugherty, Mrs. Jim 256
Daugherty, James R. Foundation 260
Davenport, Jouett Harbert "John" 119
Derby, (England) 31
Dallas, Texas 69, 75, 86, 98, 119, 136, 138, 139, 140, 156, 157, 159, 175, 185, 189, 199, 240, 256, 270, 280, 283, 286, 293.294
Dallas County, Texas 66, 140
Davis, Jefferson 5
Dearborn, Indiana 117

Delaware Hotel 226, 227, 239
Delille, Henriette 31
Democrat State Convention ix, 14, 61, 66, 115, 140, 194, 213, 219, 222, 223, 281, 286
Democrat National Convention (2016) 268, 271, 278
Denton, Texas 150, 207, 287
Derden, Dave 113, 114
Dickerson, James 95
Diest, (Holland) 31
Disciples of Christ 4
Dixie Day 237
Donovan & Wyle 151
Dooly, John 10, 14
Douglas, Dr. A.M. 114
Douglas, Stephen 18
Downs, Solomon W. 4
Drexel, Saint Katherine 31
Drummond, Dylan 189, 293
Driskell Hotel 157
Duchesne, Saint Rose Phillipine 20, 31
Ducker, Maud Peters 190
Dunklin, Irby 234, 251
D'Unger, Claude 29, 244
D'Unger, Gerald Paul 29
Dupre, Laurent 300

E

Eagleton, Thomas 271
Eastland Clark Club 167
Eastland County, Texas viii, ix, 117, 118, 119, 120, 139, 149, 157, 158, 159, 163, 167, 184, 191, 192, 194, 198, 200, 201, 275, 283, 285, 290
Eastland County Bar Association 192
Eaton, John 211
Estillette, E.D. vii, 27, 58, 61, 62, 64, 103
Eighteenth Judicial District Court 103
Eliza (no last name) and children Polk, Olivier 15
Elizabethtown, Kentucky 102
Ellis County, Texas vii, 65, 66, 71, 75, 81, 90, 118
Ellis County Museum 18
Ellis, L.A. 234
Ellis, Leigh 234, 256
Ellis, Richard 65
Evans, Charles I. 156, 157, 158
Evans & Gooch 157
Evans, Sam 103

F

Farenthold, Frances "Sissy" vi, x, 4, 5, 6, 18, 29, 32, 47, 51, 54, 65, 89, 256, 260, 261, 268, 270–273, 277, 281, 290
Farenthold, George Edward 262
Farenthold, Sissy & George family, Benjamin Dudley Tarlton
Farenthold, George Farenthold

II, Emilie Farenthold, James Robert Daugherty Farenthold, Vincent Bluntzer Tarlton Farenthold 270
Farenthold II, George 54, 268, 270, 273
Farenthold, Emilie 262, 270, 273, 293
Farenthold, Randolph Blake 269
Farenthold, Rhiley 269
Feast of the Immaculate Conception 36
Fechheimer & Co. 151
Ferris, Justus Wesley 68
Ferris & Rainey 68, 83, 84, 85, 118
Fields, Capt. W.A. 113
Fifteenth Amendment, U.S. Constitution 54
Finch, H.A. 160
Finch, Ronald 18
Fisher, H.C. 123
Flanagan, W. 115
Fleury, Sister Claire 42
Fleming, J.R. 119, 159
Fleming & Moore 119, 159
Fort Morgan 95
Fort Worth Bar Association 226, 227, 229, 250
Fort Worth Club 221
Fort Worth & D.C. Section 196–199
Fort Worth Democrat 135

Fort Worth Daily Gazette 124, 125, 136, 137, 144, 192, 284
Fort Worth, Texas v, viii, ix, 87, 89, 98, 102, 105, 122, 125, 131, 132, 135, 136, 137, 138, 139, 141, 142, 143, 144, 145, 146, 149, 150, 151, 152, 153, 155, 156, 157, 158, 159, 163, 169, 170, 171, 177, 178, 183, 187, 188, 190, 191, 192, 193, 194, 195, 196, 197, 198, 99, 200, 214, 219, 220, 221, 222, 223, 226, 227, 229, 234, 235, 236, 239, 240, 248, 249, 250, 251, 252, 256, 268, 275, 280, 282, 283, 284, 285, 286, 290
Franklin, Benjamin 12, 277, 278
Franklin Cemetery, St. Mary's Parish 234
Franklin, Louisiana 10, 11, 12, 13
Frederick County, Maryland 3, 4
Free Fall Festival 220
Free Masons 278
Freemasonry 278
Freestone County, Texas 77
Frost, J.R. 167
Fuller, Theodore 2
Fulton, Hon. B.D. 114

G

Gaines, Judge R.R. 214
Gaines v Newbrough 210, 211, 213

Gainesville, Texas 140
Galveston, Texas 114, 115, 132, 177
Gannon, J.J. 171
Garland, Henry L. 300
Garnett, M. H. 160
Garnett & Muse 160
Garrett, Hon. C.C. 123
General Land Office 97, 99, 100, 150
Gettysburg, Pennsylvania 95
Getzendaner, W. H. 68
George and wife May and family, Jimmy, Usilda, Tifford 15
Georgetown, Scott County, Kentucky 3
Georgetown University 35
Ginocchio's Hotel 135
Gone With The Wind 57
Good Government committee 281
Graham Radiator 284
Grand Coteau, Louisiana 20, 22, 23, 29, 30, 31, 33, 35, 36, 43, 44, 45, 57, 61, 71, 78, 98, 244, 256, 289
The Grand Hotel 135
Grant, President Ulysses S. vii, 56, 63
Grant Parish, Louisiana 58
Gray, Edward 140
Gray Reed & McGraw 189
Grayson County, Texas 143, 160
Greek College 32

Green, Brigadier General Thomas 23
Greene & Morgan Military Service 3
Grundy, Elizabeth 300
Guaranty Abstract Title Company 221
Gulf, Colorado and Santa Fe v M.S. Johnson 150, 160, 161
Gunn, Frederick C. 177
Gunn & Curtiss 177
Guy, R.S. 69

H

Hadge, R.P. 111
Hagarstown, Maryland 4
Hale, V. W. 140
Hanna & Hogsell 137
Hall, District Judge Joseph Marion viii, 82, 95, 96, 102, 103, 104, 105, 106–111, 114, 150, 160, 220, 238, 239
Hamilton, Katie Tarlton 265
Hanger, Senator William A. 219, 222, 223
Hannegan, Edward A. 4
Hardy, William 18, 26, 27
Hardyman, John (Administrator of Estate) 26, 27, 61
Hare, Silas 143
Harwood, T.F. 115
Hauser, Vanessa 265

Haw, Mary Eliza 35
Hayes, Steve 155, 178, 293
Head, Henry Oswald (Associate Justice) ix, 140, 143, 251, 282, 283, 285
Head, Dillard, Maxey, Freeman, McReynolds and Hay 143
Hebert, Rachael 30
Hearson, Genevieve Tarlton 263
Helsinki Watch Committee 271
Hendrick, Wallace B. 214
Higgs, Bob 150
Hildebrand, Ira P. 254
Hill County, Texas 78, 113, 114, 115, 116, 133, 141, 197, 200, 236, 279, 280
Hill, D.G. 192
Hilliard, E.T. 119
Hillsboro, Texas viii, x, 24, 65, 77, 78, 82, 88, 90, 91, 97, 98, 101, 109, 111, 113, 114, 117, 124, 125, 132, 133, 140, 193, 200, 221, 235, 251, 257, 260, 262, 280, 294, 295
Hillsboro City Cemetery 90, 103
Hillsboro Heritage League Board 78
Historic Photos of Fort Worth 146
Hobby, Governor William 245
Hockaday School (Dallas) 270
Hogg, Governor James S. viii, 68, 90, 113, 114, 115, 116, 123, 133, 134, 140, 142, 150, 163, 169, 198, 276, 285, 290

Hogg and Commission Democratic Club 113
Home Guaranty Abstract Company 221
Houssaye, Leila (Lila) de la 221
Hoover, Herbert 280
Houston Daily Post 191
Houston Post 158, 192, 202
Howell, Monsignor John 272
Howeth, Allan 125, 126, 293
Hubbard City, Texas 279
Huff, Z.T. 99, 100
Hudson, L.L. 219
Hudspeth, Judge George 55
Huff, W.L. 143, 144, 149
Humble, Mark 83
Human Rights Watch 271
Hunt, D.G. 167
Hunter, Sam J. (Associate Justice) ix, 183, 188, 191, 195, 196, 197, 198, 199, 200, 217, 218, 227, 230, 231, 277, 282, 283
Hurricane of 1919 in Corpus Christi 1, 2, 243, 290

I

Incarnate Word Academy 29
Indulgence of Articulo Mortis 36, 37
Independence Title Company, Dallas, Texas 86
Interstate Immigration convention 116

J

Jack County, Texas 143
Jacksboro Gazette 192
Jackson Walker LLP 266
Jarvis, J.J. 150
Jefferson, President Thomas 9
Jenkins & Pearson 160
"Jeremiah, the Catholic Tarlton" 3
"Jeremiah, the Protestant Tarlton" 3, 4
Jeremiah, Alfred 3, 5, 6
Jesus 31
Jesuit High School, New Orleans 50, 264
Jesuit College 32, 105
Jesuits, the Fathers of the Society of Jesus v, 20, 22, 32, 34, 42, 43, 44, 46
Johnson, Andrew 173, 174, 293
Johnson County, Texas 81, 82, 90, 96, 103, 106, 150
Johnson, Lyndon B. 281
Johnson, M.S. 161
Johnston, Joe 95
Jones County, Texas 192
Jones County Bar Association 192
Jones v Fancher 93
Jones, Dan M. 192
Jones, George Wallace 4
Jones, Sallie 120
Johnson, Henry and Adeline and family, Louis, Maria, Kitty, Susan 14, 15

Jordan, George I. 91, 97, 98, 99, 102, 294

K

Kellogg, Governor William vii, 56, 57, 59, 62, 63
Kennedy, Dr. 90
Kennedy, John F. 280, 281
Kennedy, Judge 196
Key West, Florida 1
King Judge John E., 8th Judicial District of Louisiana 27, 52, 61
Kirkpatrick, W.A. 99, 100, 102, 220
Kirkpatrick v Tarlton 220
Tarlton v Kirkpatrick 98, 103
Knights of Columbus 222, 240, 252
Knights of Pythias Lodge Hall 163
Ku Klux Klan x, 237, 238, 260, 290

L

Lacey, Francis Ann Howe 65, 66, 67, 69, 70, 79, 81
Lacey Home vii
Larissa College 77
Lawrence, A. 119
Lebane, J.F. 219
Lebanon, Tennessee 95
Lee, C.K. 237

Lee, Robert E. 141, 150, 190
Lewis, E.T. 300
Lewis, Paul M. 220
Lewis, Judge Yancey 254
Lexington, Kentucky 4
Lexington, Virginia 141
Lincoln, President Abraham 21, 24, 56
Lincoln County War, New Mexico 118
Liverpool, England 3
Littell, Ann Eleanor 35
Littell, Constance Collins 35
Littell, Isaac F. and wife, Mary Eliza Haw and family, Constance, Sarah Celeste, Suzanne Marie, Mary Eleanor and Mary E. 36, 57, 62
Littell, "Miss Nannie" (Susan Marie Littell a/k/a Mooma) 1, 57, 80, 82, 231, 251, 252, 256, 261
Littell, Dr. Moses 35
Littell, Sallie 82
Louisiana Purchase 9
Louisiana Centenary College 21
Louisiana State University 221
Love, Roland 36, 37
Lowrance, Will 78

M

Mack., Theodore 131, 132, 159, 197
Maddox, B. M. 211
Maddox, J.H. 219
Malone, L.F. 133
Manifest error, concept of 207, 237
Manassas, Virginia 95
Mansfield, Texas 91
Mansion Hotel 135
Manning, Joshua and Ann 35
Marion College 118
Martin & Brown 151, 153–157, 171
Martin, William C.C.C. and wife, Sophia Martin 10, 17
Masons 114, 238 see also Freemasonry 278
Masonic Lodge 114, 278
Martinez, Mother Superior Victorine Pizarro 33, 34, 36, 37, 40, 41, 42
Matthews, J.A. 192
Mary, the Mother of Jesus 9
Martin & Brown 151
Masonic lodge 114, 278
Massie, John J. 221
Massingill, M.L. 239
Mattingly, Ann 41
Meacham, H.C. 280
McConnell, Eli 141
McDermott, Paul 251
McDonald, Atwood 281
McDowell, E.A. 150
McErney, John vii, 56, 62
McGloin, Geraldine 29, 244

McGown IV, Quentin 146
McGregor, Judge Frank B. "Bob" 105, 106
McKay, Dr. R.B. 17, 50
McKinley, President William 158, 226
McKinnon, Capt. A.P. 91, 114
McKinnon & McCall 98, 99, 100
McLean, W.P., Jr. 219
McLean, Judge W.P. 170, 219, 227, 229, 251
McLennan County, Texas 163
McMillan, Kent 129
McWilliams Elizabeth a/k/a McWaters, Elizabeth 14, 16, 17, 25, 26, 27, 50, 51, 52, 53, 54, 55, 60
McWilliams v Dr. John Tarlton 55
Merrill, Louise 214
Merriman, Texas 118
Middleton & Daugherty 151
Millard, Dr. Edward, Dr. 5, 33, 34, 35, 36, 37, 38, 41, 42, 43, 45, 46, 57, 256
Millard, Elizabeth 80
Millard, Eleanor Littell 57
Millard, Mary Elizabeth 256
Millard, Robert F. 35
Mirror 113, 114
Mobile, Alabama vi, 5, 6, 7, 9, 49, 60, 74, 89
Mobile County, Alabama 7
Moore, Governor A. J. 95
Moore, J. M. 119, 149, 158

Moore, William Folsom, Chief Justice Texas Supreme Court 119
Moore, Walker 143
Moran, Sister Kate M. 36, 37, 39, 41, 42
Morgan, Hank (character) 278
Miracle of Grand Coteau vi, 29, 44
Montgomery, Alabama 95
Montgomery (MD) College Student Senate 269
Mooma 256, 261
Moore, J.M. 119
Morgan City Archives Commission 10
Morgan City, Louisiana 10, 11, 89
Morrow, Wright Chalfont viii, 24, 102, 251, 295
Moreland, Q.T. 219
Murphy, Rev.T.R. 240

N

Nachon, Father Francois M. 42
Nacogodoches, Texas 35
Nash, Newton J. 67
Nash & Kemble 70, 83, 84
Navarro County, Texas 90, 97, 207
Naw and wife Fancy (no last name) and family, Albera, Clara, Ellick 15
The Nervous Man 105
New Delhi, Louisiana 68

New Era 284
New Orleans, Louisiana 17, 20, 21, 31, 43, 49, 50, 56, 98, 182, 264
New York City 135
Newton, L.W. 239
Nixon, Richard M. 280
Nolan, Dean Robert M. 251
Norris J. Frank 279, 280, 290
Norris, Warner 279
Northington, Taylor County Sheriff 151
North Beach, Corpus Christi 2, 244
Novena vi, 30, 34, 36, 38, 42, 46
Noxubee County, Mississippi 91
Nueces County Courthouse 2
Nueces County Historical Society 29
Nueces Hotel 2
Nunn, John R. 106

O

Oakwood Cemetery 187, 251, 252, 256
O'Brien, Borue 89
OKeefe, Father 234
Oliver, Dr. M. H. 65, 66–71, 81, 85, 86
Oliver, Lunette 67
Oliver & Calhoun 66
Olivier, a child 15
Olivier, John Louis 44

Olivier, Frank 45
Opelousas, Louisiana 5, 21, 35, 55, 58, 63, 256
Oppenheimer, General L.M. 132, 133
The Opelousas Courier 27, 54, 58, 61, 62, 63, 73

P

Paddock, B.B. 135
Palo Pinto County 210, 213
Palo Pinto County Commissioner's Court 210, 211
Paris, Texas 214
Parker Judge Alton B. 222, 223
Parker County, Texas 141, 142, 183, 191, 200, 282
Peace Tent 271
Peale, Norman Vincent 280
Pearson, Chief Justice R. M. 81
Pensacola, Florida 95
Perrill, Judge J.W. and wife 82, 146, 147
Perryman, G.W. 119
Phillip–Charles, Duke of Aarschot, the 3rd Count of Arenberg 32
Pickwick Hotel 135, 239
Plenary Indulgence 37
Poindexter & Padelford 162
Portland, Texas 246
Poursine, Pulcherie (Novice) 42
Power of attorney 60, 125, 126
Pope Gregory XV 32

Pope Leo XIII 44
Port Aransas 2, 246
Pruitt & Smith 221
Putman, J.A.B. 140

Q

Quitclaim deed 175, 205, 206

R

Rainey, Anson 67, 68, 83, 84, 118, 191, 220, Chief Justice 5th Court of Appeals (Dallas) 220, 283
Range levy 187
Ranger, Texas 177
Randolph, Judge 150
Reavis, W. 133
Reeves County, Texas 191
Reflector 113
Regulators, The 118
Remembering Fort Worth 146
Richmond, Virginia 95
Rivercrest Country Club 221
Robert E. Lee Camp, Confederate Veterans 150
Roberts, Governor Oran M. 23, 24
Roberts v Helm 163–167
Robertson County, Texas 97
Robertson, H.G. 140
Rockport, Texas 284
Rockwall County, Texas 146, 147

Roosevelt Central Republican Club 157
Roosevelt, President Theodore 222
Roman College 32
Rose Hill Cemetery, Houston, Texas 271, 272
Ross, Governor Lawrence Sullivan 115, 116, 120
Ruback, Chad 175, 176, 293
Russell, Thomas D. 237
Rye, Edgar 284, 285

S

Sacred Heart Academy vi, 20, 22, 23, 30, 31, 33, 38, 43, 45, 257
Sacred Heart, Convent of 33
Sale of personal property, definition 208
Sale of real property, definition 126
Samuels, Sidney ("silver tongued lawyer") 231, 239
Sandoz, Leonce 63
San Antonio, Texas 115, 191, 213, 222
Sanger Bros, et al v R.M. Henderson 149, 151–158
Sayles, Henry 115
Sauder, Mollie 284
Scheuber, Charles 171
Scott, Sallie "Elizabeth" 90
Schexnayder, Bishop Maurice 44
Schmick, H.S. Sheriff 120

Schwartz, Caroline 179
Scott & Brelsford 184
Scott County, Kentucky 3, 4
Scurlock, Josiah Gordon "Doc" 118
Sebastian, W.P. 192
Senter, E.G. 214
Seven (no last name) 15
Seymour, Texas 82
Shaw, John 279
Sam Shackelford Survey 99, 100, 101
Shackelford County, Texas 159, 192, 199, 285
Shackelford County Bar Association 192
Sherman, Texas 140, 143, 144, 183, 200, 233
Shirley, Erin 10
Shoemaker, Susan 217
Simkins, Col. 170
Simkins, Professor, Judge W.S. 50, 231, 234, 237, 238
Sisters of the Holy Family 31
Slaughter, C.C. 214
Slave, slave or slavery vi, ix, 4, 5, 13, 14, 18, 24.25, 26, 31, 53, 54, 56, 58, 61, 62, 279
Slay, W.H. 231
Smith, A.L. and wife Ann P. Smith 78
Smith, Al (presidential candidate) 280, 281
Smith, Homer H. 16, 25, 26, 27
Smith, John F. 18, 58
Smith, LeRoy A. 251
Smith, S. 53
Smith, T.S. 114
Smith, W. D. 240, 251
Smith v McWaters 27, 50, 53
Smith & Tarlton 61
Snodgrass, Frank 214, 215
Snodgrass, Ex Parte 214
Society of the Religious of the Sacred Heart 31
Society of the Holy Child Jesus 31
South Texas Catholic 30
Sprouts, M.A. 156
Springfield, Texas 78
Spruance, Thomas 219
Statute of Frauds 209
Stayton, Associate Justice, Texas Supreme Court 94
Sant'Ignazio Church in Rome 32
St. Charles Borromeo Cemetery 256
St. Charles Borromeo Catholic Church 30
St. Charles College 12, 18, 19, 20, 22, 33, 34, 35, 36, 45, 46, 49, 50, 55, 61, 105, 289
St. Ignatius of Loyola 32
St. John the Baptist 31
St. Mary's County, Maryland 3
St. Mary's Episcopal Church 257
St. Mary's Parish v, vi, 3, 9, 10, 12,

13, 17, 21, 25, 26, 27, 35, 50,
51, 52, 55, 60, 74, 89.98, 214,
221, 234, 240, 257
Stafford, Mrs. Zarelda 150
Stanley, Frank B. 156, 157
Stanley, Mary 15
St. Charles College 16, 18, 21, 25,
29, 30, 32, 34, 41, 91, 271,
275, 280
St. Landry Courier 300
St. Landry Democrat 55, 299
St. Landry's Parish vi, vii, 18, 25,
26, 27, 34, 35, 50, 55, 57, 58,
59, 60, 61, 98, 275, 281
St. Theresa Benedicta of the
Cross 247
State v City of Cisco 184, 192,
282, 283
Steel, C.H. 192
Stephens, Isaac W. 140, 141, 142,
146, 149, 152, 154, 155, 156,
163, 167, 169, 173, 183, 184,
191, 195, 197, 200, 202, 219,
283, 285
Stephens, J.W. 251
Stephens County, Texas 120, 192
Stevenson, Adlai E. 163
Stewart, A.J. 158
Stewart, C.E. 219
Stolley, Scott 185, 293
Stonewall Brigade 190
Storey, JoAnn 166
Stubblefield, J.R. 192

Stubbs, James B. 115
Sulphur Springs, Texas 140
Sunset, Louisiana 22
Sumner County, Tennessee 143
Swayne, Jim 150

T

Tanzy, Marion 120
Tarantula Map 135
Tarlton, Ann 3
Tarlton, Alfred 3, 5
Tarlton, A&J (business) 6
Tarlton, Alfred Jeremiah 5
Tarlton, Amanda 3
Tarlton, Catherine 3
Tarlton, Caroline Mary Belser 5, 6
Tarlton, Caroline Belser 5, 6, 221
Tarlton B.D. v, x, 1, 3, 12, 14,
19, 24, 30, 36, 47, 49–51, 55,
57–64, 71, 73, 78–83, 89–91,
93, 94, 98, 102–106, 113–118,
123, 133, 140, 141, 149, 152,
190–194, 202, 213, 214, 218,
220, 221, 222, 225, 227, 228,
230, 234, 236–241, 247–252,
254, 256, 259, 260, 263, 265,
267, 279, 280, 281, 289, 290
Tarlton, B.D., Jr. x, 1, 224, 246,
247, 256, 260, 261
Tarlton, Caleb 3
Tarlton v Daily vii, 83, 87, 118
Tarlton, Elizabeth Wright 221, 235

Tarlton, Emily 3
Tarlton, Emma Louise 5
Tarlton, Emma Jane 7
Tarlton, Elizabeth 1
Tarlton, Fanietta 24, 102
Tarlton, Farmuba 82
Tarlton, Frances 1
Tarlton, Frances Caller 7, 10, 12, 16, 24, 51, 52, 60, 74, 262
Tarlton, Frances Celia 7, 14
Tarlton, Frank Ross 14
Tarlton, Genevieve 1, 190
Tarlton, Green Duke (G.D.) viii, 14, 19, 30, 98, 256, 257
Tarlton, Helen Collier 90
Tarlton, Huldah 90
Tarlton, Jeremiah 3, 4
Tarlton, John (son of John Belser Tarlton) 221, 225, 237, 249
Tarlton, John Belser 5, 6, 21, 89, 221, 234, 235
Tarlton, John, Dr. v, ix, 3, 4, 5, 6, 7, 10, 11, 12, 15, 16, 17, 27, 31, 33, 34, 44, 45, 51, 52, 54, 55, 57, 59, 60, 61, 7374, 75, 79, 81, 82, 88, 89, 262, 290
Tarlton v Kirkpatrick viii, 98, 100, 102, 103, 220
Tarlton, Dr. "Leo" Llewellyn Pitt 3, 6, 9, 10, 11, 12
Tarlton, Marie Lilly Delahoussaye 221
Tarlton, Mary Eleanor 80, 187, 251, 252, 256

Tarlton, Mary Martha 5
Tarlton, Meredith 3
Tarlton, M.E. 82
Tarlton, Ralph Briscoe 3
Tarlton, Peter Richardson 14
Tarlton, Richard Manning 82
Talton, Richard Toulmin 90
Tarlton, Sarah Elizabeth 90
Tarlton, Suzanne Marie 1, 256
Tarlton, Toulmin vi, 12, 19, 30, 36, Dr. Toulmin Tarlton, 44, 45, 46, 49, 57, 60, 98, 105, 256
Tarlton, Vincent 261
Tarlton & Ayers 213, 221
Tarlton & Bullock 91
Tarlton, Jordan & Tarlton 91, 97, 98
Tarlton & Tarlton 90
Tarlton, Tarlton & Morrow 102
Tarlton v Wofford 18
Tarrant County Bar Association ix, 222
Tarrant County Commissioners 177
Tarrant County Courthouse 137, 138, 144, 150, 169
Taylor, (Confederate) General Richard 23
Taylor, Bob 190
Taylor County, Texas 120, 149, 151, 157, 192
Taylor County Bar Association 192

Teche Country 21
Terry, J.W. 162, 169, 170, 171
Texas Central Railway Company v Stewart 149, 158, 159
Texas A&M Law School 188
Texas Bar Association 177
Texas Bar Convention 114
Texas Commission of Appeals v, vii, viii, 83, 104, 105, 113, 123, 124, 125, 134, 159
Texas Land News 284
Texas & Pacific Section 197, 198, 285
Texas Railroad Commission 162, 169
Texas Volunteer Guard 132, 133
Thirteenth Amendment, United States Constitution 26
Thomas, J.E. 119
Thomson, L.J. 113
Times Picayune 17, 98
Texas Bar Convention 114
The Thomahawk 284
Thurgood Marshall Law School 271
Thomas, E.A. 144
Thorne, E.P. 162
Tiger Island 10
TransMontaigne Partners 265
Todd, Charles T. 140
Tom and wife Irving, (no last name) 15
Toulmin, Theophilus L. 7
Town & Gown Club, Austin 252

Transylvania University 4, 5
Trinity University 118
Trimble, William A. 4
Trimble Tech High School 237
Truly, R.B. 119
Twain, Mark 278, 279

U

United Way 29
University of Louisiana Law School vi, 33, 49, 55
University of Texas School of Law ix, 225, 227, 229, 230, 232, 234, 235, 236, 240, 246, 249, 250, 251, 252.254, 255, 256.259, 260, 263, 266, 270, 271, 290
University of Virginia 102
Urquart v Burleson 164

V

Vassar College 270
The Vatican 30, 42, 44, 45
Vaughn, George 66–71
Vincent, R. E. 251
Vinson, Hanker 15
The Voice 45

W

Waggoman, B.L. 219
Wagstaff, J.M. 192

Warmoth, Governor Henry 56
Warren County, North Carolina 81
Warren, John D. 220
Washington Catholic Seminary 35
Washington County, Maryland 3
Washington Literary Society 142
Washington, D.C. 35, 256, 271, 280
Washington, President George 278
Washington & Lee 141
Wallace F.R. 219
Wallace, Judge 196
Walsh, Capt. W.C. 150
Watts, A.T. 214
Warren, John D. 220
Waxahachie, Texas vii, 18, 60, 65, 67, 68, 70, 71, 73, 74, 75, 82, 88, 90, 118, 141, 191, 262, 283
Waxahachie City Cemetery 73–75
W.C. Robinson v Moore 149
Wear, William Clayton 111
Webb, Sam 285
Wells, H.P. 68
Westbrook Hotel 239
West, Mary 162
West Point 5
Western Sun 284
White, Edward Douglas 50
White House 222
White Leagues vii, 61, 62, 63
White Point, Texas 246
White Settlement, Texas 221
Wichita Falls, Texas 285
Wichita Falls Herald 284
Wilson, Mary vi, 30, 32, 33, 34, 35, 36, 40, 43, 44, 45, 46, 57, 256, 289
Windsor Hotel 140
Women's suffrage 260
Woodlawn, Mississippi 91
Woollam's Lake 132
Wofford, James N. 18
World Columbian exposition 116
Wortham, Louis & Fru 231
Wright, Elizabeth Wright 221, 235
Wyly, Mr. & Mrs. J.J. 190
Wynne, Colonel R.M. 190, 219

Y

Yellow Bayou, Louisiana 78
Yellow fever 5
Yoakum's History of Texas 157
Yorktown, Virginia 95
Young, A.W. 133

Z

Zietz, Josh 279

www.ingramcontent.com/pod-product-compliance
Lightning Source LLC
Chambersburg PA
CBHW070959160426
43193CB00012B/1842